DSLR Cinema

DSLR Cinema:
Crafting the Film Look with Large Sensor Video

2nd edition

Kurt Lancaster

Focal Press
Taylor & Francis Group

NEW YORK AND LONDON

First published 2013
by Focal Press
70 Blanchard Road, Suite 402
Burlington, MA 01803
781-313-8808

Simultaneously published in the UK
by Focal Press
2 Park Square, Milton Park, Abingdon, Oxon OX14 4RN

Focal Press is an imprint of the Taylor & Francis Group, an informa business

Notices
Knowledge and best practice in this field are constantly changing. As new research and experience broaden our understanding, changes in research methods, professional practices, or medical treatment may become necessary.

Practitioners and researchers must always rely on their own experience and knowledge in evaluating and using any information, methods, compounds, or experiments described herein. In using such information or methods they should be mindful of their own safety and the safety of others, including parties for whom they have a professional responsibility.

Product or corporate names may be trademarks or registered trademarks, and are used only for identification and explanation without intent to infringe.

Library of Congress Cataloging in Publication Data
Lancaster, Kurt, 1967-
  DSLR cinema : crafting the film look with video / Kurt Lancaster. -- 2nd ed.
    p. cm.
  Includes bibliographical references and index.
  ISBN 978-0-240-82373-7 (pbk.) 1. High definition video recording.
2. Single-lens reflex cameras. 3. Composition (Photography) 4. Digital cinematography. I. Title.
  TR862.L36 2013
  777--dc23
                                                              2012021688
ISBN: 978-0-240-82373-7
Printed in the United States of America by Courier, Kendallville, Indiana

Contents

PART 1 • DSLR Shooter's Toolkit

PART 2 • Master DSLR Shooters at Work: Case Studies

PART 3 • Getting the Gear

Foreword

Shane Hurlbut, ASC

When Kurt Lancaster came to me with the idea of writing this book on HDSLR filmmaking, I was honored to be a part of it. I have been neck deep in this technology since January 26, 2009. It has been a roller-coaster ride trying to figure out this new disruptive technology from a motion picture cinematographer's perspective. Forging ahead with normal operating procedure did not translate. I had to think out of the box and teach myself about menus and picture styles, and create a new checks-and-balances ritual for shooting. There is not much that this camera system cannot do because it can be small and compact or as big as you choose to make it. The platform is so liberating that I feel like a five-year-old again—full of possibility and endless creativity.

I refer to the Canon 5D Mark II as a game-changer because the paradigm has shifted. This is the future, and as technology gets better so will the camera's data rates, processing power, and ability to do more uncompressed media capture. I shot with film for my entire career—that includes 17 movies, hundreds of commercials, many music videos, and 21 short films—because the HD landscape never attracted me. It looked plastic and too sharp, with a depth of field that felt false. I have since found that if the story and characters are engaging and the film transports you, the capture medium doesn't matter.

Why the sudden shift in thinking about HD? The Canon cameras do not look like HD. It is what I call digital film because the quality is unlike any other HD camera available to date. The image looks unique. It is its own genre—one that I believe looks and feels the closest to film. In my opinion HD video capture has finally come from the right place: the still photography platform. Canon has been working on this sensor for years.

When directors Scott Waugh and Mike McCoy came to me to lens Act of Valor (2012), I told them that I didn't want to shoot another action picture unless we were going to reinvent the action genre. Seeing the potential in this small Canon 5D DSLR, we embarked on a mission: to capitalize on the compact nature of the camera, using it to our advantage by pacing and moving it in new and exciting ways that were a completely immersive experience for an audience. I wanted the audience to see the world through the eyes of the Navy SEALs. We wanted it to feel immediate, visceral and immersive. As an audience member you became emotionally invested in the characters and their journey.

My creative journey with the camera involved a steep learning curve in 2009. The Elite Team and I made many mistakes in the beginning. Midway through the journey, everything just worked. I continued to hone my abilities with the 5D camera system and subsequent cameras by ingesting as much knowledge as

I could and share it with the film community. That is how Hurlbut Visuals was born (see http://www.hurlbutvisuals.com/).

Lydia, my wife of 23 years and soulmate wanted to showcase my fearless, pioneering, trail-blazing spirit. She and our web developer, Ryan Fritz of Ryno Technologies designed Hurlbut Visuals in the summer of 2009. Lydia convinced me that I had to change the way I think. The old rules of holding things close to your chest don't apply anymore. I began sharing everything as I was experiencing it while shooting *Act of Valor* and a variety of commercials.

Our shooting experiences became the HurlBlog (see http://www.hurlbutvisuals.com/blog/).

I answer every comment personally and give practical on-the-job learning. The unexpected benefit was the amazing dialog that occurs with our reader's input. I learn so much from the blog readers and feel excited about our forum. Lydia's vision of an intimate, personal, and heartfelt experience that was not just about an individual but about the synergy and team effort involved in creating beautiful images came alive and continues to expand.

Hurlbut Visuals has grown over the past three years. Our mission to create, innovate and educate has also expanded. We are a creative collective comprised of writers, directors, producers, camera operators, first assistants, editors and lighting technicians who have worked together for years. We are visual storytellers who use a variety of tools to achieve spontaneity and capture the best performance.

The Last 3 Minutes is where we figured out how to have Canon 5D imagery that held up on a 60-foot screen. The story is a result of the writing and direction of a very talented director Po Chan. She has passion and a clear understanding of how to get the best performance from an actor by writing a backstory to make the characters come alive. Po embraces a visual style that is not ordinary. She is visionary, and I thank her for writing and directing a short that will continue to change the way people think about this technology. In March of 2012, Po and I collaborated again on *The Ticket*, which was Po's follow up to *The Last 3 Minutes*. She wrote a beautiful and cinematic love story about getting one last chance. We used the latest in DSLR 4K capture: The Canon 1DC. This is the world that I have been trailblazing for quite some time. When the camera was delivered to Hurlbut Visuals, my Elite Team and I did various tests, using what we had learned from our collective experience with the Canon 5D MK II. After the first night of testing, one word came to mind. WOW! Canon harnessed 4K in a small footprint with the processing power to record to CF cards without external recorders. This took our creativity and visuals to a whole new level.

Lastly, a huge thank you to Kurt Lancaster for giving a voice to HDSLRs, specifically the Canon cameras, in this new book. I welcome him on the set any time after his assistance on *The Last 3 Minutes*. He jumped into action when our sound person was stuck in traffic and did excellent sound recording. Kurt was like a superhero sound guy in the night to save our project. Kudos, my man!

4 June 2012

Acknowledgments

I would like to thank Elinor Actipis at Focal Press for being intrigued enough with my email pitch for a book on DSLR cinema to ask me for a formal proposal to get the ball rolling and her insistence to update with a second edition.

Many thanks to Michele Cronin at Focal Press for shepherding the original edition from its genesis through—if not a revelation (that's for readers to decide)—but a completion. Kudos for Lauren Mattos for carrying through with the 2nd edition. Excellent work.

Thanks to all of the manufacturers, artists, and photographers—too many to name individually—for permission to use their images in this book. Without the pics, it would have just been words, which would just not have been as exciting.

Furthermore, much appreciation for the critical eye and keen advice of Julian Grant and Dave Anselmi—my deep appreciation for their comments. This book is better than it would have been without them.

Many thanks to the reviewers who gave comments at the beginning of the process: Dave A. Anselmi, Director/Producer/Instructor (PracticalMysticProductions. com), Michael Brennan, Director of Photography; Julian Grant, Producer/Director, Assistant Professor at Columbia College-Chicago; Andrew Jones, Cinematographer; Eugenia Loli, Tech reviewer, software developer, videographer (<http://vimeo.com/eugenia/videos>); Bruce Sheridan, Chair, Film and Video Department, Columbia College Chicago; Phil South, Tutor, Bristol Old Vic Theatre School.

Hats off to Diana Copsey, Nathaniel Westenhaver, and Jessica Wolfson for the transcriptions of many interviews.

Thanks also to Peter Tvarkunas, Director of Education at Canon, who was open to the project and offered much support.

I especially want to thank the international cast of filmmakers, cinematographers, journalists, and DSLR shooters who were generous with their time for interviews: First off, Philip Bloom, whose DSLR films and blog inspired me to delve into DSLR cinematography—he is a true British gentleman; American Jared Abrams at WideOpenCamera; planetMitch at planet5D.com—I look forward to his DSLR news updates every day; Rii Schroer, a German photojournalist working in England; Brazilian director Bernardo Uzeda and cinematographer Guga Millet; British ex-pat Neal Smith at Hdi RAWworks; American filmmaker and colorist Jeremy Ian Thomas (Hdi RAWworks); Kris Cabrera for insights into special effects with the Canon 7D; American writer and director

Jamin Winans; and much appreciation for Hong Kong director Po Chan and ASC member Shane Hurlbut for letting me on the set of *The Last 3 Minutes*, so I could see the Canon 5D Mark II in action, as well as the Elite Team members who offered tips and allowed me to get underfoot as they shot, and of course Lydia Hurlbut, who not only offered invaluable assistance with the manuscript, but made sure I was in the right location for shoots over the greater LA area.

I also wish to thank my colleagues at the School of Communication at Northern Arizona University who provided moral support during the writing of this manuscript as I held down a full teaching load. Norman Medoff offered advice and encouragement. Paul Helford and Janna Jones were always there with a smile. Mary Tolan was a friend who jumped at the chance to shoot a project with a DSLR and asked the right questions. Mark Neumann always provided moral support and was always open to faculty willing to push the envelope in the classroom. Peter Schwepker lent me his 5D over spring break before I decided to get mine—many thanks. I also want to thank my dean, Michael Stevenson, who offered encouragement when I took on the project; it was a boost of support during a hectic semester.

In addition, I thank my students who inspire me to do even better work—both in teaching and shooting—some of whom were willing to experiment with DSLR cinematography when I encouraged them to use DSLRs for their projects before there were any rule books: Shannon Sassone, Shannon Thorp, Danielle Cullum, Taylor Mahoney, and Margo McClellan.

I also want to thank my friend Beau L'Amour, who not only gave me a place to stay in LA, but offered detailed advice on audio and lenses, and got me contacts at Bandito Brothers.

Finally, special thanks to Stephanie and Morgan Petrie—who have been my family in Flagstaff. And of course to my mother, Judy Bennett, and her husband, Clay, who opened their cottage on Sebec Lake in Maine—providing a place to relax after the book was completed.

About the Website

The Website includes a number of additional resources, including videos of the films that are featured as case studies in the book.

Please be sure to visit!

http://booksite.focalpress.com/dslrcinema

Visit the author's DSLR Cinema blog

www.kurtlancaster.com

The HDSLR Cinema Revolution

You can go for greatness or be concerned about making mistakes. If
you're concerned about mistakes you will hold yourself back.
—(Bob Primes, ASC HDSLR workshop at Hdi RAWworks,
Los Angeles, May 1, 2010)

THE BEGINNING OF THE HDSLR REVOLUTION: PHOTOGRAPHER VINCENT LAFORET REDEFINES THE GAME

Many students and low-budget indie filmmakers shoot on video because film
cameras and film stock are too expensive (I remember paying around $50 to
purchase and develop 2 minutes of black and white 16 mm film in the mid-
1990s at NYU). Video cameras—especially with the release of Panasonic's
DVX100 that shot in 24P and allowed for gamma curve changes in cameras
priced at $3,700 in 2002—were perceived as a game changer. A lot of indies
gravitated toward this camera for their cinema projects. Then affordable HD
cameras hit the market with full HD 1920×1080 resolution by the late 1990s,
and it appeared the genie was let out of the bottle. Today, consumers can purchase mini point-and-shoot HD cameras and iPhones that James Bond could
use on his spy missions.

Yet, all of these cameras—whether HD or not, whether shooting in 24P or 30P,
whether recorded on Panasonic's P2 cards at 100 Mbps—look like video, feel
like video—that uncinematic, flat, overly sharp look that makes cinema-makers
and photographers cringe.[1] Why? Because video cameras are so crammed with
features (needed for ENG work and for ease of use for low-end consumer cameras) that it becomes everything for everyone. Video cameras can shoot family
reunions; reporters can shoot news; sporting events can be caught in full HD
glory—but none of those video cameras captures the look and feel of cinema
(without special 35 mm lens adapters). Video cameras are full of compromises,

---

[1] In the right hands, electronic news gathering (ENG) cameras and lower-end HD cameras can look
cinematic, but for the low price point, I'm not aware of any HD video camera that can look nearly as
cinematic as a Canon 5D Mark II camera.

such as high zoom ratios with fixed lenses that do not come close to the quality of the glass found in Zeiss or Canon L series prime lenses, for example.

Vincent Laforet, whose photographs have appeared in *National Geographic, Sports Illustrated, Time, Life,* and *Newsweek,* among others, remembers purchasing a Panasonic DVX100 (the miniDV 24P camera), but he quickly became "totally disinterested" in it, he tells me in an interview. "I was not impressed with lens, depth of field, and the look and feel of it" and he returned it in a week. Jeremy Ian Thomas, a colorist and editor at Hdi RAWworks in Hollywood, discusses how he felt as a former student at the Los Angeles Film School, where he was constantly confronted with the limitations of video: "I'd be shooting on these crappy DV cameras. You're looking at the image and even with HD cameras it doesn't look like a movie to me, and I immediately found out that that had to do with color. It had to do with creating looks and creating a vibe for the movie by doing certain things to the image" (interview with author).

In the fall of 2008, photographer Vincent Laforet redefined the video versus cinema game.

Laforet, one of Canon's "Explorers of Light" educators and a former Pulitzer Prize-winning photographer for *The New York Times* (2000–2006), had an appointment with David Sparer, Canon's senior manager of Pro-Products Technical Marketing. It was a Friday and the team had just unpacked the prototype Canon 5D Mark II, a digital SLR camera, that was announced on September 17, 2008. Laforet took a peek, but they wouldn't let him touch the camera until he signed a nondisclosure agreement. Indeed, when he found out it was the world's first DSLR camera to shoot full-size HD video, he begged Sparer to let him borrow one for the weekend. But the cameras were to be shipped out to other photographers for testing on Monday, so the answer was no. Laforet made a pitch.

"This camera is basically going to sit for two days doing nothing," Laforet remembers saying. "Just let me borrow it for a few hours and I'll give it right back, so I can try shooting a sample movie." They eventually agreed, and told Laforet that Canon would not sponsor the movie. "You are just borrowing the camera entirely independently from Canon, and doing your own little thing. If the movie turns out good, we'll use it—if not, we won't," Laforet remembers them saying.[2]

He came up with a scenario and shot *Reverie* over a weekend (see Figure I.1).

When Laforet first saw the results of the 5D Mark II on-screen, he knew this was different from any type of video he had previously examined. "I was literally stunned a number of times," he mused. "I could not believe my eyes. It's

---

[2]Wallach, H. Interview: Vincent Laforet. <http://www.usa.canon.com/dlc/controller?act = GetArticleAct&articleID = 1286&fromTips = 1>.

FIGURE I.1
Still from Vincent Laforet's *Reverie*, the runaway Internet hit that changed Laforet's life overnight.
(©2009 Vincent Laforet. Used with permission.)

one of the best still cameras out in the world. But between the size of the sensor and the lens choice and the way it captures light it's absolutely stunning." In short, it looked like it was shot on film. After Laforet put *Reverie* online (Canon liked it), it received over 2 million views in a week, and Laforet's life changed overnight. The day after the upload, he received three different film project offers within a day. Independent filmmakers, video journalists, and students saw the results and many dumped their video cameras and started shooting their projects on DSLRs. Canon's 5D Mark II—when utilizing the proper settings and lighting conditions—started to be utilized as a cinema camera.

Although Nikon released the first DSLR that shot HD video (the D90 with 1280×720p resolution), it was Canon's 5D Mark II that captured the hearts of filmmakers. It not only utilized full HD 1920×1080p video, but it did so with a full frame sensor (36×24 mm)—essentially equivalent in size to a 65 mm VistaVision cinema camera. But primarily, high-definition single lens reflex cameras, the hybrid DSLR (HDSLRs)—those that shoot stills and high-definition video—are designed for photographers. They're stills cameras. But thousands of DSLR shooters are using them as cinema cameras. This book shows DSLR shooters how to get the cinematic look using the video mode of DSLR cameras.[3]

---

[3]The book uses *HD-DSLR*, *HDSLR*, *hybrid DSLR*, and *DSLR* interchangeably, but mostly *DSLR* for the sake of simplicity. Furthermore, most of the examples covered in this book were coincidently shot with Canon 5D Mark II (predominantly) and the Canon 7D, as well as Canon's Rebel T2i. There's one example of a Panasonic GH1 utilizing a Steadicam Merlin. Nikon deserves mention, but no one I came across was using them. There are many manufacturers making DSLR cameras that shoot good HD video, but it seems that most of the independent filmmakers and journalists shooting with DSLRs are mainly opting for the Canon.

"I was literally stunned a number of times," Laforet mused. "I could not believe my eyes. It's one of the best still cameras out in the world.

Ultimately, the difference between ENG video cameras and DSLR video cameras seems to revolve around the fact that DSLRs did not come out of the ENG video camera world: they came from the stills camera world, from where cinema originally evolved—an important distinction for Shane Hurlbut, ASC.

SHANE HURLBUT, ASC, EMBRACES THE CANON 5D MARK II

Hurlbut, who most recently DP'ed *Terminator Salvation* (2009) and *Act of Valor* (2012), was originally trained on ENG cameras—a number of years ago as a student in mass communication at Emerson College in Boston. One eventful summer made him change his "religion." Over a summer break, one of his friends returned from USC film school and asked him to help shoot a movie in their hometown in upstate New York. He reminisces, "So I thought, 'All right I'll help Gabe out and learn.' It was all nights, so I started working on that project and fell in love with film. I just started looking at it and it was so different than TV video and I thought 'my God this is it.' So I went back that next semester and I changed everything I had from TV and mass communication to film and then I did a four-year film degree in one year."[4]

At the time, video just did not look like film. HD (at least at the prosumer level) may have been a game changer for news, sports, and event videographers—but not for many filmmakers.

The American Society of Cinematographers—that elite group who will give membership only by invitation—sponsored an event to show off the Canon 5D Mark II at Sammy's Camera in Los Angeles in February 2009. Hurlbut, among other ASC members, attended. "I went to Sammy's, and everyone was playing with it," but many weren't convinced at first, because of the stills camera form factor, and weren't sure on how to best harness its potential as a cinematic tool.

But Hurlbut saw the potential right away. "They had Vincent Laforet's film, *Reverie*, playing up there on a monitor. And I looked at that spot, and I thought, 'Whoa, that came from this camera?' And then I put the 5D in my hand and a light bulb went off. I knew that this was going to change everything. I was all in" (speech at Hdi RAWworks, 1 May 2010). He bought the Canon 5D Mark II that evening. "I realized that this is a game changer. I thought it was revolutionary. Then my mind just started thinking completely out of the box, 'What if we could do this, this, this, this, and this,' and it began

---

[4] All interviews with Hurlbut were conducted by the author (in March 2010), unless otherwise noted.

to inspire me even more as a filmmaker." He worked his way through the various menu functions and taught himself how to use the camera. When McG, the director of *Terminator Salvation*, called Hurlbut and asked him to direct and shoot a series of webisodes to promote the movie—all based around a first-person perspective of a helmet cam—Hurlbut was all over it. It would allow him to take advantage of the Canon 5D Mark II. "The cameraman was the actor," Hurlbut says. "It was so exciting." Bandito Brothers Productions produced the webisodes for Warner Brothers. Bandito Brothers directors were very impressed with the look of the *Terminator* webisodes, so they asked Hurlbut to DP their feature, *Act of Valor*, about the elite Navy SEALs where Hurlbut got to experiment more with the 5D—75% of the feature all of the action scenes was shot with Canons DSLRs. (Speech at HdiRAWworks, May 1, 2010.)

"Where did the idea of motion pictures come from?" Hurlbut asks. "It came from a brilliant individual, Louis Lumière. When he looked through his pinhole camera, he asked himself the question, 'I wondered what it would look like if this image moved?' SHABANG!! Motion pictures were born. Why were the keys to the castle given to the ENG manufacturers to design our HD platform? Their specialty is capturing the news and sports. When I look at their images they don't look cinematic. I feel that the HD platform has now come from the right source, still photography." For example, Hurlbut explains, "I like to shoot a shallow depth of field, so the audience is drawn to what's in focus."

Hurlbut saw the potential right away. "They had Vincent Laforet's film, *Reverie*, playing up there on a monitor. And I looked at that spot, and I thought, 'Whoa, that came from this camera?' And then I put the 5D in my hand and a light bulb went off. I knew that this was going to change everything. I was all in."

Why were the keys to the castle given to the ENG manufacturers to design our HD platform? Their specialty is capturing the news and sports. When I look at their images they don't look cinematic. I feel that the HD platform has now come from the right source, still photography.

Up to this point, the HD video camera chip technology just doesn't quite do it for Hurlbut because the video looks overly sharp and has way too much depth of field. "New make-up is being designed, diffusion is being added, new LUTs (lookup tables) are being engineered all to try and make HD look good," Hurlbut says. "The Canon does all of this automatically without all the re-invention. You need to think much more out of the box, stop looking at all the numbers and drink the DSLR Kool-Aid, along with its limited color space and digital compression. This is what makes it look cinematic and organic, I call it digital film."

FIGURE I.2
Shane Hurlbut, ASC, looks at his field monitor as he adjusts the focus ring on the Canon 5D Mark II for *The Last 3 Minutes*. "I light to the monitor," Hurlbut says. Note the red tape on the monitor setting the 1:85 aspect ratio; the 5D Mark II does not output HD when shooting in live mode, but standard definition.
(Photo by Kurt Lancaster.)

FIGURE I.3
The shot from *The Last 3 Minutes* that Shane Hurlbut set up as seen in Figure I.2.
(©2010 Hurlbut Visuals. Used with permission.)

Because of this, Hurlbut embraces the DSLR over the high-end HD video cameras. "If I am shooting anything else, then I am shooting film," Hurlbut states. He often gets some strange looks when pulling out his 5D, especially when he hands it to the Technocrane technicians. "When I grab my 5D Moviemaker package, people who never worked with the still photography platform before view it like [a] UFO has just landed," he laughs.

But despite its alien look in the film world, Hurlbut tries to keep shooting simple. "What I like to do is try to keep it as close to the process of exposing film as possible." In the short produced for Canon, *The Last 3 Minutes* (see Figures I.2 and I.3), he notes how he used "my lighting monitor which becomes my viewfinder. It is intimate and my portal to view the light and composition." Not a big black tent with tons of wires running out of it, with waveform monitors, computers, and large HD monitors inside, nor did he utilize a digital image technician (DIT) seen on the set of *Battlestar Galactica*, for example. By embracing the simplicity of the Canon technology, he was able to keep the production simple, small, and intimate with the director and the actors, not a big circus. The camera becomes the DIT as well as the video playback technician. "Small footprint, big vision," he smiles.

As Shane Hurlbut says, the camera "is exciting to me. And I think out of all this it's going to start a massive revolution."

Neil Smith, one of the pioneers of all-digital postproduction for the RED camera was not so easily convinced as Hurlbut and Laforet about the potential DSLR cinema revolution.

NEIL SMITH'S TAKE ON THE DSLRS CINEMA REVOLUTION

Neil Smith, a white-haired Englishman who retired from Microsoft, financed a grad school degree in neuroscience and became a documentary filmmaker. A few years ago, he started the former all-digital postproduction house, Hdi RAWworks, specifically for digital file-based workflows down in The Lot in Hollywood.

He attended the Collisions conference about the merging of filmmaking and DSLR cameras near the end of August 2009 at the Los Angeles Film School. Not only did Smith observe Shane Hurlbut, ASC, and Vincent Laforet speak, but Smith's Hdi RAWworks company put together their material that was to be projected at the conference. He looked at the work on a 60-foot screen and remembered thinking, "This is serious; this is cinematic-quality images."[5]

Rodney Charters, ASC, also convinced Smith to consider the potential of DSLRs as a cinema camera. As the DP on the TV series *24*, Charters purchased a Canon 5D Mark II and used it primarily for effects plate shots in the series. Neil Smith met him when he was shooting a CBS pilot, *Washington Field*, on a RED camera. He used Smith's posthouse for the postproduction work. Charters needed to get shots of the White House, Smith explains. "You try to film out in the streets of Washington, DC, anywhere near the White House with a RED camera and see what happens when an SUV with dark windows pulls up and six beefy chaps get out and beat the crap out of you," Smith laughs. Charters, Smith continues, took the stealth approach. "He and his AC got his 5D Mark II, went outside, and took some background shots of the White House. He pretended to be a museum tourist. He got a shot where a cop car goes right in front of him, and nobody is stopping him," Smith adds.

---

[5] All interviews with Smith in this chapter were conducted by the author in March 2010.

Smith wondered how the HD video capabilities of the Canon 5D Mark II would compare to the 4 K resolution of a RED camera. Would it be cinematic or look as though it painfully stood out with a video aesthetic? Back in a screening room down at The Lot in Hollywood, they projected Charter's White House footage on a $100,000 2 K DLP projector. "We put it on the 20-foot screen downstairs," Smith remarks, "and I looked at it and I said, 'Ooh, that doesn't look as bad as I expected to look.'"

"We are a RED house," Smith continues, "we know image quality; we graded the first 4 K images off of the first RED. We understand all about color space and resolution." So even to consider using a hybrid DSLR that line-skips its images because the CMOS sensor processor is too slow to handle it was more than a leap of faith. It was, for the digital purist, like asking the ugly duckling to dance after turning down the prom queen (see Appendix 1, "Image Resolution"). But in the right hands, the ugly duckling can shine. Smith asked Charters to do the ultimate test. Shoot a series of demo shots at The Lot with the RED One, Canon 5D Mark II, and the Canon 7D and intermix the footage and see whether anyone could tell the difference.

They presented the work at the HD Expo in New York in the fall of 2009 in front of 200 filmmakers, Smith explains. "We asked everybody, 'If you can guess absolutely correctly which is RED, 5D, and 7D, we will buy you the best meal you ever had,'" Smith challenged. "We have not had to buy a meal." Despite the numbers and resolution charts, the 5D and 7D hold up against the RED—at least in the 2 K world. However, 4 K resolution is an entirely different story. Smith felt that Canon would beat out the other dedicated video cameras due to Moore's Law—faster, better, cheaper—the HDSLR cameras can only get better, plus Canon has the sales distribution and mass market on its side.

> We asked everybody, "If you can guess absolutely correctly which is RED, 5D, and 7D we will buy you the best meal you ever had," Smith challenged. "We have not had to buy a meal." Despite the numbers and resolution charts, the 5D and 7D hold up against the RED—at least in the 2 K world.

> In the end, Smith feels that the DSLR model for shooting movies "is a new form of filmmaking. This is cinéma vérité reborn." He adds: "There is something about the form factor about these cameras which allows you to work with actors in a totally different way."

Greg Yaitanes, a director of the TV series *House MD*, agrees with Smith. When they used the Canon 5D Mark II to shoot the last episode of *House* in spring 2010, he said in an interview with Philip Bloom, "This was beyond a cinematic look. It gave a new level of being able to pull the actors out of the background and pull them right to your face, and give an intimacy that I haven't seen in digital or film."[6]

In addition to its size, Smith says the Canon sensor has a certain cinematic look to it. "To me, these HD digital SLRs have a 35 mm film aesthetic—there is something about the sensor and the color science," Smith muses. "You know, Canon had been making good 35 mm [still] film cameras for years; they've been making good 35 mm digital cameras for years. There is something in the sensor design, something in the spirit of the machine, the soul of the machine that is very organic. There is something that Canon engineers do with these sensors and their color science that produces a very film-like aesthetic."

Smith feels that due to "the form factor, the price, the image quality, and the new techniques of filmmaking" that it will "revolutionize anything with a micro budget. Anything under a million dollars where they used to consider a large HD camera they will now consider two or three HDSLRs." Due to Moore's law, Smith explains, "faster, better, cheaper" HDSLRs will just get better. Because Canon has the R&D and the marketing, he feels it will remain king of the HDSLR cinema world.

LUCASFILM TAKES ON DSLRS–WITH THE HELP OF PHILIP BLOOM

Lucasfilm apparently agrees with Smith. Independent filmmaker Philip Bloom, who, like Smith, dismissed the value of the Canon 5D Mark II, bought one and tossed it aside because he couldn't control some of the features manually. As a professional DP, he wanted that control. But late in the spring of 2009, he saw the potential. He started shooting some projects with it. He wrote about his experiences and put samples of his work on his blog (philipbloom.net). People noticed. Within several months, he became one of the key HDSLR experts, being invited to give workshops and asked by Canon and Panasonic to test out cameras for them. Rick McCallum, the producer of *Star Wars* (episodes I–III) noticed as well and invited him out to Skywalker Ranch in Marin County, California, in October 2009. Mike Blanchard, the head of postproduction at Lucasfilm, called him up. They wanted to know how far the cameras could be pushed cinematically—can a DSLR be used as a cinema camera?

Bloom arrived with his equipment and shot around the countryside of Skywalker Ranch (see Figure I.4). He converted the files to Apple ProRes overnight and cut together a rough edit by morning. The big guys wanted to see it projected on a 40-foot screen. That was the true test. Bloom knew the work

---

[6]Bloom, P. (April 19, 2010). Exclusive: In-depth interview with Greg Yaitaines. *PhilipBloom.net.* <http:// philipbloom.net/2010/04/19/in-depth-interview-with-executive-producer-and-director-of-house-season-finale-shot-on-canon-5dmkii/>.

FIGURE I.4
Still from Bloom's *Skywalker Ranch*, a test video he shot for Lucasfilm to see how it would look blown up on a 40-foot screen. "My heart was racing," Bloom says. "I watched as the edit played and they loved it."
(©2009 Philip Bloom. Used with permission.)

looked good on his computer screen. And his stuff looked good on the Web—but on a cinema screen? That was the true test.

For George Lucas and his team, Bloom says, "If it looks great on the big screen then that is the most important thing. Not codecs, limitations, bit rates, et cetera. All those are very important, but the most important thing by far for them is how it actually looks and it passed with flying colors. That is what they really care about."[7]

Bloom blogged about his experience at Skywalker Ranch:

> I was nervous. Never having seen my work on a big screen as good as this, but also George Lucas came in to watch and also the legendary sound designer Ben Burtt. My heart was racing. I watched as the edit played and they loved it. My favorite moment was when the star timelapse came on and Ben Burtt said 'Hey, now, hang on!!' This was a very quick ungraded draft edit knocked together from a crappy grey day as a test, not supposed to be shown as an example of my work! Then Quentin Tarantino came in as he was due to talk at a screening of *Inglourious Basterds* and George said to Quentin, come see this. Quentin waxed lyrical, calling it Epic and William Wyleresque and was shocked it was shot on a DSLR. He had no idea you could shoot HD video on them or they were so good.

[7] Bloom, P. (December 12, 2009) The tale of Lucasfilm, Skywalker Ranch, Star Wars and Canon DSLRs on a 40 foot screen! *PhilipBloom.net.* <http://philipbloom.net/2009/12/12/skywalker/>.

Bloom passed the test and Lucasfilm used Canon 5Ds on selected scenes of *Red Tails* (2012), a story about an African American fighter squadron in World War II. Mike Blanchard, Lucasfilm's head of postproduction, wasn't sure if the footage would hold up on-screen. "Certainly when we just look at the footage and put it on a big screen it holds up way better than it has a right to," he says. A lot of people get caught up in the numbers game, comparing one type of camera to another, he continues, such as the argument that "film is 4 K, blah, blah, blah. You know, it's really not, because nobody ever sees a projected negative.[8] So by the time you do a release print and [put it] through its paces, it's no way near [what] a lot of people claim that it really is. So the great part about working at Lucasfilm, for people like Rick [McCallum] and George [Lucas]—working for them—is that you just show them things and that's where it ends. We don't do little charts about how it doesn't have that or it doesn't do that. We make it work. And that's just a beautiful way to do work, because it opens up everything" (Interview with Jared Abrams, 15 April 2010; http://www.cinema5d.com/news/?p = 3216).

HOLLYWOOD EMBRACES DSLR

When the finale of *House MD* (2010) was shot, director Greg Yaitanes and his team went with the Canon 5D Mark II. They previously shot on film. He noted that there is a stark difference between those who are shooting stories and those who are shooting test charts: "Somebody could sit there and say to me, 'Well, you know, I looked at the specs and this doesn't line up and this and that.'" But Yaitanes said the proof comes from working "out there in the field." We "told a story and people have had an emotional reaction to that story, and, frankly, again, that trumps everything"—and they continued to use the 5D in the 2010–11 season.[9]

The HDSLR cinema movement forced video camera companies to change how they approach their camera designs. In order to stay in the game—the demand for DSLR video was that big—they designed and released large sensor video cameras with interchangeable lenses. Initial cameras included the Sony FS-100 and Panasonic AF-100, with some bloggers announcing them as "DSLR killers." Not so fast. The DSLR killed the prosumer video camera market and they evolved in order to stay in the game. And they've got game. Steve Lawes, the DP for the British television series, *Sherlock*, shot *Convergence* on a Sony PMW-F3 (~$14,000 body), and as can be seen in Figure I.5, the color rendition and shallow depth of field looks like it was shot on a DSLR.

---

[8]The raw negative can go up to 6,000 lines of resolution, whereas a projection print (analog) is typically around 2,000 lines (but digital intermediate scanned films can go higher).

[9]Bloom, P. (April 19, 2010). Exclusive: In depth interview with Greg Yaitaines. *PhilipBloom.net.* <http://philipbloom.net/2010/04/19/in-depth-interview-with-executive-producer-and-director-of-house-season-finale-shot-on-canon-5dmkii/>.

FIGURE I.5
A still from Martin Scanlan's *Convergence*, cinematography by Steve Lawes. Note that shallow depth of field, low light capabilities, and color rendition. It looks like it was shot on a DSLR, but it's Sony's high end video camera sporting a large sensor and interchangeable lenses. (See Scanlan, M. and Lawes, S. (2011). *Convergence.* Vimeo.com. <http://vimeo.com/16898584>.)
(©2011 Steve Lawes and Martin Scanlan. Used with permission.)

Furthermore, Canon, in a challenge to RED, introduced 4K cameras in 2012, producing a video camera and DSLR model. In an interview with Shane Hurlbut at the 2012 National Association of Broadcasters in Las Vegas, he still emphasized the fact that all of the new cameras—from HD DSLRs to 4K—coming out are tools. Start with the story, he says:

> When you read a story, when you read that script and that script speaks to you, that script will tell you exactly the right tool to use. You used to only have two or three tools. Now you have twenty some odd tools at your disposal. As a cinematographer, I'm good at using multiple tools. So it's not just an Arri Alexa. Now it's the Arri Alexa mixed with the Canon C300, mixed with the 5D, mixed with the 7D. So it's like multi-formatting these wonderful tools to best tell your story. And I think right now we're at a crossroads. This is the next chapter and 4K is going to blow people's mind.

In the world of 4K, the clarity of the images is in no doubt.

"4K capture on Canon's 1D-C DSLR or the C500 is the closest that I've ever seen video look like film," Hurlbut exclaims in excitement. "And it's looking like Kodak film." After comparing RED and the Canon 1D-C 4K DSLR side by side, he felt that Canon had the edge: "It looked like I was watching 35 mm motion picture on the 1D-C, while the RED looked a bit more like video."

Hurlbut, continuing his interview, feels you're getting the best of both worlds with Canon's new cinema DSLR. "You're able to get all the beauty of the 5D sensor, but now in something that's even cleaner, faster, sporting a Canon log file, so you're able to have twelve and a half stops of latitude, and then it's something that looks and feels so cinematic and so sharp." The detriment to such a high resolution, however, is that it "shows all the cons of a face, and all the imperfections," he adds. But because Canon used JPEG compression, Hurlbut feels that it "rounds all of that incredible 4K sharpness off, just enough to make the skin look alive" without worrying about using a diffusion filter to help hide blemishes.

In the end, Hurlbut feels that it will depend upon the story whether it should be shot in 4K or some other tool. "The future is whatever tool best tells the story," he says. He feels that you need to "formulate a visual landscape and navigate it with the proper tools in order to tell that story best."

The Canon 5D Mark II and the Motion Picture Industry

Jared Abrams http://wideopencamera.com/

The Canon 5D Mark II has truly revolutionized the motion picture industry. Ironically, the camera's video capability was all done by mistake. A video engineer was visiting the stills camera division of Canon when he was shown the new Canon 5D Mark II. He simply said, "If you like, I can add video to that camera."

Here in Hollywood alone many major productions have adopted the Canon 5D MK II or Canon 7D as their A, B, or C cameras. It all started with the movie *Iron Man 2*. The 2nd Unit DOP was using the camera for stunt work. At $2,500 it was better than risking a camera operator's life and cheaper to have it destroyed during a stunt than any other camera available at the time. There were major flaws with the camera when it first came out. There was no manual aperture control, and it shot only true 30 P. Canon sent two engineers to the set, and within two weeks, they were able to add manual aperture control to the camera. The frame rate was the same but now the camera was a better tool for video work.

DOP Shane Hurlbut was also using the 5D Mark II as an additional camera for a Navy Seals movie (Act of Valor) he was shooting with multiple cameras and formats, ending up shooting most of the movie with 5Ds and 7Ds.

Philip Bloom was contacted by Rick McCallum of Lucasfilm to consult on using the Canon 5D Mark II for plate shots and eventually became an additional camera operator on George Lucas's new film *Red Tails*. DOP Rodney Charters of the hit show *24* was using the Canon 5D Mark II for plate shots and car mounts around Los Angeles.

The camera started popping up everywhere. By the spring of 2010, HDSLR fever had hit Hollywood. Ken Glassing, the Second Unit DOP for *NCIS*, had been using the Canon 7D for all kinds of work, such as motorcycle shots and POV shots from the trunk of a car. DOP Crescenzo Notarile had been using the 5D Mark II for B camera work on the *Ghost Whisperer*. *Californication* had one spinning on 2nd Unit, replacing a 16 mm Bolex. AMC's *Mad Men* began using a PL Mount Canon 7D for their new episodes. It now seemed as though everyone was using this new tool in his or her kit.

Then Gale Tattersall, the DOP of the show *House MD*, and Director Greg Yaitanes decided that the camera was a perfect fit for the small sets on an upcoming episode. This was the real test for the camera. Would it hold up under broadcast conditions for one of the most popular shows in the country? It passed with flying colors. The final episode was a hit, and everyone in the HDSLR community rejoiced.

Now it is no longer news if a show is shooting with HDSLRs. The Canon 5D Mark II, with its full-frame still sensor, has a certain aesthetic that cannot be achieved with any other camera. The use of shallow depth of field to help tell the story had been missing from the video toolkit for some time. There was a short time of DOF lens adapters, but that was only a temporary solution. Now with the shallow DOF of the Canon HDSLRs, we have that tool, and it comes at a bargain price. Anyone with a good story and a good eye can produce high-quality imagery with these cameras.

WHAT THIS BOOK IS ABOUT

This book is designed for people who want to open up the possibilities of using DSLRs and other large sensor video cameras as a cinema camera—whether they're shooting a wedding, a student thesis film, a documentary, video journalism, an independent film for a festival, or a feature. It's designed to help the DSLR shooter create cinema-quality HD video with the fewest possible people and least equipment—to maintain a small footprint of the one-person shooter, if needed, but with the ability to maintain a big vision, as Shane Hurlbut noted earlier.

Ultimately, video shooters can learn how to make their work look better by reading this book, but hooking that cinematic look to a good story is more than key. It's essential. It's what will impact an audience.

Philip Bloom, one of the gurus of DSLR cinema, best sums up the purpose of this book, as he explained to me the DSLR vision over breakfast at Venice Beach's Sidewalk Café:

> Suddenly we are giving people an affordable tool to make high-quality imagery, and it's releasing potential in people they never realized they had. There are people out there who never thought that they would be able to shoot high-quality images like this, that they would have the opportunity to do it. And they will go out and do it and they may not do it as a full-time job—and most of them [won't]—but it's the passion brought out in people that is just incredible.

This book is about taking that passion, that desire to shoot HD video with a large sensor camera, as if they were shooting film—and not as if they're shooting on an ENG or prosumer video camera. These cameras don't function like one of those. Instead, you must think like a cinematographer, rather than a videographer.

The simplicity of pointing and shooting a DSLR camera as if you were shooting a video camera with everything automatically set is not the way to go.[10]

---

[10] I'm exaggerating here. Many video users shoot everything manually, but the difference with a DSLR is that it reflects the purity of shooting on film—set lens with depth of field, set your lighting, meter it, set the f-stop, focus, and shoot.

And shooting a large sensor video camera in a point-and-shoot mode can be just as disastrous. Just as a cinema camera requires a solid understanding of lenses, focus, composition, depth of field, exposure, lighting, ISO (film exposure speed), color balance, and separate recording of audio, the large sensor shooter needs to approach projects in a similar way.

WHAT'S COVERED IN THE BOOK

This book assumes you already know how to shoot and edit. At the same time, the importance of basic cinematography will not be assumed, and even if you already have this knowledge, the review may be beneficial because the examples draw mainly from a DSLR perspective, with some large sensor video camera examples, as well. In either case, the first part of the book covers what I call the *cinematographer's toolkit*, the tools needed by shooters to attain a cinematic look, the "film look"—or at least a large sensor cinema aesthetic that sets your work apart from normal video.[11]

Chapters 1 through 5 include either a checklist or a set of steps, so you can plan each element as you begin to master it, or use each checklist as a helpful reminder. All the chapters include working examples from some of the best shooters in the field to illustrate the technical and artistic expression of cinematography. It's not an exhaustive overview of DSLR and other large sensor shooters, however. Only a few were selected for this book—based on availability and the author's sensibilities. In this edition, I include samples from my work—from using Magic Lantern in my Occupy Wall Street video (covered in Chapter 5), as well as a case study for a project my students and I did for the National Park Service in Utah (Chapter 13). In addition, I included a case study from one of my students using puppetry, so that student work could be represented in the book. There are many, many others that just could not be included. Chapter 6 covers postproduction workflow—updated for Final Cut Pro X, as well as Adobe Premiere—while Chapter 7 provides an overview and exercises on storytelling so you can quickly think about the number one reason to get a DSLR in the first place: to tell good stories.

The goal isn't to master the entire art and craft of cinematography in these chapters, but to expose you to some of the basic principles so you can begin shooting projects cinematically. Ultimately, the film look is actually different from the cinematic look of DSLRs, which can be referred to as a *DSLR cinema aesthetic* or a *large sensor video aesthetic*; however, I do refer to the film look throughout the book as a shorthand, a simple way to explore cinematic look that's far different from conventional video.

---

[11] Most of the examples and workflow discussion revolve around HDSLRs, because the focus of this book is really for low-budget shooters, who tend to shoot with DSLRs, and those who can't really afford high-end large sensor cameras. In either case, the principles are the same, whether you're shooting on a $600 Canon Rebel or a or a $5,000 Sony FS-100 or a $16,000 Canon cinema DSLR: Light and shadow, story, and proper camera settings.

Part 1, "DSLR Shooter's Toolkit: A Cinematographer's Guide to Crafting Astounding Images and Telling Better Stories," includes the following chapters:

1. "Composition, Blocking, and Camera Movement." This chapter provides the basics, the first tools needed to begin to master what it means to make cinema. It examines the golden mean in composition, the importance of working with actors to tell a story visually through body language, as well as why camera movement is one of the most powerful elements in cinematography.

2. "Lighting Your DSLR Shoot." Without an understanding of light and shadow, the DSLR shooter will never break out of the flat video aesthetic. Lighting sets the mood of every scene, and just because large sensor cameras are good in low light doesn't mean you should ignore the most important tool in cinematography.

3. "Exposing Your Shots with DSLRs" This chapter describes technical geek stuff, but cinematographers wouldn't consider themselves cinematographers without an understanding of how to utilize these tools to shape the look and feel of their digital films. A mastery of the tonal scale will teach you how much light to use on your subject and in the background. Exposure will help you determine not only how much light hits the sensor, but how much depth of field you'll have, while the ability to use a variety of lenses already sets the DSLR shooter's work apart from many video shooters.

4. "Using DSLR Picture Styles" Shane Hurlbut, ASC, says that with DSLR cameras, you have to get the picture close in-camera because there's not much latitude for color grading in post. Picture style is one of the most powerful tools DSLR shooters can use to get their look before shooting. The chapter also covers the use of flat and superflat settings, in addition to exploring how to change color temperature in-camera. Furthermore, the chapter has been updated to include Technicolor's CineStyle for my project, *Grand Canyon Winter*.

5. "Recording Quality Audio with DSLRs: Yes, It's Possible!" Not enough can be said about the importance of getting clean audio. It's more important than capturing a good picture. Poorly recorded sound will prevent an audience from seeing your film. This chapter goes over some of the technical aspects of microphones and includes recommendations for equipment. It also includes the best way to get the cleanest sound for DSLR shooters: the external audio recorder. It includes workflow for using Magic Lantern, a firmware hack that allows Canon DSLR shooters to get audio meters, headphone jacks, and focus assist in-camera—a really important tool for run-and-gun video journalists.

6. "DSLR Postproduction Workflow and Techniques" This chapter still details the steps required to convert DSLR footage into a form friendly for editing and color grading using Squared 5's MPEG Streamclip or Cineform's NeoScene, but these are not as important now, since Apple's Final Cut Pro X does it on import (into PreRes 422 in the background), and Premiere

5.5 and 6 allows you to edit these files natively without any conversion. In addition, it includes steps for using DualEyes, the software that will sync external audio recording with in-camera sound, but for those using Final Cut Pro X, it will sync files in one step. Furthermore, the chapter includes the fundamental steps for color correction in Final Cut Pro, as well as a basic overview of Magic Bullet, an easy-to-use and powerful color-grading software tool.

7. "Telling Better Stories with Your DSLR." This chapter is for those who want to make good on their traditional storytelling skills. It's one thing to buy a DSLR camera and start shooting, but to enter the world of professional cinema, a mastery of storytelling is essential. The chapter provides the basics of the three-act structure, covers the importance of visual storytelling through the actions characters take, and provides tips on writing good dialog. It uses Vincent Laforet's *Reverie* and Jamin Winans' *Uncle Jack* as case studies. In addition, it includes exercises on how to get good story ideas.

Part 2, "Master DSLR Shooters at Work: Case Studies," presents seven international case studies of master (and student) DSLR shooters at work. It includes examples of short fiction and short documentary projects.

8. "Crafting the Film Look with Postproduction" *Casulo* (2009), directed by Bernardo Uzeda, Brazil, 17 min. A team of Brazilian filmmakers put together one of the most visually attractive DSLR projects to date. The film, *Casulo*, was shot on a Canon 5D Mark II and earned the top Brazilian cinematography award in 2010. The director of the film, Bernardo Uzeda, told me that after a screening (the work was transferred to 35 mm film), some experienced postproduction people felt the print contained "such sharpness and rich colors that it looked as if it was shot in 65 mm. I think this kind of a result for a camera that costs even less than the lenses and accessories we were using is quite a revolution." For those with an eye for film, the Canon 5D Mark II stood out due to its VistaVision-size sensor. The before and after shots of postproduction noise removal and color grading included in this chapter reveal the importance of taking the time to do it right in post.

9. "Crafting the Film Look by Building a Rapport with Characters: *16 Teeth: Cumbria's Last Traditional Rakemakers* (2009), directed by Rii Schroer, England, 2:29 min." This short but sweet piece of documentary journalism by German photographer Rii Schroer shows not only how a one-woman team can get superb results when using a Canon 5D Mark II, but the care taken to build a rapport with her subjects actually helped achieve a cinematic feel, which was also shaped by avoiding the standard TV news style of shooting and narrating with a reporter's voice.

10. "Crafting the Film Look with Cinema Lenses: *A Day at the Races* (2010), directed by Philip Bloom, United States, 6:00 min." Neil Smith, mentioned earlier in this introduction, wanted Philip Bloom to shoot a project on a Canon 7D fitted with a special PL mounting plate that can take cinema lenses. Lenses are important to the DSLR shooter, but this project shows

what kind of look can be attained by using $20 K Cooke lenses. It reveals Philip Bloom's signature style with close-ups of faces in and around horse stables and a racetrack.

11. "Crafting the Film Look with Location and CGI: *The Chrysalis* (2010), directed by Jeremy Ian Thomas, United States, 6:54 min." The importance of getting the right location is highlighted in this case study, as Jeremy Ian Thomas shows off the capabilities of the Canon 7D in the salt flats of Death Valley, California; it also showcases how digital 3D graphics become incorporated into DSLR footage. In addition, it includes details from the preproduction meeting I observed before the team went out to shoot.

12. "Crafting the Film Look with Light, Composition, and Blocking: *The Last 3 Minutes* (2010), directed by Po Chan, director of photography Shane Hurlbut, ASC, United States, 5:18 min." I was on set during the shooting of this ambitious film shot over a period of five days with 18 different locations. This heart-rending story that flies by quickly shows off the power of cinematic storytelling with the Canon 5D Mark II. The chapter includes interviews with the writer-director, Po Chan, as well as with Shane Hurlbut, ASC, the cinematographer on the project.

13. "Crafting the Film Look with Sound Design" The Timpanogos National Monument, Utah: *Hansen Cave* (2:44 min) *Middle Cave* (2:09 min), and *Timpanogos Cave* (3:32 min), directed by Kurt Lancaster, United States."

14. "Crafting the Film Look with Puppets and Miniature Sets: *Gods of the Flies* (2012), directed by Danger Charles, United States, 5:53 min." is an examination of the crafting and shooting of puppets based on an Argentinian author's short story about how flies perceive heaven and hell. A solid example of capturing cinematic images using miniature sets and puppet work.

Part 3, "Getting the Gear," comprises the last two chapters of the book and breaks down what kind of equipment you can get on low budgets.

15. "DSLR Cinema Gear for Low Budget Shooters" provides a list of recommended gear for those shooting on a budget. It breaks the budget into three categories: one for students, one for video journalists and documentarians, and one for low budget fiction. The list is about affordability and small crews. It's no longer a large list as provided in the first edition, but rather the minimum needed to shoot. I don't go into supporting gear mounts, but recommend a camera, microphone, audio recorder, a tripod, and monopod for most situations. Keep the set-up simple and focus on the story.

16. "Conclusion: From Film to Low Budget Large Sensor Cinema." The final chapter details where we are and where we are going with HDSLR cinema.

This is one of the most exciting times to be a filmmaker. Potential filmmakers and students got excited with miniDV and the later prosumer HD, but these didn't really break through to the cinema world, other than with a few exceptions. When it comes to the HDSLR cinema revolution, there's been nothing like it in the history of cinema. The closest we got was the break-through by Richard Leacock and Robert Drew, who developed a portable 16 mm sync-sound film camera that changed how documentaries were made (see, for example, *Primary*, 1960).

What kinds of projects and what styles of filmmaking will develop from large sensor cinema? You, as a visual storyteller will pave the way for a new kind of cinema, a cinema that could never have been previously attained on such a small equipment budget.

Show us what you can do.

PART 1
DSLR Shooter's Toolkit

A Cinematographer's Guide to Crafting Astounding Images and Telling Better Stories

We bring a light into the darkness. We find the magic and structure the movie.

(Gordon Willis, ASC, Cinematographer of *The Godfather*)[1]

The importance of cinematography and its relationship to storytelling—whether you're shooting shorts, feature fiction, documentaries, news, weddings, or music videos—cannot be underestimated. To be a good shooter, you need to think like a cinematographer (whether or not you're doubling as the director). And cinematographers are fundamentally storytellers—the ones who translate a writer's words into images that draw viewers into the world. Without a compelling story, you simply have disassociated images. Beautiful images without a story may look good, but to get an audience to watch your digital film, the story is key, even if that story is a visual poem (such as Philip

---

[1] Fauer, J. (2008). *Cinematographer Style: The Complete Interviews, Vol. 1*, (p.395). American Society of Cinematographers.

Bloom's "People" series or his compelling short doc, *A Day at the Races*, featured in Chapter 10, or a short story with no dialog, such as Vincent Laforet's *Reverie*). Indeed, not-so-perfect images tied to a compelling story will hold an audience more than strong images linked to a poorly conceived concept or story. If you need to cover the basics, including tips on writing good dialog, take a look at Chapter 7, "Telling Better Stories with Your DSLR."

Cinematic style is essentially the way to express yourself through filmic language. Just as authors use words to describe a scene, a character, and action or a painter uses pigments and dyes to give form, shape, and color to a canvas, a director and cinematographer will use camera movement and lighting to express themselves. Indeed, the words *cinematography* and *photography* are interrelated—meaning to write with movement and light (*graph*: write; *cinema*: movement; *photo*: light). Shooting with a DSLR—a digital tool that approaches the mythic film look more nearly than any other video camera preceding it— you need to think about shooting your projects by means of camera movement (and stillness), as well as by light (and shadow). These are your fundamental expressive tools in telling your story.

If you ask cinematographers how to attain the cinema look, likely they'll respond against your expectations. You're really not attempting to create a mythical "film look," but rather trying to create the look and feel of the story you're trying to tell, cinematically. The first part of this book examines how to create the best possible image for your story. It includes several setups as described by working cinematographers who have created a look that matches their story's intent.

> The desire to attain a cinematic look with video was born out of the stark and flat pixilation of the video image, as opposed to the sharp but creamy soft look of film. One of the main reasons filmmakers have avoided using video cameras to shoot their movies (despite the potential huge savings) revolves around the inherent quality of the video look—an aspect of resolution and sensor property when it exposes light digitally. Furthermore, the video look also stems from an established way we perceive video in broadcast television—such as very contrasty images, facial tones not as natural as in film, very little details that can be seen in the shadows—so everything is often lit evenly, brightly, and results in the "video look."

This book shows you how to move away from the video look and will help you attain a cinematic look with DSLRs. But the ability to attain this look is highly subjective and what some people may tolerate as acceptable, others may cringe; however, very few can deny that a good story, well executed, trumps any kind of look. As a DSLR shooter, your goal should be to help reinforce the look and feel of a story through better cinematography. Not only are the stories you choose to tell up to you, but how they look and feel to an audience derives from the choices you make when shooting; the shot will feel different if your protagonist wears red versus green, for example. As Jon Fauer, ASC, says, the style—the look you're trying to attain—is what will grab an audience's attention. In a commercial, he notes, "You are trying to sell a product or idea, but you are also trying to grab people's attention, with the cinematography, the lighting, composition, and camera movement."

Allen Daviau, ASC, cinematographer for such films as Peter Weir's *Fearless*, Stephen Spielberg's *Empire of the Sun*, *ET: The Extra-Terrestrial*, and *The Color Purple*, among others, discusses one way he works with a director to get the "look" of the story: "looking at films, stills, paintings, and tear sheets out of publications." He continues by discussing how Raoul Coutard, cameraman for Jean-Luc Godard, used a similar approach:

> For a scene that shows a gentleman walking through a door, the left side of Godard's frame might have been inspired by a genre noir film from the '20s and the right side of the frame might have come from a poster he saw that morning on the Metro.

Just as there is no formula for writing a script or directing, there is no formula for cinematographers to create the look of a film—it's drawn on art, storytelling, a passage from a poem, a photograph, a poster, a visit to a museum, and much more. The inspiration and art come first. The technology—like the painter's brush—is used in service to the art.

The cinematographer for such television shows as *Malcolm in the Middle* and *Dawson's Creek*, Levie Isaacks, ASC, says that a cinematographer creates "the look of the film" by how "[y]ou select your film stocks. You select the kind of camera movement that you want to do. You select your lighting style: contrasty or not contrasty and the colors. Out of all those elements, you create the look of the film."

Andrew Laszlo, ASC, cinematographer for *Shogun*, explores the look of the film as a way to choose a style. This style, or look, should be drawn from "the subject matter," the story of the film, he says. After reading the script, Laszlo notes how "images begin to form in your imagination and in your vision." He wants to "impact the audience" with these images, so he "enhances" this reality:

> I have to bring something to that reality that will affect the audience as they look at the picture. Is it a happy day? Is it a sad day? What can I do to create an impression, an emphasis? Techniques and tools come into play—lenses, film stocks, filters, focal lengths, all kinds of gimmicks that an individual artist may come up with and say, "This is what I feel; this is what I'll do to enhance the image so it will serve the story best, as depicted by the script."

Like Isaacks, Laszlo realizes that the tools of the cinematographer are vast: film stock, lighting style, camera movement, lenses and focal lengths, filters—not to mention the time of day, the use of scrims, flags, and reflectors, lighting ratios, tone and color, and so on. Filmmaking—even more so than theater—is one of the most difficult art forms to master. A painter paints, a novelist or poet writes, a sculptor sculpts—all arts that are conducted in one medium (most of the time). In film, many different art forms and technology comprise the cinematographer's palette.

As a video shooter, you need to consider shooting like a cinematographer, not a videographer. So the first few chapters of this book cover the main elements you need to consider to make Canon DSLR video look more cinematic, and give you these techniques on a low budget. You don't need the full equipment package of a Hollywood production team (although that can help), but you can achieve this shooting solo, if needed. So the information in this book is useful not only for independent filmmakers, shooting both documentaries and fiction, but also for event and wedding shooters, video journalists, as well as students.

The first three chapters provide the foundation, the basic tools needed for shooters to craft a cinematic look with large sensor video—from composition to exposure. The fourth chapter describes how you can shape a cinematic look by manipulating the picture styles of DSLR cameras. Chapter 5 covers audio recording—one of the most important aspects in making a good film, while Chapter 6 presents the postproduction workflow. As I define these tools of the cinematographer, I include examples of how shooters approach them in their projects. The goal isn't to master the entire art and craft of cinematography in these chapters, but to expose you to some of the basic principles so you can begin shooting projects cinematically, to help express the film look.

The final chapter of this part, Chapter 7, "Telling Better Stories," is one of the most important, for if you do not know how to craft a good story, then your images will contain little meaning and will unlikely attract an audience. There are many books on telling stories, but this compact chapter provides you with core information so you can start telling better stories right away.

CHAPTER 1

Composition, Blocking, and Camera Movement

Composition, blocking, and camera movement are the building blocks of your story. They're intertwined like DNA. You cannot have one without the others, so this first chapter begins with defining these three elements and showing examples of how shooters compose their image along the golden mean, how they tell a story through the blocking of performers, and how they utilize camera movement poetically.

COMPOSITION

Your three-dimensional subjects and the scene they're in are composed through your lens. This composition relies on many factors, including lenses and shot sizes, as well as camera angles. But one underlying principle can't be understated: the *golden mean* appearing in nature, a ratio studied by mathematician and philosopher Pythagoras (whom you might recall from that high school geometry class). Many cameras are equipped with rule-of-thirds grid lines, which provide a decent way to compose your images—keeping eye lines on the top third of the image and your subject in either the right or left third, for example. But photographer Jake Garn argues that the Rule of Thirds isn't as naturally dynamic as the use of the golden mean, which we can see in one of his photos in Figure 1.1—the girl in the foreground composed along the golden mean.

Garn explains how Mario Livio explores this topic in his book, *The Golden Ratio: The Story of PHI, the World's Most Astonishing Number* (Broadway Books, 2003). The ratio provides a spiral and rectangular pattern that reflects a pattern found in nature and, when used by photographers and cinematographers, can create powerful compositions.

If you want to learn how to do this and train your eye to compose your images around the golden mean, the Shutterfreaks team—a group of photographers who have created a website with tips and tricks (shutterfreaks.com)—offer a Photoshop application that allows you to take stills of your compositions and

FIGURE 1.1
Jake Garn's photo with the golden ratio symbol laid out on top of it by the photographer.
(Photo ©Jake Garn [http://jakegarn.com]. Used with permission.)

see how well they fit within the golden mean. You may download Shutterfreak's application for Photoshop, so you can analyze a still within a golden mean grid; see http://www.shutterfreaks.com/Actions/RuleOfThirds.php.

Vincent Laforet's *Reverie*, shot on a Canon 5D Mark II was the first sensational DSLR web hit that highlighted the low-light capabilities of the camera. It features a man longing for a girl, failing to find her during a late-night rendezvous. Let's look at a few random stills and apply Shutterfreak's golden mean app in Photoshop, just to see how it holds up compositionally along the golden mean (see Figures 1.2–1.4).

Another aspect of composition includes creating the illusion of three dimensions by providing depth to a scene. The woman in Figure 1.4 appears to stand out from the background due to the fact that lights are on in the background—this gives the scene depth. Also, you may stage background and foreground characters and move them along different planes of action to signify the sense of depth as well.

Practicing with depth, light, and placement of your subjects is the best way to train yourself for good composition. Ultimately, there are no rules, only what looks and feels right for the story. But an understanding of where and why these rules work—and a mastery of them in your shooting—is important if you want to create powerful shots. Don't break the rules until you know how to use each of them well.

FIGURE 1.2
In the opening shot of Laforet's film, we can see how the man and woman kissing become the compositional center point, the naturally occurring spot on the "canvas," placing the Brooklyn Bridge in the background into balance. If Laforet had composed the characters dead center, the choice may not have been as compositionally powerful as the one he chose. Whether or not Laforet was conscious of it, the golden mean used as a tool helps provide compositional resonance to the scene.
(Still from Reverie. *©2008 Vincent Laforet. Used with permission.)*

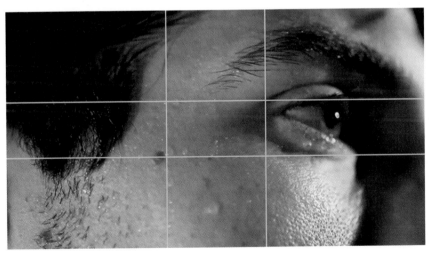

FIGURE 1.3
In this tight close-up, we can see again how Laforet's compositional choice resonates with power around the golden mean.
(Still from Reverie. *©2008 Vincent Laforet. Used with permission.)*

FIGURE 1.4
The woman waits for the man, but he'll be too late. Whether or not he was conscious of it, Laforet composed her along the golden mean, providing strong composition to the scene as the camera tilts up. Note the back light placement causing a rim light glow, as well as her shadow to fall across the ground right across the golden mean line, presenting a strong compositional vertical for the shot. (Three-point lighting setup is covered in the next chapter.)
(Still from Reverie. ©*2008 Vincent Laforet. Used with permission.)*

Checklist for Composition

1. Who owns the story and/or who owns the scene? Your compositional choice may revolve around your central character or characters. Know who they are so your composition can reflect the central power, point of view, and/or ownership of the scene.
2. What is in the frame? What you see is what you get. If you don't want something in the frame, get it out of the way or move your subject(s) until everything you see is meant to be there.
3. Place your main characters along the golden mean for strong composition. Follow the general principles of framing a character screen left if they're looking right and screen right if they're looking left. Keep eyelines around one-third from the top as a general rule. Break these rules when your story demands it.

Golden Mean Application

To use the Golden Mean application from the Shutterfreaks team in Photoshop, first download the app from http://www.shutterfreaks.com/Actions/RuleOfThirds.php.

How to Install the Actions
1. Open Photoshop.
2. If you haven't already done so, extract all the files from the ZIP file into a folder on your hard disk.

3. Click and drag the .atn file from that folder to your Photoshop window. If you look in the Actions window in Photoshop, you will see the action set appear there.

Using the Actions
Open the action set by clicking the little arrow just to the left of the name RuleOfThirds. You may need to scroll down in the Actions window to see the actions.

Open a photo you want to analyze.

Highlight one of the actions by clicking it, and then run the action by clicking the Play Selection arrow at the bottom of the Actions window.

The actions will make changes to a duplicate of your file so that you can protect your original.

Notes

1. If the Action window isn't visible, you can show it by going to the Photoshop menu and selecting Window/Actions.

2. If you'd like an action that will help you crop your images to conform to the Rule of Thirds and the golden mean, check out our Rule of Thirds Pro Action (http://www.shutterfreaks.com/Actions/RuleOfThirdsPro.html).

3. If you are new to using Photoshop actions, http://www.shutterfreaks.com/Tips/GettingStartedPS.html offers an introduction to the basics.

4. If you see an error similar to "The Command Make is not currently available," you may be running the action on a 16-bit image in an older version of Photoshop that doesn't support layers in 16 bits. To correct the problem, convert your image to 8 bits before running the action.

Your Shutterfreaks Team (Used with Permission)

BLOCKING

Blocking is where, when, and how subjects are placed and move in the composition, whether working with actors or characters in a documentary. How they are placed, when they move, where they move from, and where they go are dependent on the story. There should be nothing random because these movements (the blocking of the performers) need to be motivated; otherwise, random movements not grounded in the story will appear weak on-screen. The job of the director is to shape or choreograph the blocking (see Figure 1.5), while the cinematographer needs to capture these movements with the camera.

Po Chan's approach to blocking in *The Last 3 Minutes* (featured in Chapter 12) is as precise as her direction on all aspects of the short: "All elements in this short film, from casting and the music to the wardrobe; from makeup (the choice of lipstick color) to the hairstyle and hair color; from the patterns and textures of the set dressing pieces to the looks of the crystal itself, are all carefully chosen so that they all work in harmony to tell the story," she explains to me in an interview on set.

In the scene, Po takes time to set up the physical actions for actor Harwood Gordon, as his character William Turner has a heart attack and collapses to the floor. Po knows what she's looking for. She understands very well (and is glad) that Gordon has had no such experience before. She goes into extreme detail and wants Gordon to convey the pain in this moment. She explains to him the different layers of emotions that should be inside him in this scene. By doing so, she keeps the actor fresh in his imagination, and the physical action conveys that naturalness she's looking for. Some actors may be hands-off with the director, but Po says she looks for actors she can communicate with, heart to heart, look into their eyes, and know their feelings: "I trust them and I want them to know that they can trust me."

Every gesture Gordon does, every expression he makes, is carefully observed by Po. In this scene there is no dialog, so the physical actions are the main vehicle

FIGURE 1.5
Po Chan directs the blocking of William (performed by Harwood Gordon) in the opening sequence from
her short, *The Last 3 Minutes*.
(Photo © 2010 by Kurt Lancaster.)

to convey the story. "I trust my instinct within—it's always correct," she says.
She puts herself emotionally into the scene as she directs: "If my actor cries,
I cry. I apply myself to them. Even though I can only live one life, I can experience many more different lives through the art of cinema." Figure 1.6 shows
how the blocking in this scene is tied to the shots.

> There are several possible combinations of blocking with a camera:
>
> - A performer can stand still and the camera remains locked down.
> - A performer can stand still and the camera moves.
> - A performer can move and the camera is locked down.
> - A performer can move and the camera can move.

Each of the combinations described above changes the dynamics of the scene.
There is no "right" choice since it depends on an understanding of the story
and what you want to convey to the audience. Each scene has an emotion shift,
a change that alters the emotion of the scene, and an understanding of when
this change occurs will help you make the better choice.

For example, in this particular scene (refer to Figure 1.6), the camera remains
fairly static (with slight handheld motion, but no dolly or crane shots), and

FIGURE 1.6
A series of shots from the opening sequence of *The Last 3 Minutes* (Dir. Po Chan) reveal how her blocking visually reveals the story. The movements and position of Harwood Gordon's character, William, on-screen provides the information for an audience to understand what is going on; Shane Hurlbut's shots support the blocking by conveying these emotions through shot sizes, composition, and lighting.
(Stills from The Last 3 Minutes *©2010 Hurlbut Visuals. Used with permission.)*

the character moves. In the second image, we see a low camera angle looking up before it cuts to the third image, when Gordon drops into a tight close-up frame of the camera. These two shots contain the shift in the scene—conveying to the audience the suddenness of his heart attack in the first, while the close-up expresses his surprise and pain. This is the first time the tight close-up is used in this scene. It's the crux, the point where the scene shifts into a new direction. In the beginning of the scene, William is mopping the floor, alone with his thoughts. But in the close-up, we see his pain and struggle, and the scene shifts as he struggles for a meaningful heirloom in his pocket and his life flashes before his eyes. The filmmakers could have added camera movement at this point to emphasize this point, but it may have come across as melodramatic or overly manipulative, whereas the low angle followed by the tight close-up does the job in this particular instance.

In summary, blocking is the visual depiction of the story by actors' bodies—their body language, gestures, and movement through space—and this blocking must be tied to the shot, whether the camera is locked down or moves. In the opening sequence to *The Last 3 Minutes*, we can see how the story is fully told by not only how the character of William is composed in space, but how he moves and how the camera captures his movements. Whatever decision you make as a cinematographer when shooting be aware that blocking and camera movement are intrinsically tied together (see the next section on camera movement).

> Blocking is the visual depiction of the story by actors' bodies.

Checklist for Blocking

1. Who owns the scene—the point of view character? This is the character who, perhaps, has most to lose in the scene or the character impacted by the events in the scene. When you know who owns the scene, then, as the director, you can determine what the emotional state of this character is at the beginning of the scene and at the end of the scene: where does this change occur? You need to know this to be able to effectively block the scene (and determine how you'll emphasize this moment—through shot size/angle changes and/or camera and/or actor movement).

2. Set up your camera so that you capture not only the action of this character, but more importantly, the reaction of the character to the events occurring in the scene—especially where the scene change occurs. The character's actions and reactions will motivate where and what you capture on camera—and will help immensely in editing. The choices for blocking and the use of the camera include these four combinations:
   - A performer can stand still and the camera remains locked down.
   - A performer can stand still and the camera moves.
   - A performer can move and the camera is locked down.
   - A performer can move and the camera can move.
   The choice you make should be dependent on the needs of the story; this takes analysis (see Chapter 7 on stories for more details).

3. Make a list (mental or physical) of the shots you need to tell the story—and for editing, especially as it relates to the scene's emotional shift. Think about the actions of the characters and what they're doing from shot to shot. What shots do

you need to tell the full story when you edit? Where do the performers' eyelines take us? This is one good clue in choosing shots to edit, and a good shooter needs to capture these eyelines. What will the shots look like as you edit? Do you have enough shots? Can you condense several shots into one shot with camera movement? Documentary filmmakers the Renaud brothers mention how important it is for shooters to be editors: "We started out as editors as I believe all young filmmakers should do. If you can become a good editor first, it is easy to become a good shooter."[1]

CAMERA MOVEMENT AND STABILIZATION

If blocking expresses the movement in the composition of a scene, the camera movement moves the composition and will result in strong visual dynamics. Just as a character needs to be motivated before moving on-screen, the camera needs to be motivated in its movement. The camera's movement needs to be tied to character motivations and movements because the camera captures emotions and actions through its lens.

To quickly attain an amateur look in your DSLR projects, just handhold the camera and move around a lot. Controlling the movement of a camera takes discipline and proper tools. And DSLR cameras are less stable than typical video cameras; they're shaped for photography, not for handheld video movement. When you are engaging in handheld movement, the cameras are awkward and difficult to keep stable for longer sustained shots. One of the problems with handheld work is that it's hard; it's easy to make the movements unprofessionally shaky! Move in slow motion and make the camera feel heavy. It's easy to whip a light camera around and make it jiggle too much as the body of the DSLR shooter fails to remain still. You must Zen your body and focus your attention on the shot. In many of the shots of *The Last 3 Minutes*, Shane Hurlbut, ASC, handheld the camera, but his body was rock steady and the movements of the camera were slight and were never jerky.

Several companies have designed a variety of handheld and shoulder-mounted stabilization devices for helping with handheld shots. But they can still provide poor results if you're moving around and bouncing too much. Holding still, moving in slow motion, and moving as if you're carrying weights will help your handheld work. Proper stabilization, whether using a tripod or Zacuto's "Target Shooter," for example, when properly practiced, will help provide a professional cinema look.

When handholding shots, you may tilt up and down along the vertical axis (yaw) or move side to side, left to right (pitch). A roll occurs when you move front to back like a ship riding waves at sea (rarely used).

---

[1]Lancaster, K. (2010). Shooting in Haiti: an interview with the Renaud brothers. *Documentary Tech.* <http://documentarytech.com/?p=3489>

It's easy to whip light cameras around and make it jiggle too much as the body of the DSLR shooter fails to remain still. You must Zen your body and focus your attention on the shot.

One of the safest ways to get a clean shot is to use a tripod … when the story warrants it. It's one of the best ways to get stable and acceptable shots for DSLR projects, but the shots may appear too static, so some slight motion may be needed. Again, let your story determine the best way to convey the emotion you want in a scene. You may pan or tilt on a tripod (whether on a tripod or handheld), but be sure to move in slow motion to minimize shakiness and the "Jell-O effect" of the camera's CMOS sensor— when vertical lines shift diagonally while panning when you move the camera fast because the sensor speed is too slow to keep up with the movement. Also, remember that the longer the lens, the faster the apparent motion and the more unstable the shot will be when handholding. It may be best to use a tripod when using a long lens.

Panning a DSLR and the Jell-O Effect

A lot of video tests revealing how a fast pan can cause verticals to shift have been posted online. Critics point to these shifts as a weakness to the camera. At the same time, however, this issue doesn't seem to impact many professional filmmakers. Shane Hurlbut, ASC, says he's rarely encountered the problem. Vincent Laforet (dir. *Reverie*) recently said this about it:

> While the "Jell-O effect" exists with any CMOS sensor given their design, I didn't find it to be a factor in this project—or, for that matter—on any of my other productions. It's important to keep in mind that any camera out there, film or digital, has limitations on how fast you can pan it—especially when projected onto a large screen. In general,

a DP will always plan for this on any camera moves they are directing the speed of the camera's move. It's important to remember that a pan may look just fine on a 17″ monitor—but the same pan may be a bit painful for the audience's eyes on 50 foot silver screen. Unless you are doing dynamic and fast moving action sequences, where you are purposefully moving the camera at extremely high rates (*whip pans, running sequences, etc.*), I would say it's unlikely you will encounter issues with the "Jell-O effect."[2]

In the end, it's the DP's responsibility to know the strengths and weaknesses of his tools and to know how to shoot around those limitations.

Camera movement includes

- Pan: left to right on the tripod axis (see Figure 1.7a)
- Tilt: up and down on the tripod axis (see Figure 1.7b)

---

[2]Laforet, V. (2010, June 1). VW Spec Ad posted with behind scenes video. *Vincent Laforet Blog* <http://blog.vincentlaforet.com/2010/06/01/vw-spec-ad-and-canon-digital-learning-center/>, accessed 02.06.2010

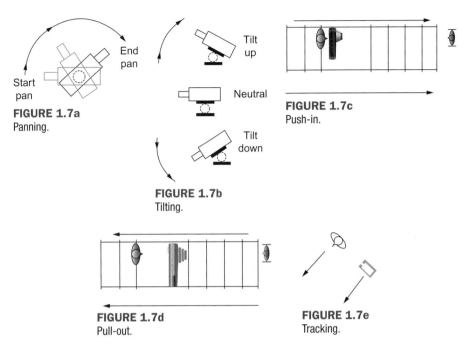

FIGURE 1.7a
Panning.

Tilt up

Neutral

Tilt down

FIGURE 1.7b
Tilting.

FIGURE 1.7c
Push-in.

FIGURE 1.7d
Pull-out.

FIGURE 1.7e
Tracking.

- Push-in through space (see Figure 1.7c)
- Pull-out through space (see Figure 1.7d)
- Tracking (or dolly): lateral movement through space (see Figure 1.7e)
- Crane: up and down movement through space

Despite the suggestion of using a tripod, one of the most powerful tools to create the film look revolves around camera movement—that poetic push-in or tracking shot that moves the viewer smoothly through the space of the cinematic world. But getting a dolly that works really well will blow the budget (let's face it, cheaper tripod dollies—tripods with wheels attached to them—just don't cut it). And the skateboard dolly or wheelchair trick goes only so far (and requires a smooth surface). Laying down tracks just isn't doable for most DSLR shooters, either.

However, there's an affordable way to get that high-end filmic look: the Kessler Crane Pocket Dolly Traveler, a fairly inexpensive device that can produce high-end results. In Philip Bloom's short, *Salton Sea Beach* (http://vimeo. com/10314280), he masterfully attains tracking shots by using this dolly (see Figures 1.8 and 1.9).

High-end dollies can be bulky and expensive. For low-budget DSLR shooters—especially those one man- and one woman-band shooters—the 25-inch pocket dolly (see Figure 1.10) becomes a portable solution that can be thrown in a tripod bag.

If the Pocket Dolly Traveler adds a rhythmic beat like a line of poetry, Ken Yiu's use of Tiffen's Steadicam Merlin presents a song. He achieved amazingly

FIGURE 1.8

Two stills from *Salton Sea Beach*, showing how subtly Philip Bloom slowly pushes in on a shot using the Kessler Crane Pocket Dolly Traveler, which allows for Hollywood-type dolly/track camera movements both laterally and in and out. (Note the change in the sides of the shot—the 2 × 4 in the bottom screen left is no longer visible above.) The slow push-in offers poetic power around its smooth rhythmic beat. Push-in shot from 1:31. Film shot on a Canon Rebel T2i with a variety of lenses. Color grading with Magic Bullet software. (©2010 by Philip Bloom. Used with permission.)

smooth handheld shots in *Wedding Highlights* with a Panasonic Lumix GH1 with kit lens (see Figure 1.11).

WEBLINKS

"Merlin Cookbook"
http://www.merlincookbook.
com/MerlinBetaBalInstr1-27.pdf
"Magic Formula"
http://www.merlincookbook.
com/formula.php

Tiffen's Steadicam Merlin balances the camera on a handheld support device, providing the ability to shape smooth handheld shots. It requires perfect balance based on the camera's and accessory's weight—so windy days are not good when using this tool outdoors. The "Merlin Cookbook" is a website that assists Merlin users to achieve balance with their particular camera. Instructions can be found there as a PDF file: http://www.merlincookbook.com/MerlinBetaBalInstr1-27.pdf. The site also includes a metric and English measurement scale to create the "Magic Formula" for balance; see http://www.merlincookbook.com/formula.php.

FIGURE 1.9
Philip Bloom sets up a tracking shot in his short, *Salton Sea Beach,* using the Kessler Crane Pocket Dolly Traveler on his tripod. By moving the camera on this micro dolly, the DSLR shooter can achieve high-end Hollywood-style cinema motion.
(©2010 Philip Bloom. Used with permission.)

FIGURE 1.10
The 25-inch Kessler Crane Pocket Dolly Traveler (version 1) used by Philip Bloom in *Salton Sea Beach*. The image in the foreground shows the product with the crank and belt. Bloom recommends the one with the crank because he feels it's "definitely smoother … and is quiet. I don't actually use the crank on the Pocket Dolly," he notes. "I find I get better results using it by hand, but the addition of the crank and belt system makes it smoother than the non crank one and I was able to get first takes almost every time" (Bloom, P. (2010, May 5). Kessler Crane's Motorized dolly tripod system now shipping. *PhilipBloom.net.* <http://philipbloom.net/2010/05/25/kessler/>)
(©2010 Kessler Crane. Used with permission.)

FIGURE 1.11
Ken Yiu achieved amazingly smooth motion in his *Wedding Highlights* using the Panasonic Lumix GH1 and the kit lens (14–140 mm, f/4-5.8) with Tiffen's Merlin Steadicam. Color grading with Final Cut Pro (see Yui, K. Lumix GH1-Wedding Highlights. *Vimeo.com*. <http://vimeo.com/6272661>.)
(©2009 Ken Yiu.)

FIGURE 1.12
Tiffen's Steadicam Merlin used by Ken Yiu on his poetically smooth project, *Wedding Highlights*.
(© Tiffen Corporation.)

Ken Yui's setup for his wedding shoot includes these settings (they only make sense for Merlin users who've read the manual; see Figure 1.12):

> GH1 + stock lens (+ low profile quick release)
> Front: |)
> Bottom: ||)
> Arc: −1
> Stage: −2
> Gimbal position: 32 mm
> Z: −5

Vladimir Chaloupka of Santa Fe, New Mexico, presents a video tutorial using a Canon 5D Mark II on the Tiffen page at http://www.tiffen.com/merlin_canon5d_qtmovie.html.[3]

WEBLINK
Merlin video tutorial using a Canon 5D Mark II
http://www.tiffen.com/merlin_canon5d_qtmovie.html

However smooth the Merlin may be, it does take considerable practice, including support, to make it really shine. For longer-duration shots, you may need some sort of wrist and/or waist support. Redrock Micro may also offer a more affordable way to go, but if you're really on a low budget and want the steadicam look, the do-it-yourself steadicam may prove useful (http://steadycam.org/). It costs about $14 in parts, but after having built and used one, you do get what you pay for: bulky and too heavy.

THE FRANKEN-CAMERA

By Travis Fox, 5 June 2010

Recently, a couple people have asked me about my (and these are not my words) *ghetto fabulous* or *franken-camera* Canon 7D video system (see Figure 1.13). In some ways, the DSLR system for me simply represents a better camera, not a fundamental

FIGURE 1.13
Travis Fox of Travis Fox Films (travisfox.com)—and formerly a video journalist for *The Washington Post*—didn't like the feel of DSLR cinema rigs, which to him felt as though he was carrying a shoulder-mounted video camera. He missed the feel of his Sony Z1U "cradling it like a baby or a football as is my practice," he says.
(Photo by Mark Mann ©2010 Travis Fox Films. Used with permission.)

[3]Chaloupka, V. On Steadicam Merlin and Canon 5D Mark II still camera. *Tiffen.com.* <http://www.tiffen.com/merlin_canon5d_qtmovie.html>

shift in video storytelling. Over the years, I've changed cameras when technology changed and quality got better but my style has more-or-less remained constant.

The biggest reason I had for not adopting the DSLR sooner was ergonomics. I could deal with the lack of timecode, the audio fixes, and the overheating, but I simply couldn't handhold the thing steady and interact with my characters at the same time. I wanted a DSLR built like the Sony Z1U, which I used lovingly for years. I checked out all the standard "rigs," the Zacuto and the Redrock Micro, but they seemed to push me towards holding the camera like a Betacam [shoulder-mounted camera], not cradling it like a baby or a football as is my practice.

In the end, I ended up saving money and getting a fit I could deal with. An $8 bracket (it's literally the cheapest flash bracket that B&H stocks) holds the Ikan monitor out in front to the left of the lens just like the Z1U. I splurged on the other bracket (it was a hundred bucks), which holds the audio gear and balances the camera out by moving weight to the back of the camera. …

With the ergonomics worked out, one of the first assignments I had was a series of stories with NPR's Adam Davidson in Haiti for *PBS/FRONTLINE*. As soon as I headed out in the hot Haitian sun I was soon confronted with a series of new issues to work out. The biggest surprise was the overheating. I had worked with 5D in the Chihuahuan desert in July, so I thought I was prepared, but in Haiti the 7D would shut down sometimes only after 30 minutes of shooting in the heat of the day. I quickly changed the way I work in order to minimize this DSLR flaw. (Fox, T. (2010, June 5). The Franken-Camera. *Travis Fox Films*. <http://blog.travisfox.com/>)

Philip Bloom, in *Cherry Blossom Girl*, utilized a variety of lenses, as well as Zacuto's tactical shooter around the streets of Chicago (see Figure 1.14).

Unlike the Merlin, where we see how Ken Yiu engaged smooth handheld movement while walking, Bloom stands still, allowing for a slight bobbing movement of the camera as the Tactical Shooter is braced against his body (see Figures 1.15 and 1.16). He's in full control of his 5D Mark II camera.

FIGURE 1.14
Still from Philip Bloom's *Cherry Blossom Girl* (see http://vimeo.com/5223767) was shot handheld with Zacuto's Tactical Shooter. Shot on the Canon 5D Mark II. The Tactical Shooter has since been replaced by a newer model, the Target Shooter.
(©2009 Philip Bloom. Used with permission.)

FIGURE 1.15
Bloom stabilizes his Canon 5D Mark II with Zacuto's Tactical Shooter (replaced by the Target Shooter
model), giving him the ability to engage fairly stable handheld shots. Attached to Bloom's 5D is the
Zakuto Z-Finder eyepiece for the camera's LCD screen and a Rode Video Mic. (Bloom, P. (2009, June 18).
Cherry Blossom Girl. *PhilipBloom.net.* <http://philipbloom.co.uk/2009/06/18/new-web-series-and-new-
short-film-on-canon-5d-mkii-the-art-fair/>)
(©2009 and courtesy of Philip Bloom.)

FIGURE 1.16
Zacuto's Target Shooter (the later model of the Tactical Shooter used by Philip Bloom in *Cherry Blossom
Girl*). Attach a Z-Finder, and you'll have an essential eyepiece for outdoor shooting. It not only adds
another point of contact to the body when shooting (for better handheld stabilization), but allows for
better viewing of the LCD screen because it includes either a 2.5× or 3× magnification.
(© 2010 Zacuto; http://store.zacuto.com/Target-Shooter.html.)

Checklist for Camera Movement and Stabilization

1. What does your story demand? Your story—the emotional intention you're trying to express in your shot—should indicate whether the shot should be locked down on a tripod or contain smooth movement (such as with the Pocket Dolly) or a little bit more rough (perhaps the Zacuto Target Shooter). Also, take note at what point in a scene the camera should move or stay still. This should convey the emotional shift in the story.

2. What angle of lens are you using? Long lenses = tripod in most cases. Normal and wide lenses = handheld and handheld stabilizers.

3. What kind of shot do you need? If you want the handheld look, providing a sense of immediacy or presence to the scene, then utilize a handheld stabilizer—such as the Steadicam Merlin—with a wide to normal lens. If you need a stable shot, no matter the lens size, then lock down the camera on a tripod.

4. Are you short on time? Do you need to "run and gun"? For video journalists and documentary filmmakers on the move, the handheld stabilizer, such as Zacuto's Target Shooter or Striker, or Redrock Micro's nano—RunningMan—will be best for quick setups and to get in and out of a scene quickly.

If the composition, blocking, and camera movement shapes the visual look of your film, lighting determines what the look *feels* like. No matter your lens choice, proper exposure, and ISO setting, a lack of understanding how to utilize light will destroy your cinematic look. A cinema-like camera will not provide a film look alone. Lighting is your most powerful ally in helping you sculpt a film look. Vilmos Zsigmond, ASC (*The Deer Hunter*), says that the "type of lighting we use actually creates the mood for the scene."[1]

This mood is what you, as the shooter, must try to shape and capture with your camera. It helps provide visual depth to your picture. If you shoot an off-white subject against a white wall, there's not much contrast—not much light and shadow—and the picture appears flat. If you shoot somebody white against a dark background, the person stands out, and if you add background lighting to the scene, the depth increases. Because of the large sensor of DSLRs and some advanced video cameras—along with high ISO settings for DSLRs and the video camera's comparable gain settings—they maintain a strong advantage over small chip video cameras because of the capability to shoot in natural and practical low-light situations. Fewer lights are needed on set.

The quality of light refers to what it *looks* like and what it *feels* like. What it looks like is what you see on the surface. The feel, on the other hand, conveys the emotion shaped by lighting. You can craft the look and feel of a film by paying attention to:

1. Light quality
2. Light direction
3. Light and shadow placement
4. Color temperature

Craft the look and feel of a film by paying attention to:

1. Light quality
2. Light direction
3. Light and shadow placement
4. Color temperature

LIGHT QUALITY 1: SHOULD IT BE HARD OR SOFT?

Hard light is direct, producing harsh shadows, and results in a high level of contrast. This can come from a sunny day or an unshaded light pointed directly

---

[1] Fauer, J. (2008). *Cinematographer Style: The Complete Interviews, Vol. 1.* (p.332). American Society of Cinematographers.

FIGURE 2.1
Steve Lawes utilizes a soft three-quarter frontal key light while utilizing a shallow depth of field using a Sony PMW-F3 Super 35 mm HD video camera in *Convergence*, directed by Martin Scanlan. In addition a hard light source is utilized as a three-quarter rear "kicker", the harsh light providing tonal contrast to the shot, due to the stark brightness opposed to the soft quality key coming from the left front. Shot on a Sony PMW-F3. (See Scanlan, M. and Lawes, S. (2011). Convergence. Vimeo.com. <http://vimeo. com/16898584>.)
(©2011 Steve Lawes and Martin Scanlan. Used with permission.)

at a subject. Hard lights are especially effective as backlight and rimlight sources, such as the example in Figure 2.1.

Soft light is indirect, created by reflecting or diffusing the light—an overcast day or a scrim or sheet dropped between the light source and the subject, or simply bouncing light off a white art board, or even reflecting light off a wall or ceiling. This type of light provides low contrast to the image (see Figure 2.2).

One of the counterintuitive properties of light is the fact that as the lighting instrument is brought closer to the subject, the softer the lighting gets, while farther away, the harder it is because it becomes more of a point source, causing the hard light quality to stand out. A diffused light source from farther away may convey a harder light quality than a low-watt Fresnel lamp up close.

LIGHT QUALITY 2: DIRECTION

The direction of the light will determine the placement of shadows and, consequently, the physical texture of objects and people. There are fewer shadows when the lighting is on-axis of the camera (the front). Shadows increase as the light shifts off-axis of the camera and to the rear of your subject. Light from the side will increase the texture of the scene. When lighting is "motivated," it refers to a light from a particular source, such as a fireplace, window, lamp, or the sun. In the medium close-up of Evie Bicker in the still from Scanlan's *Convergence* (see Figure 2.2) shot on a Sony PMW-F3 HD video camera with a Super 35 mm

FIGURE 2.2
A woman sitting at an outdoor cafe in Martin Scanlan's short, *Convergence*, director of photography by Steve Lawes. A high three-quarter key highlights the left side of her face, while soft shadows sculpt her cheekbone with soft-quality light. Shot on a Sony PMW-F3. (See Scanlan, M. and Lawes, S. (2011). *Convergence*. Vimeo. com. <http://vimeo. com/16898584>.) *(©2011 Steve Lawes and Martin Scanlan. Used with permission.)*

sized sensor, a high three-quarter key highlights the left side of her face, while soft shadows sculpt her cheekbone with soft-quality light, the light motivated by a sunlight. Her dark clothing and well-lit face provides high contrast in the scene, making her expression stand out. (The bright pink scarf also punches the scene with color, again making her stand out in the scene.) This light was likely scrimmed providing a soft look and feel on the woman. If the scene expressed hard light and shadows a totally different feel would shape the scene. As an additional note, the saturation of color is more prominent when the source is from the front, while colors become desaturated when the lights are placed in the rear.

Light Placement Terminology

- Key: The main light source of the scene (a window, a table lamp, overhead lighting, a fireplace, and so forth). Know where your motivated light source is and add lights, if needed, to reinforce it accordingly. Can be hard or soft quality.
- Fill: Lights used to fill in shadows caused by the key light. Usually a soft quality.
- Back and Rim: Lights placed behind characters to separate them from the background. A rim light specifically is placed high with the light falling on a character's head, her hair lit in such a way as to differentiate her from the background.
- Background: Lighting occurring in the background of the set, designed to separate it from the foreground, giving the scene visual depth. These could be street lights, lights in a store, a hallway light inside, and so forth.

Following are a series of stills from a variety of DSLR and large sensor video shooters' work, each one illustrating a different light source direction.

Light Source Direction: Side

A side key light on the front of the face brings out the main features of the character, the emotions expressed by the face (see Figure 2.3).

FIGURE 2.3
In Philip Bloom's *San Francisco's People*, he utilizes practicals from street lamps to light his subject. (See Bloom, P. (2009). *San Francisco's People*: Canon 5DmkII. <http://philipbloom.co.uk/dslr-films/san-franciscos-people-canon-5dmkii/>.) Shot on a Canon 5D Mark II; 50 mm f/1.2 lens with Zacuto Z-Finder (eyepiece adapter).
(©2009 Philip Bloom. Used with permission.)

Light Source Direction: Side

FIGURE 2.4
In this still from Rii Schroer's *16 Teeth: Cumbria's Last Traditional Rakemakers* (featured in Chapter 9), we see how Schroer utilizes side lighting to highlight the features of her subject. Side lighting brings out texture because it reinforces shadows, as we can see with the man's wrinkles (on-axis light will lesson shadows). Fill light reflects back onto the man's screen-right face to help ease out the shadows (light from a window). Backlighting provides a sense of depth to the frame. Shot on a Canon 5D Mark II. Canon 24–70 mm/2.8 lens. (See Schroer, R. (2009). *16 Teeth: Cumbria's Last Traditional Rakemakers*. Vimeo.com. <http://vimeo.com/4231211>.)
(©2009 Rii Schroer. Used with permission.)

Light Source Direction: Back

FIGURE 2.5
Steve Lawes utilizes the backlight of street and city lamps (in a shallow depth of field), creating a silhouette of the two leads in *Convergence*. Backlight from a low angle, rear, provides a colored rim light around his performers shaping a colorful shot with the cityscape in the distance. Shot on a Sony PMW-F3. (See Scanlan, M. and Lawes, S. (2011). *Convergence*. Vimeo.com. <http://vimeo.com/16898584>.)
(©2011 Steve Lawes and Martin Scanlan. Used with permission.)

Light Source Direction: ¾ Rear

FIGURE 2.6
A three-quarter rear key provides a hard quality light source on the face of Neil Henry sculpting strong shadows on his face. A fill light from the left side removes some of the shadows. Shot on a Sony PMW-F3. (See Scanlan, M. and Lawes, S. (2011). *Convergence*. Vimeo.com. <http://vimeo.com/16898584>.)
(©2011 Steve Lawes and Martin Scanlan. Used with permission.)

Light Source Direction: Front

FIGURE 2.7
This frontal key light from Scanlan's and Lawe's *Convergence* brings out the full emotion of loss and longing in the character (performed by Neil Henry), with just the hint of a soft shadow screen right. Notice the eyes contain a glint in them. Frontal lights make characters come alive through eye lights. Some cinematographers will add an eye light to bring liveliness to the shot. Shot on a Sony PMW-F3. (See Scanlan, M. and Lawes, S. (2011). *Convergence*. Vimeo.com. <http://vimeo.com/16898584>.)
(©2011 Steve Lawes and Martin Scanlan. Used with permission.)

Light Source Direction: ¾ Frontal Key

FIGURE 2.8
This still from Vincent Laforet's Reverie utilizes a ¾ frontal key (Profoto 7B head with reflector and modeling lamp with bare head) from a high angle, emphasizing the beauty and dramatic look of the woman. Backlighting is shaped from available (practical) street lamps and also causes shadows to fall into the foreground of the shot. The higher the backlight, the shorter the shadow on the ground (but not the face). Shot on a Canon 5D Mark II, 50 mm lens at f/2. (See Laforet, V. (2008). *Reverie*. Vimeo.com. <http://vimeo.com/7151244>.)
(©2008 Vincent Laforet. Used with permission.)

FIGURE 2.9
The setup for the shot featured in Figure 2.8. Vincent Laforet, screen right, sits behind the camera, while we can see the break lights on the vehicle casting red light onto the model. *(Photo courtesy of Vincent Laforet.)*

FIGURE 2.10
In the opening sequence to Laforet's *Reverie*, we can see how he crafted a night look for this scene. Soft light (with a blue gel to color the scene) from above left lights the actor's face, while one from the front hits his feet. The light is tightly controlled, minimizing spill, so as to enhance the shadows in the space. The lack of a backlight also helps accent the darkness and provides the night-time feel. Shot on a 5D Mark II. (See Laforet, V. (2008). *Reverie*. Vimeo.com. <http://vimeo.com/7151244>.) *(©2008 Vincent Laforet. Used with permission.)*

Note: If you're shooting in the daytime and need to make it look dark, use blue gel filters with a high hard light (representing the moon) and desaturate the colors.

LIGHT QUALITY 3: LIGHT AND SHADOW

Shadows bring out drama and are essential when creating a night scene (see Figure 2.10). Related to light direction is the placement of shadows. The direction and height of the light determine how shadows fall in the cinematographer's composition. Lights from the front will minimize shadows, whereas lights from the rear will increase the amount of shadows seen on camera. The higher the light source, the shorter the shadow. If you want long shadows, shoot at sunrise or sunset, or place your lights low, instead of high, in the background. Side lighting will increase texture.

LIGHT QUALITY 4: COLOR TEMPERATURE

Digital sensors see lights differently than people do. Computer chips are not as smart as human perception and have a hard time adjusting precise and subtle differences in color caused by different kinds of light sources. Different chemicals burn at different wavelengths, producing different color qualities depending on whether the lamp is halogen, tungsten, fluorescent, sunlight, and so on. Also, sunlight changes its color temperature depending on the time of day and whether or not it's cloudy (see Figure 2.11). Color temperature is measured in degrees Kelvin (K).

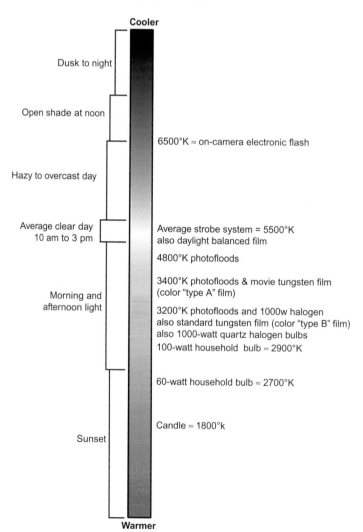

Color temperature, daylight & light bulbs

Cooler

Dusk to night

Open shade at noon

6500°K ≈ on-camera electronic flash

Hazy to overcast day

Average clear day
10 am to 3 pm

Average strobe system = 5500°K
also daylight balanced film

4800°K photofloods

3400°K photofloods & movie tungsten film
(color "type A" film)

Morning and
afternoon light

3200°K photofloods and 1000w halogen
also standard tungsten film (color "type B" film)
also 1000-watt quartz halogen bulbs
100-watt household bulb ≈ 2900°K

60-watt household bulb ≈ 2700°K

Candle ≈ 1800°k

Sunset

Warmer

FIGURE 2.11
An overview of the color tones during different times of day. Sunset can also refer to sunrise. The warmer and cooler label refers to the quality of the tones, not to actual temperature.
(Based on image from http://www.freestylephoto. biz/camerakh.php, accessed 28.02.2010).

Our eyes adjust to these varying color temperatures automatically. Indoor settings for cameras are usually set at 3200 K, whereas outdoor settings are usually at 5600 K; both of these numbers are averages for indoor tungsten lighting and outdoor daylight. Even though cameras have automatic white balance systems, the white balance setting of your camera allows you to adjust the setting manually. You may set your camera to manual mode and adjust it with a white or gray card. The Canon 5D and 7D, as well as the Panasonic Lumix GH series, include adjustable color temperatures you can select with the dial (Philip Bloom refers to this as "dialing in the color temperature"). Balancing correctly is important so that you can control your image. Sometimes you may want to experiment with color temperature as a way to change the look of the scene, but you should always control this important element of lighting (see Figure 2.12).

Cinematographer's Tip

Color Temperature
Shane Hurlbut, ASC

You have to get the in-camera look as close as possible to the final vision for the project. It's an 8-bit color space, 4-2-0. It is compressed and that color space can be limiting. I find it is the compression that makes it look the closest to film, so embrace it. As a cinematographer, you really need to micromanage the color temperature. If you want a day exterior to feel consistent throughout a day from morning till sunset, you need to start with your color temperature so that it is consistent with that of the sun. In the morning it could be around 3400 degrees. To keep the light looking white and not orange, you will need to set your color temp at 3400 Kelvin. By midday it should be around 5200 to 5500 Kelvin. You repeat the same approach at sunset. We had a sequence in *Act of Valor* on a dry lake bed that posed for a landing strip in the Horn of Africa. We started before the sun came up and were there until it went behind the Sierra Nevada at around 7:45pm. I used this micromanaging approach and the image is so consistent. In the final color correction we hardly had to do any manipulation other than dialing in contrast. (Hurlbut, S. (2009, Nov. 9). Collision Conference. *Video.* <http://shanehurlbut.smugmug.com/Professional/CollisionConference/10137672_ia4ZS#697099091_Bqx5z-A-LB>, accessed 28.05.2010).

In addition, many of these cameras allow you to create presets for the picture look. Several DSLR shooters have mimicked the look of a variety of film stocks to create different looks as well. (See Chapter 4 for details on adjusting color temperature, as well as steps for shaping your picture style.) In addition, post-production color grading allows you to further shape the look of your project (Philip Bloom, for example, uses Magic Bullet software to utilize color grading plug-ins to achieve his looks).

There is no one way to determine color balance. Do you balance for tungsten if you're indoors near a window, do you just go with the camera's preset (daylight, indoor, outdoor shade, and so forth), or do you dial it in? You need to look at the image and think about how it relates to the story to best determine

FIGURE 2.12
Three shots of the same model using three different color temperatures. The middle one is "correct." The first one is too blue, and the third is too warm for the standard look. However, the color temperature is a guide; you may decide the warm image is the color temperature you're looking for to capture the feeling of your story.
(Photos by Kurt Lancaster.)

White Balance Tip
Do not manually white balance during a sunrise or sunset because you would be adjusting the nice golden flow into white, and you don't want to lose the golden glow! During the sunset scene in *The Last 3 Minutes*, Shane Hurlbut, ASC, dialed in his color temperature at 4700 degrees K (see Figure 2.13).

FIGURE 2.13
Shane Hurlbut, ASC, dialed in the color temperature to 4700 degrees Kelvin for the beach scene from *The Last 3 Minutes* (featured in Ch. 12). Shot on a Canon 5D Mark II. (See Chan, P. and Hurlbut, S. (2010). *Last 3 Minutes*. Vimeo.com. <http://vimeo.com/10570139>.)
(©2010 Hurlbut Visuals. Used with permission.)

what you need. Shane Hurlbut, ASC, dials in his color temperature by eyeballing the monitor or the camera's LCD screen and getting the look as close as he can get it before turning it over to postproduction. Others suggest using the presets for consistency depending on the lighting type you're in, and setting manual white balance only when in a mixed lighting setup (halogens, fluorescents, incandescents in one room, for example). The Canon 7D tends to go a little red when shooting indoors with the incandescent setting.

SAMPLE LIGHTING SETUPS

The following stills and diagrams with brief explanations show basic setups for shooting outdoor day, outdoor night, indoor day, and indoor night as tied to the idea of composition and light quality.

Outdoor Day (Soft and Hard)—Philip Bloom's *Cherry Blossom Girl*

When shooting outdoor locations, time of day and weather are the two most important factors to consider; they determine your light source and shadows. Big-budget films may use generators with daylight lamps, but when shooting a documentary or an outdoor wedding, for example, you need to be aware of the sun's location because it will be the primary light source (see Figures 2.14 and 2.15). Mornings and afternoons tend to provide better shooting because the color temperature will provide warmer skin tones; it will also provide

FIGURES 2.14 AND 2.15
In these two stills from Philip Bloom's *Cherry Blossom Girl*, we see how he utilized the position of the sun to light the same subject in two different ways. In the first, we see the woman lit from the side with soft-quality lighting, reflected sunlight causing fill light on her right side. In the second shot, Bloom places the woman so she's lit by a high key sun from ¾ back, acting as a hard rim light, which causes a glow around her hair and shoulders. The sunlight reflects back onto her face, acting as a soft fill. (See Bloom, P. (2009). *Cherry Blossom Girl*. Vimeo.com. < http://vimeo.com/5223767>.)
(©2009 Philip Bloom. Used with permission.)

long shadows, so you can shape the look around this light and shadow placement. However, when shooting during the "golden hour," you'll have less time to shoot and a bit more challenge in post to match the color temps from shot to shot (and sometimes within the shot) because the lighting is changing quickly (and thus the color temperature). In addition, to soften the quality of the light, you may want to use a scrim to remove the harshness of the light on a subject's face, or you may want to bounce light off a reflector to provide fill light.

Indoor Day—Philip Bloom's *Cherry Blossom Girl*

FIGURE 2.16
In this shot, Bloom utilizes an open doorway to provide a key light on his two subjects inside. The rear side lighting lights the screen left side of the couple, while a bit of reflected light on screen right helps add a bit of fill to the scene. Notice the color temperature of warm hues, compared to the cooler tones of the woman in Figures 2.14 and 2.15. Shot on a Canon 5D Mark II. (See Bloom, P. (2009). *Cherry Blossom Girl*. Vimeo.com. <http://vimeo.com/5223767>.)
(©2009 Philip Bloom. Used with permission.)

Outdoor Night—Martin Scanlan's and Steve Lawes' *Convergence*

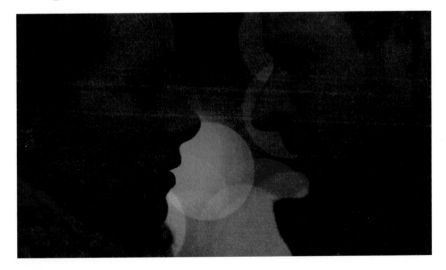

FIGURE 2.17
In this shot from Scanlan's and Lawes' *Convergence*, we see a tight close-up of Evie Bicker and Neil Henry as they are about to kiss. The shot is sculpted with a shallow depth of field, creating bokeh from the out of focus lights in the background. Due to the different colored lights, this effect creates a romantic feel for the scene, with soft red and bluish lighting used faintly on the performers' faces, the lighting designed to reflect the lighting seen in the background. Shot on a Sony PMW-F3. (See Scanlan, M. and Lawes, S. (2011). *Convergence*. Vimeo.com. <http://vimeo.com/16898584>.)
(©2011 Steve Lawes and Martin Scanlan. Used with permission.)

FIGURE 2.18
Rii Schroer utilizes sunlight from a window as her key light in *16 Teeth: Cumbria's Last Traditional Rakemakers.* The light bounces off the back wall and ceiling, acting as fill light on the characters. A fireplace also adds backlighting screen left. For additional details, see Chapter 10. (See Schroer, R. (2009). *16 Teeth: Cumbria's Last Traditional Rakemakers.* Vimeo.com. <http://vimeo.com/4231211>.) *(©2009 Rii Schroer. Used with permission.)*

Indoor Day—Rii Schroer's *16 Teeth: Cumbria's Last Traditional Rakemakers*

In shaping the interior during the day, many cinematographers will use windows for short shoots (see Figure 2.18). They may add in a daylight lamp from the direction of the window on longer shoots, so as not to lose light direction when the direction of the light changes over the course of a day.

Indoor Night—Vincent Laforet's *Reverie*

FIGURE 2.19
Beauty dish light from above with grid. TV light in front with blue screen. Rim light with bare bulb from behind couch. Lens: 1.2, 85 mm at f/2. (See Laforet, V. (2008). *Reverie*. Vimeo.com. <http://vimeo.com/7151244>.)
(©2008 Vincent Laforet. Used with permission.)

Checklist for Lighting

1. The *quality* of the light: hard or soft; direct lighting or bounced (or scrimmed) lighting for each light you're going to use.

2. The *kinds* of light you're using: key, fill, back, background. (Yes, there are many different types of lights—from sunlight with a reflector to hardware store halogen work lights, but you need to determine how they're going to be utilized.) Many scenes will have all four of them, but there's no rule. Sunlight with a reflector may be all that's required. With DSLR cameras, Philip Bloom says that he tries to use as much natural and practical light as possible before bringing in other lights. When necessary, he uses LED and Kino Flo Divas, and he stresses the importance of some LED light in front to light the eyes of the performers. But he's an experienced shooter. If you're more of a beginner, practice with three-point lighting until you can really "see" the light around you and how you can use it to your advantage and use such material as bouncing light off a white t-shirt, for example.

3. Light *placement* of each light. A frontal ¾ key will make the scene look different than a rear ¾ key with a frontal fill light. Lighting placement will determine shadow placement, all of which will convey a different mood.

4. Lighting zones or *contrast* range
   A. Will everything be lit evenly?
   B. Will there be some contrast between bright and darker areas?
   C. Will there be great contrast between the light and shadows?
   D. Will you need to scrim the lights to dim them, use a dimmer, move lights closer or farther away from the subject?
   E. Do you have shutters on the lights to control where the light falls?
   F. Do you have blackout scrims (flags) to control where the light and shadows are placed?

5. If you're shooting outdoors, what *time of day* will provide the best mood for the scene? Because sunlight is your key light source, it will determine to a large extent the mood of your scene. A high-contrast scene with harsh light might be best during late morning through early afternoon, while early morning or early evening will provide the golden hour look with long shadows and rich sunlight hues. Use of reflectors and scrims will help you control outdoor lighting. Night shots may require additional lighting setups if there aren't enough practical lights (from storefronts and streetlamps, for example).

6. Control your *color temperature*. Indoor lighting is different than outdoor lighting. A fluorescent light will look different than an incandescent bulb. Know your primary light source and adjust your white balance accordingly.

CHAPTER 3
Exposing Your Shots with DSLRs

THE ZONE SYSTEM, HISTOGRAMS, AND ISOs

One of the tools to shape the ratio of light and shadow revolves around the zone scale—an arbitrary scale indicating the tonal values from dark to light in an 11-step black–grey–white gradation, numbered 0–10 (0 = black; 10 = white; see Figure 3.1). Zones 0–3 represent black and deep shadow values (details and texture in an image can begin to be seen in zone 2, while 3 shows dark details and some texture, and 4 reveals landscape shadows and dark foliage). In addition, zones 4–6 represent face tones (from dark-skinned to Caucasian facial tones). The mid-gray of 5 represents brown skin tones and sky; this is also the value of an 18% gray card used for white balance. Zones 7–9 hit lighter greys and highlights (an 8 would reveal texture in snow, whereas 9 would represent blown-out highlights, and 10, pure white). Each zone number indicates a doubling in brightness from the previous zone; the gray in 6 is twice as bright as the gray in 5; the gray in 7 is four times brighter than 5 (each step is a multiple of two). The black in 1 is half as bright as in 2. The doubling and halving of the grey scale is similar to the doubling and halving of the exposure range in f-stops.

Shane Hurlbut, ASC, explains, "Film has about 13.5 stops of latitude. Eight of these fall in the over-exposure (highlights) while 5.5 falls in the underexposed areas (the shadows)." The Canon 5D Mark II "goes in the other range,"

FIGURE 3.1
Zone scale from 0–10, referring to a quantification of a black-to-white gradation. One zone is twice as bright as the next when moving toward the white, while it's half as bright when moving toward the black. This matches the changing values of f-stop settings.
(Based on Zone System. Wikipedia.com. <http://en.wikipedia.org/wiki/Zone_system,> accessed 28.02.10)

Hurlbut explains. "It's got 7 in the under and 4–5 in the over." He adds: "So you're not able to handle highlights as well" as in film with the 5D.

Simply put, the zone scale is a tool filmmakers can use to train their eye in controlling how much light should be in a scene—to properly shape the exposure range of cameras. Don't use it as a technical tool for every shot, but practice with it so you can begin to see the potential range of darks to brights and learn where your camera can handle the exposure range.[1]

SHOOTING TIP FOR ADVANCED DSLR SHOOTERS

For those who really want to master this material and get the most out of postproduction imaging—especially if you want to use Magic Bullet Looks, shoot in a "flat" mode (such as Technicolor's CineStyle for Canon DSLRs), making the image low contrast; don't crush the blacks and avoid blowing out the image. The shot may look flat in-camera, but in post, you can make it shine. If you have a laptop on set, you can test the flat look, shoot an image, and color grade it to see how it looks. You could also switch to a different non-flat picture style to test the look. Shooting flat will give you the most flexibility in post. Details on how to engage a "flat" picture style are covered in the next chapter, "Using DSLR Picture Styles: Pitfalls of Presets and Creating Custom Styles."

---

[1]The dynamic range refers to the luminance range of the setup—the ratio of brightest to darkest areas of the shot. In general, video has about a 4½ zone scale range (different formats will go higher or lower, whether you're using miniDV—less, or DigiBeta—more), whereas DSLR cameras with large sensors can double that. Generally, video can express a contrast latitude ratio of 25:1, whereas film has 256:1 ratio (each zone is a doubling of brightness, so four zones is 16 times difference, 8 zones is 256 times difference). Knowing this, you can make choices as to proper exposure for a person's face; for example, lighting the set accordingly so that your ratio stays within four to five zones and letting the rest fall off. And if you want the audience to see details throughout the shot, you can set up your lights so that everything stays within four zones, for example. The contrast ratio for video cameras reflects their small chip sizes ⅓ to ½ inch. Such DSLR cameras as the Canon 5D and 7D contain much larger chips, the 5D provided the largest, allowing over eight zones of exposure according to Shane Hurlbut, ASC. Jeremy Ian Thomas, a colorist at Hdi RAWworks in Hollywood, says he can get two stops of latitude in the shadows with the Canon 7D if it is shot "superflat," a picture style mode that provides low contrast.

Each of the camera's exposure settings (the f-stop or T-stop), matches the change in the zone scale; a stop down will halve the value of the exposure, whereas opening one stop will double the brightness. So the filmmaker can take advantage of the zone system by either setting up lights and adjusting exposure or using natural lighting and adjusting exposure. The f-stop doesn't measure tonal values; it's simply a representation of how much light is reflected on the surface of what's being shot—the light coming through the lens. Looking at an image doesn't reveal the f-stop setting, but when you use the zone system, you can get a fairly accurate read of the tonal values to the point that you could re-create the look of the shot.

The typical place to start with exposure is to measure your primary subject in the setup with an 18% gray card. Set your ISO and take the measurement. This will set your proper exposure (you'll get the correct f-stop setting), placing it in the middle (zone 5). If you control the lights, you could also go the other way. Open the aperture all the way and then adjust the lights until you have the 18% gray card at the proper exposure.

Let's look at an indoor night shot from Laforet's *Reverie* to see how we can use the zone system practically. In Figure 3.2, we see tonal values of 0–6—black to brightly lit skin tones.

FIGURE 3.2
We could re-create Laforet's interior night shot using the zone system by quantifying the tonal range of black-gray-white. To accent the darkness, Laforet lets the blacks fall off, revealing little to no detail in much of the setup (0–1). We can begin to see details in the 2–3 range, while 4 and 5 allow us to clearly see the patterns on the pillow, the texture of the t-shirt, the man's arm and hand, as well as the table. Zone 6 is typically the value of Caucasian skin tones, and, save for the soft focus on his feet, we would clearly see the detail. The screen-right side of his face is shadowed, and we lose detail here, whereas the screen-left side of his face reveals details in the skin tone, edging on being a bit bright (7). The blue's brightness (tint and shade) changes depending on the tonal values; it's really dark in the background (where the 3 is), and a bit brighter in the zone 5 areas, to being really light in zone 6.
(Still from Reverie. *©2009 Vincent Laforet. Used with permission.)*

By keeping the dynamic range within six stops and exposing the brightest part of the face at 6, Laforet is able to shape the rest of the scene around the blacks, letting the exposure of the man's body fall down to 0; blacks dominate the scene (stressing the nighttime feel of the shot). He allows the Caucasian skin tone to shine the brightest with the face and feet, while part of the arm and hand to hit zone 5, and leaving the shadows falling off into the blacks.

The ISO setting of the DSLR camera allows you to change the "speed" of the film—the higher the number, the less light you need to expose it (but it will get noisier—putting grainy patterns in your shots); the lower the number, the more light you need.

Tip: Zone Scale in Practice

A typical Caucasian face has a reflectivity of 36%; a brown face, about 16%; a black face, 10%. Green leaves have a 14% reflectance, while black velvet is at 2%. Light grays reflect 70% of light, while off-whites reflect 80% (see Viera, D., & Viera, M. (2005). *Lighting for Film and Digital Cinematography*, (p.54). Wadsworth).

If you want to expose for zone 5 (the "correct" exposure for an 18% mid-range gray card), set your lights and place your subject, angle the 18% gray card so that it reflects the same light as your subject, and take your reading. The 18% gray card refers to the reflection and absorption of light (18% of the light is reflected, while 82% is absorbed). If you get an exposure reading of f/5.6 on your light meter for your particular ISO setting, then that's your f-stop setting, and the rest of the tonal range will fall off or increase depending on the amount of light in other areas of the shot. If you're trying to control the amount of detail in the shadows and/or highlights, you can adjust your lights accordingly. (The light

meter in the Canon DSLRs provide an average exposure in video mode—if you need a spot meter, install Magic Lantern covered in Chapter 5, or, even better, purchase a light meter.)

Most independent filmmakers and video journalists will usually just eyeball the exposure so that the image on the LCD screen looks right. But if you're really trying to control the image and know that you want the audience to see details in the background, you could plan for it to be two stops dimmer than your main subject in the foreground (which you've exposed at f/5.6 on zone 6), for example. You would light the background for zone 4, and you would know you're in zone 4 when you get a metered reading of f/2.8 at the same speed (ISO setting). At the same time, if you want your audience to see details in the highlights, you could keep the exposure of your highlights in zone 7 (one stop above your main subject of 6, setting your lights and scrims so your meter would not go above f/8).

Tip: Lighting and the Zone Scale

A fast way to set your lights so as to brighten or dim your subject is to remember the inverse square law as a main property of light. Doubling the distance of the light from your subject (by either moving the light or your subject) drops off the brightness four times. If you halve the distance, the brightness increases by four. So if your subject is being lit inside by a window, and she's too bright for your exposure range, you can move the subject farther away (or scrim or place a gel filter on the window). If you're using lights, then you can simply move the lights farther away or closer to the subject to change the intensity (or you could use a dimmer on the light—although this will tend to change the color temperature of the light, thus impacting your white balance).

In either case, moving the light or moving the subject toward or away from the light source will change your zone scale.

Most small image sensors in video cameras have about a 4½ to 5 stop range (meaning you can expose along nearly five zones; film contains at least 8 stops), but large sensor cameras, such as the Canon 5D Mark II, have achieved around 9 stops, according to Philip Bloom. So choosing which zone to expose provides an idea of where your highlights and shadows will fall out of the exposure range. Choosing to properly expose at zone 5, for example, allows you to capture a fair amount of detail when exposing in zones 4–8 or 3–7.

Tip: The Histogram

If you don't have a light meter, you could use the histogram graph found on most cameras to "read" the range of tonal values in the shot, and adjust the camera's exposure or ISO setting accordingly (see Figure 3.3). The histogram represents the amount of your scene that's bright or dark (the tonal values). If the meter shows a high amount on the left side of the screen, the image is overall dark, showing the image to be "crushed" (a lot of detail lost in the blacks); high values on the right side of the meter reveal the image to be mostly bright and could be blown out. The gray values fall in the middle, so the 18% gray card reference representing the midrange point will be equivalent to a histogram reading in the middle of the graph. When applied to the zone scale, the readings on the left 40% of the graph would represent 0–3 (the dark grays and blacks), 4–6 (the middle gray tones) would fall into the middle of the graph (20–30%); while brighter gray tones, highlights, and white would fall along the right 30–40% of the graph.

FIGURE 3.3
The Canon Rebel's histogram, which indicates the spread of darks to brights—the shadows to highlights from left to right. Essentially, it allows you to quickly monitor whether the blacks have been crushed or the highlights blown out. Most DSLRs don't include the histogram when recording. Install Magic Lantern, covered in Chapter 5, if you want this capability. Regular video cameras have this feature built in.
(Photo courtesy of Canon.)

Photographer Michael Reichmann tells his students that when he shoots, "I'm barely even aware of the image on the LCD; it's the histogram that commands my attention." Perhaps this is an exaggeration because getting good composition is key, but once the composition has been chosen, getting proper exposure is just as important, and the histogram is one of the tools to show what your image looks like across the tonal range. Reichmann believes that there is no "bad" histogram because it's simply giving you what the reading is. Histograms are valuable for showing you how much of an image is blown out or crushed. But you can adjust your light and shadows accordingly if you're trying to place your subject in the middle of the histogram exposure zone. (See Reichmann, M. Understanding Histograms. <http://www.luminous-landscape.com/tutorials/understanding-series/understanding-histograms.shtml>).

Furthermore, if you're using a low-contrast picture style for postproduction work, the histogram becomes a useful tool for you to engage in order to watch whether or not you're crushing blacks or blowing highlights.

EXPOSURE AND DEPTH OF FIELD

Exposure represents the amount of light allowed to fall on a camera's sensor—and it also determines the depth of field of the focal plane—what's in focus.[2] Manual prime lenses, such as the Zeiss and Leica, have f-stops placed on the barrel of the lens, and you adjust the stop manually rather than through the in-camera setting (see Figure 3.4). An iris—like the pupil of your eye—controls this. When it is opened all the way (low f-stop number), more light falls in. When it is nearly closed (high f-stop number), less light enters (see Figure 3.5).

For DSLR cameras, the range of the aperture opening is measured with f-stops[3] : 1, 1.4, 2, 2.8, 4, 5.6, 8, 11, 16, 22, 32 (most video cameras don't have the 22 or 32, but many DSLR cameras do). F/1 (or the lowest number available on the lens) represents the iris opened all the way, whereas 32 (or the highest available on the lens) is nearly closed. Each number in the sequence represents a doubling of light when opening up (f/1.4 lets in twice as much lights as f/2), while a stopping down of the exposure halves the amount of light (f/2 receives half as much light as f/1.4; see Figure 3.6 for the iris range of a Zeiss Contax 50mm f/1.4 lens).

FIGURE 3.4
This Zeiss Contax 50mm/1.4 prime lens places the f-stop settings on the lens itself. This lens has an f-stop range from f/1.4 to f/16.
(Photo by Kurt Lancaster.)

---

[2] For a technical rundown of video versus film exposure, as well as dynamic range, see Appendix 3.

[3] T-stops are also used in this terminology; f-stops are determined mathematically (focal length divided by the diameter of the aperture), whereas T-stops are similar but take in effect the light absorption quality of lenses. For practical purposes, they're nearly the same. The author uses f-stops throughout this book.

Furthermore, different f-stop settings will also influence the depth of field of your lens. The lower the f-stop, the more shallow the depth of field becomes. Higher f-stops increase the depth of field. You can download a depth of field calculator for a portable device (such as an iPhone), as well as use the one on this website: <http://www.dofmaster.com/dofjs.html>. You input the type of camera, the distance to the subject in inches, feet, centimeters, or meters and it'll calculate the proper distance. (Choose the 7D camera from the dropdown menu when using a Canon 60D or Rebel (550D/600D), since the sensor size is the same.) See Figures 3.5. Note how the depth of field increases with the

f/1.4

Distance ~4' f/1.4: DoF = 1.92" (from 3.92'–4.08')

f/2

Distance ~4' f/2: DoF = 2.64" (from 3.89'–4.12')

FIGURE 3.5
The f-stops represent the opening and closing of the iris of a camera. The lower the f-stop, the more open it is, letting in more light. The higher the number, less amount of light enters. Each f-stop number represents a halving (closing) or doubling (opening) of light. An f/2.8 prevents half the light of f/2, whereas f/11 allows twice the light of an f/16. In addition, the f-stop setting determines the depth of field, as can be seen with the focal plane changing in the corresponding images with Preston the dog. At f/1.4, 2, 2.8, and 4, the background chairs are out of focus, while they begin to get sharper at f/5.6 and above. Depth of field calculation based on 5D Mark II, Zeiss Contax 50 mm/1.4 at a distance of approximately 4 feet (using the depth of field calculator at: http://www.dofmaster.com/dofjs.html
(Photos by Kurt Lancaster; model: Preston.)

f/2.8

Distance ~4' f/2.8: DoF = 3.84" (from 3.85'–4.17')

f/4

Distance ~4' f/4: DoF = 5.4" (from 3.79'–4.24')

f/5.6

FIGURE 3.5 (Continued)

Distance ~4' f/5.6: DoF = 7.68" (from 3.71'–4.34')

f/8

Distance ~4' f/8: DoF = 10.92" (from 3.6'–4.51')

f/11

Distance ~4' f/11: DoF = 15.6" (from 3.45'–4.75')

f/16

Distance ~4' f/16: DoF = 22.68" (from 3.27'–5.16')

FIGURE 3.5 (Continued)

corresponding higher f-stop values. Also note, as the distance to the subject decreases the depth of field decreases and with a subject farther away, you'll also get increased depth of field. For example, a subject 20 feet away with a 50 mm lens at f/1.4 has a depth of field of 4.15 feet, while a subject at two feet has a depth of field of less than half an inch!

Most people eyeball the exposure by using the LCD or an external monitor, but this approach will not provide an accurate reading. Philip Bloom doesn't recommend it. "Don't use the LCD screen to expose," he says. By using the camera's metering system, Bloom feels you can get a more accurate read—important for professional use. You can meter an average exposure with Canon DSLR cameras, but the spot meter doesn't work in video mode.

FIGURE 3.6
The same shot with three different f-stop settings. The top image is at f/8, the middle is f/11, and the bottom is f/16, each one letting in half the light as the one previous. F/8 is the proper exposure where you can still see some details in the shadows without the subject's face being blown out. Notice that the depth of field of the subject is sharp throughout, because of the high f-stop settings providing a depth of field between 2.11' to 4.64'. Zeiss 25 mm, f/2.8. (Photos by Kurt Lancaster.)

CINEMATOGRAPHER TIP

Film Look with Exposure, Shutter Speed, and Filters

Shane Hurlbut, ASC, says, "Making HD video look like film has a cocktail and one of the essential ingredients to this flavorful recipe is neutral density (ND). You have to keep your exposure on a [Canon 5D Mark II] around a 5.6 to get that beautiful shallow depth of field. The 7D should be around a 2.8, and the 1D around a 4.0. This gives the focus puller a chance and still retains a beautiful fall off of focus."

The 7D has close to a 35mm sensor so you would shoot around a 2.0/2.8 split to give a decent focus range but keep the background out of focus enough to battle aliasing and moiré issues. Use a shutter speed of 1/50 or 1/40 all the time. I do not like to go above it. When you go at a 1/60 or higher it starts to look like video, and it's too sharp for me. I use the motion blur at a 1/50 and 1/40 to help with the crispness of HD and make it look more like film.

In addition, Hurlbut, who shot *Terminator Salvation* (2009) and *Act of Valor* (2012), recommends using neutral density filters to change the exposure value without altering the f-stop setting). "Tiffen's Water White NDs and Water White IR NDs looked the cleanest of all the available filters. This filter was specifically designed for the HD world. It is very pure glass to give you the best image for your post color correction. The filters that were originally made for film had brown and green in the glass that was no problem to dial out in film because of the uncompressed 4:4:4 color space. But now with HD 8-bit compressed color space [of DSLRS and many video cameras], you do not have that range of manipulation in color correction. In addition, by using neutral density at higher levels to achieve a shallow depth of field, you must deal with the problem of infrared (IR) pollution. The Water White IR NDs counteract this issue and give an image that does not have so much pink/magenta. As a cinematographer, I want to limit this contamination because it ends up showing in the blacks as well as skies in day exteriors." (Shane Hurlbut, personal notes. See Hurlbut, S. (2010, Feb. 10). Filtration: Beware of the Reaper of Cheap Glass. *Hurlblog*. <http://hurlbutvisuals.com/blog/2010/02/10/filtration-beware-of-the-reaper-of-cheap-glass/.>)

Tip
If you need the exposure wide open for best shallow depth of field work, then you may want to add neutral density filters so you can lock your iris open. If you don't have an ND filter, then you can increase shutter speed—it'll make the image sharper, but you'll maintain a shallow depth of field.

Use a light meter to determine the precise value of the exposure, moving it if you want to get a reading on another part of the scene. A small exposure index meter on the bottom of the LCD screen provides a meter with a center scale indicating proper exposure with a latitude of two stops in either direction—another tool to use in your zone scale if you don't have a spot meter (see Figure 3.7). However, it provides an *average* exposure based on the lighting in the composition of the entire scene. The spot meter function does not work in video mode. Installing Magic Lantern (covered in Chapter 5) will give you a spot meter in percentages (0% for black 100% for white).

FIGURE 3.7
Canon's exposure meter on the bottom of the LCD screen provides an average exposure of your composition. The spot meter function does not work in video mode. The scale is set at 1/3 increments and can go up to plus two or minus two stops. When you press the shutter halfway, a bar below the exposure index will appear, indicating where your average exposure is—it will flash when it falls below −2 or above +2. By adjusting the f-stops and/or ISO, you can find the average center point. You can also force over- or underexposure by turning the quick control dial while pressing down the shutter halfway. *(Image courtesy of Canon.)*

Get the Canon 5D or 7D? It's the Chip Size that Offers a Smoother Tonal Range for Shane Hurlbut, ASC

"The 5D is the king of the hill," Hurlbut says. "And the 7D and the 1D are climbing that hill and they don't even have a rope. The 7D is not bad, but it's a 24 mm sensor. And you're not able to get that depth of field you get with the 5D—to have the ability to go really shallow. In a shot from *The Last 3 Minutes* with that carpet line, I've never seen anything like it. 35 mm never gave me that line before—it was extreme. And the camera was at f/5.6 with the ISO at 320, and shot with a Canon L 100 mm Macro lens. So when you need the added f-stop, you can go there; you can go shallow. (see Figure 3.8)

Hurlbut feels that the 5D provides a "broader range of visual creativity" than the 7D. The 7D "has [...] more depth of field for [a] filmmaker that doesn't have a focus puller," Hurlbut explains. What makes the difference, Hurlbut argues, is the pixel size. "The Vista Vision-size sensor on the 5D is 2.3 times the size of the 7D sensor. So the image, the pixel sizes—they are larger. The bigger the pixel, the easier it is for light to enter and give a more graduated fall off into the shadow areas, so it looks more filmic."

What does he mean by this? The larger pixel sizes, Hurlbut explains, relate to "how the contrast range falls from light hitting somebody on the face and then the shadow area that goes underneath their chin, for

FIGURE 3.8
A shot from *The Last 3 Minutes* reveals the potential narrow depth of field with the Canon 5D Mark II. Canon 100 mm L, aperture set at f/5.6, and ISO 320.
(©2010 Hurlbut Visuals. Used with permission.)

example. But the 7D is going to see that more like a black diamond run on a ski slope." The 5D will graduate into the shadow area and make more of a filmic fall off because of the pixel size and its light-gathering ability, which would feel more like a bunny slope. The 7D has the advantage of slow motion, a film gate that's closer to regular 35 mm film, and a depth of field that isn't as hard to fight with as the 5D Mark II. (Notes from personal interview, March 2010.)

CINEMATOGRAPHER TIP

Jim Mathers, president (and co-founder) of the Digital Cinema Society, discusses how he approaches exposure:

> With exposure tests, what I'm basically looking for is the sweet spot somewhere between two competing extremes of underexposure on one side, where the image would start to become unacceptably noisy; and on the other, the point where I would start to clip, or lose detail in the highlights. It would seem logical to flatly expose a chip chart, then simply count out the number of steps

between the two limits to find the median value. However, I find that this is not always the exact center between these poles; it can be more of a creative choice, and it can vary depending on the subject. And while it would be nice to assign a corresponding ASA/ISO number to a given sensor, this also depends on the shooting situation. For example, in a high contrast daylight exterior, I might tend to rate the sensor a little higher, looking to protect the highlights, which would lead me to allow less exposure to reach the sensor. However, in a low key setup I might be looking to capture shadow detail, treating the sensor as if it is less sensitive, allowing more light to pass through to help insure my shadow areas stay free of too much noise. Now, I'm way too pragmatic to have a different meter setting for every scene, but I have found two or three different ratings varying with the broad category of the shot to be appropriate, just as I might shoot a movie on two or three different stocks.

(*Digital Cinema Society Newsletter*. 26 March 2010: #6.2)

CINEMATOGRAPHER TIP

Shane Hurlbut, ASC, discusses the importance of ISO settings on the 5D Mark II and how it relates to compression of the color bit depth:

> In the beginning, I was scared to go above 500 ISO but 500 ISO is actually noisier than 1600 ISO. You have to give this sensor light. If you don't give the sensor enough light, then your 8 BIT compressed color space will go down to 6 BIT then 4 BIT then 2 BIT color space at which point you have no control in post. It is better to feed it a little more light and then adjust your color and contrast in post.
>
> (Jan. 5, 2010 newsletter: http://hurlbutvisuals.com/newsletter_archive.php)

Hurlbut Visuals conducted a series of ISO tests and determined that the best settings for reduced noise levels for Canon's 5D Mark II and 7D are ISO 160, 320, 640, 800, and 1250. (See Appendix 2.)

However, Josh Silfen, a cinematographer in New York, offers a different explanation about this:

> So, if the 160-multiple ISOs are not the native ones, why are they cleaner, and how are they derived? Well, it is correct that the 125-multiple ISOs are the noisiest because they are derived by a digital exposure push. ISO 125 is actually ISO 100 with a 1/3 stop digital exposure push, ISO 250 is ISO 200 with a 1/3 stop digital exposure push, etc. However, the 160-multiple ISOs are actually the cleanest not because they are "native", but because they are a result of a digital exposure pull. This pull brings down the exposure of the entire image, and hides much of the noise that would be visible at the next higher ISO. ISO 160 is the cleanest because it is the native ISO 200 with a 1/3 stop digital exposure pull, yielding even less noise. ISO 320 is actually ISO 400, with a 1/3 stop exposure pull, etc.

Because ISO 320 is actually ISO 400 pulled 1/3 of a stop, that means that the highlights are going to clip at exactly the same point as they would at ISO 400. The 1/3 stop pull is just making that point 1/3 stop darker than pure white. The entire image at ISO 320 is 1/3 stop darker (and may be less noisy) than the image at ISO 400, so the blacks lose detail 1/3 stop sooner, but you don't get that 1/3 stop back at the highlight end of the range—it's still gone. Therefore, at ISO 320 you're losing a net 1/3 stop from the total usable dynamic range that you would have if you were shooting at ISO 400.

If you need more exposure, you're better off going up to the next exposure-pulled ISO, or the next native ISO, rather than shooting with the increased noise and decreased dynamic range that comes along with the pushed ISOs. In general, if I am shooting a bright scene with a large contrast range, such as a daytime exterior, I will prefer to use the full-stop, native ISOs. In that situation, since I will likely be using the lower ISOs (100 or 200), noise really isn't much of a factor anyway, and I will prioritize dynamic range to prevent the highlights from blowing out as much as possible. If I am shooting a dimly lit scene, I will likely be using the higher ISOs where noise is more of an issue. In that case, keeping the highlights in check isn't usually a problem, so I will prefer to use the 160-multiple ISOs (320, 640, or 1250) so I can get more exposure with less noise.

(Silfen, J. (2010). Canon HD DSLR "Native ISO". Shootin' The Shoot: Camera Tech Talk and General Pontification. Accessed 11 March 2012. http://shootintheshot.joshsilfen.com/2010/05/13/canon-hd-dslr-native-iso/)

High ISO settings lead to noise, as can be seen in the test conducted by Hurlbut Visual (see Appendix 2). With the release of Canon's 5D Mark III in 2012, the engineers shaped their ISO in the sensor so there's less noise. In a comparison test between the Canon 5D Mark II and III shot by Saika, he set the ISO at 12800 (see http://vimeo.com/37879608), and when compared to the 5D Mark II, there is a significant difference in the noise level (see Figure 3.9).

CINEMATOGRAPHER TIP

Lens and Sensor Size on the Canon 5D Mark II

Shane Hurlbut, ASC, says, "The 5D's sensor is the size of the 70 mm Vista Vision. Focus is nearly impossible at a f/1.4 or a f/2 unless you are shooting lock-off shots with little or no motion. Shooting the 5D at a f/5.6 is equivalent to a f/1.4/2 split on 35 mm film. Nobody shoots movies at a 1.4/2.0 split because the focus puller does not have a chance to get anything in focus. If you shoot action or move the camera around with a bit of handheld, you will not have a prayer" (Notes from personal interview, March 2010).

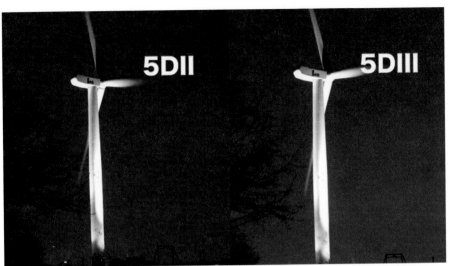

FIGURE 3.9
Saiko's side by side comparison of the Canon 5D Mark II and III at ISO 12800. The Mark II's image contains a lot of green noise. Although noise still can be seen in the Mark III image, it is significantly less. Saika. (2012). *Eos 5D Mark III ISO 12800 Movie*. Vimeo.com. <http://vimeo.com/37879608> Accessed 25 March 2012

USING NEUTRAL DENSITY FILTERS

Filters can change the quality of a lens, diffusing an image to make it slightly soft. The most important ones are designed not only to protect your lenses from scratches, but filter the amount of light hitting the lens; they are called neutral density (ND) filters. This type of filter allows you to keep the aperture open under bright light conditions; the filter essentially stops down the f-stop aperture setting—without closing the iris—the amount depending on the type of filter used, allowing the filmmaker to keep the shallow depth of field of an open iris. Filters can be screwed onto the lens or dropped in front of the lens when using a matte box, or they can be conveyed electronically if the camera has a built-in neutral density function; none of the current HDSLRs have electronic ND filters.

Filters are assigned different numbers depending on their density, their ability to block out light. ND2 will be labeled 0.3, providing for a one f-stop equivalent reduction (see Table 3.1). Companies also make variable ND filters (called ND faders) so you can adjust the filter without having to switch them out.

In addition, when you're choosing an ND filter, consider getting one that includes infrared filtration. The IR is especially useful for DSLR cameras because they're sensitive to infrared, causing oversaturation of red, as well as focusing interference issues.

Table 3.1	Filter Name, Density, and f-Stop Reduction	
ND Filter Type	**Density**	**f-Stop Reduction**
ND2	0.3	1
ND4	0.6	2
ND8	0.9	3
ND16	1.2	4
ND32	1.5	5
ND64	1.8	6

Questions to Consider When Using Filters

1. What is your exposure latitude? Are you shooting in bright sunlight, for example? Set your ISO level where you want it and then set the exposure. If you're blowing out the highlights, then it's too bright. Adding a neutral density filter will change your exposure latitude and allow you to get the shot you need.
2. Do you need shallow depth of field in bright light? Use an ND filter when you want to open up your iris and maintain shallow depth of field without overexposing your shots.
3. How much light do you want to come through? The density determines the strength of the filter. The higher the number, the less light will come through. Be aware of the changing exposure latitude with ND filters. A 0.9 filter, for example, provides 3 stops of exposure across your entire range. So if you're using an ND filter only to prevent a blowout of the highlight, be aware that your shadows will deepen, and you may lose detail, although before the ND placement, it was fine. You'll need to brighten the shadow if you don't want to lose the detail.

CINEMATOGRAPHER TIP

Philip Bloom recommends using variable neutral density filters. He prefers the Singh-Ray 77 mm screw-on because it dials in 2 to 8 stops of neutral density by rotating the filter. (Personal notes from Hdi RAWworks workshop, March 2010.)

In addition, if you're shooting flat/superflat, use filters only to change the light quality, such as ND filters, ND graduated filters, and polarizers. Other filters, such as soft and frost, and so on can be applied in postproduction using Magic Bullet, for example.

CONSIDERING SHUTTER SPEED

Typically, you would follow the 180-degree shutter speed rule. The shutter in a film camera would normally be half a circle (180 degrees), so if the film speed is 1/24 of a second (24 fps), you would double that to get the shutter speed (1/48). NTSC video shoots at 30 fps, while PAL (European standard) is 25 fps, so with NTSC you would typically shoot at 1/60 of a second shutter speed. Shane Hurlbut, ASC, however, considers this "a recipe for delivering images that look like video, not film":

> I use a 1/40th or a 1/50th of a shutter. You never go above that. Anytime you go above, it starts looking like video. By just going up to 1/60th of a second it instantly takes a beautiful 5D that gives filmic images and turns it into a video camera. The more you sharpen the image, the more it looks plastic. I use the motion blur to soften the crispness of HD video. Shooting at a 1/50th is like shooting with a 200 degree shutter. I shot the whole *Rat Pack* (1998) on a 200 degree shutter—I loved that look.[4]

So setting the proper shutter speed is important in helping to attain the film look with DSLR cameras.

CONSIDERING FRAME RATES

Before addressing in-camera settings, I want to address frame rate. Currently, film has a 24 frames per second rate, and provides one of the benchmarks for getting the film look (video shooting at 24p), which engages a judder effect when shooting (and that's part of the film look).

However, such filmmakers as James Cameron offer a different opinion. He feels that unless you're transferring your project to film or have it projected on a 24 frames per second (fps) player, then you don't need to shoot 24p. In an interview with David Cohen of *Variety*, Cameron actually argues for a faster frame rate in order to create a smoother quality of the image:

> I've run tests on 48 frame per second stereo and it is stunning. The cameras can do it, the projectors can (with a small modification) do it. So why aren't we doing it, as an industry?

> Because people have been asking the wrong question for years. They have been so focused on resolution, and counting pixels and lines, that they have forgotten about frame rate. Perceived resolution + pixels = replacement rate. A 2K image at 48 frames per second looks as sharp as a 4K image at 24 frames per

---

[4] Red centre #056. *fxguide.com.* <http://media.fxguide.com/redcentre/redcentre-056.mp3>, accessed March 24, 2010

second with one fundamental difference: the 4K/24 image will judder miserably during a panning shot, and the 2K/48 won't. Higher pixel counts only preserve motion artifacts like strobing with greater fidelity. They don't solve them at all.[5]

Cameron argues for 48 frames per second because the quality doesn't vastly increase at a higher number and it's compatible with film projection (doubling the standard 24 frame rate). Indeed, Peter Jackson shot *The Hobbit: An Unexpected Journey* (2012) using Red cameras at 48fps—which he feels will provide a smoother look to the 3D film.

For DSLR shooting, 24p will best represent the film look because that's the current aesthetic of film and best engages the film look when shooting with video. But getting the film look isn't just about shooting 24p. You need to sculpt light and shadow and work within a specified dynamic range, engage smooth and stable camera work, choose lenses and filters, and get proper exposure at the proper shutter speed when telling your story as powerfully as possible.

Checklist for Exposure

1. Set your camera to *manual* video mode.
2. Determine your *exposure latitude*. Knowing your latitude range from shadows to highlight will help determine how much light you need for your subject, foreground, and background. If you know the dynamic range of the camera, you can determine how much light and light blockage you need to control the amount of light throughout your entire exposure range. A light meter is helpful for this process, but you can also use the histogram to see the dynamic range from dark to bright. And you can use the exposure meter in the camera to get an average reading. As you practice with image, light, and shadow, you'll be able to eyeball the exposure range for your particular camera.
3. How rich do you want the image? The *ISO level*—the "speed" of the exposure—determines the richness of the image. The higher the number, the more light sensitive it will be but will result in more video noise; the lower the number, the richer the image will look but will require more lighting. Outdoor daylight will allow for ISO 100, whereas outdoor night shots will require a high ISO setting. The lower the setting the lower the noise. Increasing the ISO will add more noise to the image. Recommended indoor ISO = 320, 640, 1250 (or 200, 400, 800 on Rebels 550D/600). Recommended outdoor day ISO: 100 or 200.
4. How much light do you want? Set your aperture's *f-stop* (the lower the number, the more open the iris, letting in more light; higher numbers close up the iris, cutting off the amount of light falling on the sensor). Neutral density filters are used to cut out light without changing your f-stop. (See page 53.)

---

[5] Cohen, D. S. (April 10, 2008). James Cameron supercharges 3-D. *Variety*. <http://www.variety.com/article/VR1117983864.html?categoryid51009&cs51>.

5. How much *depth of field* do you want? When the aperture is more open, you'll have a shallow depth of field; when the aperture is more closed, the depth of field will increase. If you need shallow depth of field and you're too overexposed when the aperture is wide open, decrease your ISO setting and/or use neutral density filters—or as a backup, increase your shutter speed.

6. Set your shutter speed. It should remain at 1/40 or 1/50 of a second to maintain a nonvideo look and get you closer to the film look.

LENSES

The human eye can see about 240 degrees with peripheral vision. Lenses do *not* reveal what the natural unaided eye sees. Rather, the cinematographer uses lenses as a way to shape the *emotional equivalency* of what the human eye perceives and feels. If you stand within typical talking distance from someone, this is what may translate on film as a medium shot. If the person is in a wide or long shot, this may be equivalent to someone standing on the other side of a room—shouting distance. A close-up would be equivalent to an intimate conversation, a kiss or a fight—where you are inches from someone.

Different lenses render how we perceive the subject and setting descriptively and emotionally. Practically, a variety of lenses allow us to change the angle of what can be seen; they're measured by the focal length (a wide angle lens on a 35 mm camera would be a 20 mm focal length), and a long lens might contain a 100 mm focal length; a "normal" lens would be 35 mm or 50 mm focal length. The focal length on a DSLR camera is simply the distance of the lens to the imaging sensor when the focus is set to infinity.

A short focal length lens (a wider convex lens) bends the light sharply, bringing the image in focus only a short distance from the lens, but the image is smaller and therefore can capture more of the scene (and place much of the foreground and background in sharp focus). A long focal length lens is less convex, bending the light at a smaller angle, placing the focal distance farther away, making the image larger (with less of the foreground and background of the scene in focus).

As a comparison, the angle of view can be broken down to a 25 mm lens containing a field of view of 80 degrees, 50 mm at 46 degrees, 100 mm at 24 degrees, and 180 mm with 13 degrees.[6] In effect, the sharper the angle, the closer the view you can capture with the lens, if the camera is placed at the same distance (see Figures 3.10–3.14).

---

[6] The field of view ultimately depends on the lens size and the size of the sensor chip of the camera. A 35 mm on a 7D has a 1.6 times difference in the field of view than a 35 mm on a 5D, for example. The 35 mm on the 7D will be similar to a 56 mm on the 5D. See Collins, M. (2010). 5Dmk2/7D lens comparison test. <http://vimeo.com/14832168>.

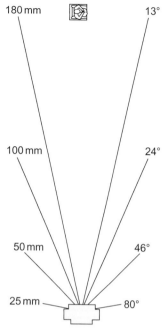

FIGURE 3.10
Angle of view illustration for
Figures 3.11–3.14

FIGURE 3.11
Zeiss 25 mm. About six feet from the subject.
(Photo by Kurt Lancaster)

FIGURE 3.12
Zeiss 50 mm.
Same distance
(Photo by Kurt Lancaster)

One of the selling points of shooting HD video with DSLR cameras (and now many large sensor video cameras) is the ability of the cinematographer to use a variety of lenses to shape the look of the project. While most prosumer HD video cameras allow for good HD clarity, digital filmmakers were limited by the fixed zoom lenses and small sensors. Larger sensors and removable lenses of the hybrid DSLR cameras was one of the main reasons filmmakers gravitated

FIGURE 3.13
Zeiss 100 mm.
Same distance.
(Photo by Kurt Lancaster)

FIGURE 3.14
Leica 180 mm.
Same distance.
(Photo by Kurt Lancaster)

to DSLRs—opening up important creative elements not readily available on standard HD video cameras (without complex and expensive 35 mm lens adaptors). Some prosumer video cameras evolved to include interchangeable lenses. The ability to play with depth of field with large sensors opens up the possibilities of utilizing more of the cinematographer's film tools to craft better and stronger visual stories.

In Laforet's *Reverie*, for example, the opening shot (see Figure 3.15) and a shot later in the film (see Figure 3.16) are from the same setup using the same lighting conditions and position. However, the angle of the lens is different. Laforet uses a tilt-shift lens (45 mm shot at f/2.8) in Figure 3.15, which allows for selective focus. The first one looks as though it utilizes the shallow depth of field of a longer lens but was used with the tilt-shift lens (see Figure 3.17), allowing Laforet to change the depth of field in the shot, placing the background out of focus, while his main subjects (the man and woman kissing) are in focus. If you look closely, you can see that in this moment of the shot (which changes focus over time), the arms of the man and woman are sharply focused while the heads are in soft focus. The second shot (Figure 3.16) reveals the woman waiting, and the Brooklyn Bridge and skyline are in sharp focus.

FIGURE 3.15
Laforet uses a tilt-shift lens (45 mm, f/2.8) to attain selective focus. Light from above on Profoto 7B with a head and beauty dish and grid. Modeling lamp from 7B head only. A small LED flashlight was used from the ground for backlight—a rim light glow edging along the woman's back.
(Still from Reverie. *©2009 Vincent Laforet. Used with permission.)*

FIGURE 3.16
Laforet uses the same tilt-shift lens as in Figure 3.15, but alters the selective focus to bring the entire shot in focus, similar to the effect with a wide angle lens. Same lighting as in the previous shot (Still from Reverie. © 2009 Vincent Laforet. Used with permission.)

In addition to the focal length and depth of field of lenses, another important factor is the speed of the lens. A "fast" lens has a wider maximum open

FIGURE 3.17
Canon's 45 mm tilt-shift lens used by Laforet to change physical alignment of the lens and thus a shifting focal plane. A low-cost alternative to the tilt-shift lens is the Lensbaby.
(Image courtesy of Canon.)

aperture (iris). Less light is needed to expose the film—better for low light and night setups (and allowing for shallow depth of field). A "slow" lens means that it contains a narrower maximum aperture opening; more light is needed for proper exposure (with increased depth of field). A fast lens could be f/1.4 or f/2, for example, whereas a slow lens would be f/5.6. The difference in the two is significant: an f/1.4 lens lets in 16 times more light than an f/5.6 lens! The terms *fast* and *slow* refer to the shutter speed when taking still shots. Typically, a slow lens would need to keep the shutter open longer to let in the same amount of light, whereas the fast lens allows for less time to let in light, thus a faster shutter speed.

The Director's Lens App for iPhone

To help you make the right lens choice, you could use Artemis, the director's digital viewfinder iPhone app, which allows you to set the format and angle of the lens, the iPhone acting as a viewfinder, including settings for the Canon 5D and 7D (see Figure 3.18).

The formats, with more in development, include:

- 16 mm Standard, Super, and 1.3 Anamorphic
- 35 mm Standard, Super, and Anamorphic
- 65 mm
- 35 mm Digital (ARRI D-21, RED One, Sony F35, Panavision Genesis)
- 2/30 Digital (Sony F23, Thompson Viper, Panasonic Varicam)
- 1/20 Digital (including Sony EX3 & EX1)
- 1/30 Digital (including Panasonic HVX200)
- 5D Mark II and 7D

FIGURE 3.18
Screen shot from the Artemis iPhone director's digital viewfinder app. It provides lens size, angle, and a visual outline representing the field of view onscreen. Developed by Chemical Wedding (http://www.chemicalwedding.tv/artemis.html)
(Image used with permission.)

The type of lens determines not only what you will see, but how much light will be exposed, as well as the potential depth of field. With most prosumer HD video cameras, filmmakers are stuck with the fixed zoom lens. Expensive adaptors allowed for the addition of a 35 mm lens, but with DSLRs, changing lenses is now a standard option—as it is now the case with some of the advanced prosumer video cameras. A zoom lens may be good for shooting documentaries, but many of these lenses adjust the exposure speed. Zooming all the way in requires more light to expose, whereas zooming back out to the widest angle requires less light. Many lenses have fixed angles, so when you place a 50 mm lens on your camera, the only way to change the size of the composition would be to move the camera closer or farther away from the subject. The type of lens determines not only what you will see, but how much light will be exposed, as well as the potential depth of field.

> The type of lens determines not only what you will see, but how much light will be exposed, as well as the potential depth of field.

Checklist for Lenses

1. Zoom or primes? Cheaper zoom lenses change the aperture speed rating. For example, an f/4–5.6 means that the lens pulled wide will provide the greatest exposure of f/4; zoomed all the way in will provide the widest exposure of f/5.6. Effectively, this means that you need to expose everything for f/5.6 or higher because you should not change the f-stop when shooting a scene (or the shots will look different). If you have the budget, more expensive zoom lenses will maintain their aperture rating all the way through the zoom—such as Canon's L series lenses.

2. Prime lenses have a fixed focal length and aperture rating. These are the best lenses but can be limiting in documentary and video journalism work because you may want to change lens angles quickly without having to change lenses.

3. What is the manufacturer's brand? Different lenses require different mounts to fit different brands and different lens sizes. PL mounts are used for cinema lenses. The Panasonic GH1 uses a micro 4/3 mount, whereas the Canon 5D uses a full-frame 35 mm EF mount, and so forth. It's recommended that you do not buy a camera with the kit lens, but invest in high-quality zooms and a couple of primes. What to look for: does the focus ring stop or is it mushy—free spinning past the point where it should stop? If you're using DSLRs in cinema projects with focus pullers or shooters needing precision, getting a lens type that stops is essential, especially when using different manufacturers' focus assists. Zeiss primes, for example, are designed for manual focusing with a lower turn ratio (a half turn usually covers the full focal range). Also, image stabilization is important because a slight shake or vibration can cause ruined shaky shots, especially on longer lenses. Furthermore, when swapping out lenses, be aware of dust. You should get into a car or go inside if the wind is blowing or cover your camera with a jacket.

4. How much of the scene do you want the audience to see? Wide angle lenses present a wider field of view, whereas long lenses narrow what can be seen.

5. How much of the scene do you want in focus? Wide angle lenses put more of the scene in focus, whereas longer lenses decrease depth of field and narrow what's in focus. Both of these questions are answered by the length of the lens and the placement of the camera. If you want the audience to see more of the scene, then use a wide angle lens. If you want them to see less, use a long lens. If you want more of the scene in focus, then use a wide to normal length lens; if you want a shallow depth of field, then use a long lens.

6. Decide the speed of the lens. A fast lens (such as f/1.4) will allow you to shoot in low and natural light, better than a slow lens (such as f/4). Faster lenses will also allow you to lower the ISO setting, giving you more room to choose a richer look. Fast lenses allow you to open wide and get shallow depth of field, while slower lenses limit your depth of field choices.

Now that we've covered some of the basics of cinematography, the next chapter will examine how you can shape the picture style of Canon's DSLRs, so you can get the look you want in-camera before you begin shooting.

CHAPTER 4

Using DSLR Picture Styles

PITFALLS OF PRESETS AND CREATING CUSTOM STYLES

There's no fixed formula for creating a cinematic look, but there are widely agreed-on parameters that should be considered. As you saw in the previous chapters, there are tools cinematographers use to create the mood they want the audience to feel in a particular scene of a story. When shooting with video, the first consideration revolves around how to offset the video look. If filmmakers are not shooting with film but using high-definition video, then they need to know the differences between the two. Indeed, many young cinematographers may have never shot on film and, consequently, may not know why video looks different than film. There are reasons why many cinematographers and directors of photography have avoided the use of video in the past, despite video being available for decades, and much cheaper than the film. If film is considered soft, creamy, as well as smooth and sharp (mainly created by a good-quality lens), and sometimes grainy, then video usually feels harsh, sharp, noisy, and sometimes juddery (when it's captured wrong).[1] The video look mainly revolves around overly sharp resolution (as well as how the signal is processed for television).[2]

> There's no fixed formula for creating a cinematic look, but there are widely agreed-on parameters that should be considered.

The attempt to control your image in-camera is one of the important tools in removing the video look and beginning to achieve a cinematic look. In this chapter, you'll learn how to engage a cinematic style with Canon DSLRs by utilizing picture-style and color balance tools.

SHOOTING THE IMAGE FLAT

What precise picture style to recommend—as well as what presets to use (such as monochrome, faithful, neutral, landscape, portrait, and standard, found in Canon DSLRs) or whether or not to create your own picture style—is highly subjective. Yet, few cinematographers would disagree that shooting in anything

---

[1] If video is captured wrong, motion-blur will need to be added to attain the 1/48 look.
[2] Television broadcasts utilize interlaced scan lines, such as 60i in a camera. If not corrected in post, websites will show these horizontal lines as video artifacts, which ruins the image.

but a modified Neutral setting may take away the cinematic look you're trying to attain.

Some cinematographers will even take the image to the extreme and shoot in "flat" or "SuperFlat"modes—especially if they're engaging in a high amount of postproduction color grading. Indeed, Technicolor scientists, consulting with Canon engineers, spent a year developing a flat picture style, Technicolor CineStyle—designed to be the best flat look for Canon DSLRs (see "Grand Canyon Winter" case study later in the chapter). Jeremy Ian Thomas, a colorist and editor at Hdi RAWworks in Hollywood, discusses the possibilities in shooting in a flat mode:

> I can actually show you some of the SuperFlat and how much information I'm pulling out of it. It's incredible. There's at least two stops in the shadows, at least. And the thing about these cameras I discovered when talking to Rodney Charters, ASC, is to expose for your highlights, because if you lose the highlights in this camera, they're gone forever. They go into the abyss of pixels and they never come back. Now, the low end I can get back. Especially if you're shooting in a flat, neutral profile. If you expose and get a beautiful sky and you want this guy's legs or his torso, I can get that back out of the shadows, but I can't get it out of the highlights.
>
> (Interview with author, March 9, 2010)

Some people warn against shooting SuperFlat because it destroys the skin tones in post, but others argue just the opposite.[3]

> By shooting the image flat, "saturated colors blossom" when properly graded in post.

Thomas feels you can get a good look with Canon DSLRs without playing with picture styles: "Skin tones, overall color saturation, and color separation with these cameras [are] pretty incredible right outta the box. It's really amazing." But he also feels that as a colorist "these cameras" are great when using "the flat profiles."

So despite the concerns of some DSLR shooters when using SuperFlat, Thomas feels that it provides the most latitude in getting the image to look good if you're going to do a lot of manipulation in post. "It'll look like milk and honey in post," he says, and by shooting it flat, "saturated colors blossom" when properly graded in post. He also prefers that the camera be set in the Adobe RGB color space, because "there's a lot of info there" for postproduction work. If you're not going to shoot SuperFlat (a parameter only recommended if you're not going to do a large amount of color grading), then Philip Bloom recommends shooting it flat—which means setting the camera's picture style to

---

[3] See Why Shoot Flat? My Definitive Answer: <http://www.elskid.com/blog/?p = 981&cpage = 1>;
Flatten your 5D: <http://prolost.com/blog/2009/8/3/flatten-your-5d.html>;
They Shoot ~~Horses~~ JPEGs Don't They?: <http://photocinenews.com/2010/04/26/they-shoot-horses-jpegs-dont-they/>;
Shoot flat or not?: <http://www.canon5dtips.com/2010/04/shoot-flat-or-not/>;

Neutral and dialing everything back (setting sharpness to 0, contrast to 0, color tone to 0, and saturation to −2).

You may also just simply choose the Neutral picture style and use the histogram and shoot flat with that—making sure there's data in all the ranges of the tonal scale. The RED One camera shoots flat because that camera is designed to go through a heavy post-process

> Choose the Neutral picture style and use the histogram and shoot flat with that—making sure there's data in all the ranges of the tonal scale.

Due to the subjective nature of color grading and getting the look of your shoot, *your first step always should be to test before shooting a real project.* Test it all the way through the postproduction phase to make sure you're getting what you want. Jeremy Abrams, who runs WideOpenCamera.com, agrees that testing is crucial. Just as cinematographers shooting on film "test lenses for color temperature [and] test the film stock for latitude," you need to do a similar thing with DSLRs. "You can't just run out and shoot. Preview before you shoot—shoot an image or a series of images and go back and look at [it] on the big monitor to see if you like what you see" (interview with author, March 2010).

> Your first step always should be to test before shooting a real project.

And if you're going to be transferring to film, it is even more important to test. What does the film processing company recommend for the settings of the camera you're using? Can you shoot test shots in all your locations with similar lighting setups and have the film processed and projected? This kind of testing may be crucial for a professional film shoot, especially on a large-budget project.

CINEMATOGRAPHER TIP

Shane Hurlbut, ASC, recommends setting the contrast and color tone at Neutral zero but knocking the sharpness to 0, saturation down one notch to −1 (and keeping the contrast and color tone at 0) when shooting with the Canon 5D Mark II (see Figure 4.1; http://hurlbutvisuals.com/blog/category/cinematography/).

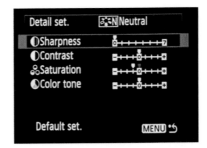

FIGURE 4.1
Shane Hurlbut, ASC, recommends setting Canon 5D Mark II's sharpness to 0 and saturation at −1 (with contrast and color tone at 0). Keep the contrast and color tone at neutral 0.
(Image courtesy of Hurlbut Visuals.)

> ### CINEMATOGRAPHER TIP
>
> Philip Bloom recommends the following settings for the Canon 5D Mark II and 7D (as well as the Canon Rebel T2i and 60D):
>
> - Sharpness: 0 (all the way to the left)
> - Contrast: 0 (middle)
> - Saturation: −2
> - Color tone: 0 (middle)

Figures 4.2 through 4.9 show examples of Canon's picture styles. Figures 4.2 through 4.5 show the pictures you should *never* use when trying to shape the cinematic look with Canon DSLRs: standard, portrait, landscape, and faithful. Rather, starting with the Neutral setting (as in Figure 4.6) and adjusting the sharpness, contrast, saturation, and color tone, you can begin to shape a more cinematic image (see Figure 4.7). Be aware that when you're looking at the small screen of the camera, the image will look better than when it's on a large screen.

Figures 4.8 and 4.9 are examples of SuperFlat and ExtraFlat settings (before any postproduction color grading). Be aware that the SuperFlat and ExtraFlat are designed to be adjusted in postproduction; using Magic Bullet plugins, for example, provides a lot of latitude in adjusting flat styles. If you're working with color correction tools, be sure to practice before committing to a particular picture style. Do test shots and take them through post!

FIGURE 4.2
Standard. Zeiss 100 mm, f/3.5.
(Photo by Kurt Lancaster.)

FIGURE 4.3
Portrait. Zeiss 100 mm, f/3.5.
(Photo by Kurt Lancaster.)

Picture Style: Standard (see Figure 4.2)

- Sharpness: +3
- Contrast: 0 (middle)
- Saturation: 0 (middle)
- Color tone: 0 (middle)

Notes: This picture style is too sharp and oversaturated; not good for attaining the cinematic look.

Picture Style: Portrait (see Figure 4.3)

- Sharpness: +2
- Contrast: 0 (middle)
- Saturation: 0 (middle)
- Color tone: 0 (middle)

Notes: The sharpness makes the image look worse and will move your image away from the cinematic look and maintain a video feel.

Picture Style: Landscape (see Figure 4.4)

- Sharpness: +4
- Contrast: 0 (middle)
- Saturation: 0 (middle)
- Color tone: 0 (middle)

Notes: As sharpness increases, the image tends to look worse for cinema projects. This picture style is designed to provide color accuracy, especially for the subject, but it'll likely look too much like video.

FIGURE 4.4
Landscape. Zeiss 100 mm, f/3.5.
(Photo by Kurt Lancaster.)

Picture Style: Faithful (see Figure 4.5)

- Sharpness: 0 (all the way to the left)
- Contrast: 0 (middle)
- Saturation: 0 (middle)
- Color tone: 0 (middle)

Notes: This picture style is designed to provide color accuracy, especially for the subject. But when you shoot Neutral or flat, you'll be able to pull these colors out in post.

FIGURE 4.5
Faithful. Zeiss 100 mm, f/3.5.
(Photo by Kurt Lancaster.)

Picture Style: Neutral (see Figure 4.6)

- Sharpness: 0 (all the way to the left)
- Contrast: 0 (middle)
- Saturation: 0 (middle)
- Color tone: 0 (middle)

Notes: This picture style is designed for the most leeway in post-production color grading. It provides you with room to play in post without burning in the video look as most of the other picture styles tend to do. You should begin with this setting and then adjust and test the settings you need for your look.

FIGURE 4.6
Neutral. Zeiss 100 mm, f/3.5.
(Photo by Kurt Lancaster.)

Picture Style: Hurlbut (User-Defined)
see Figure 4.7)

- Sharpness: 0 (all the way to the left)
- Contrast: 0 (middle)
- Saturation: −1 (one click to the left)
- Color tone: 0 (middle)

Notes: This is probably one of the best picture styles you can play with. Use it as a basis and experiment. This is the setting Shane Hurlbut, ASC, recommends on his blog. In *The Last 3 Minutes*, he bumped the Contrast to −4 and Saturation to −2—the basic settings for shooting your image flat, which reinforces the point that you need to test and adjust until you have the look you want.

FIGURE 4.7
User-Defined: Hurlbut. Zeiss 100 mm, f/3.5.
(Photo by Kurt Lancaster.)

Picture Style: SuperFlat (User-Defined) (see Figure 4.8)

- Sharpness: 0
- Contrast: −4 (all the way to the left)
- Saturation: −2 (two clicks to the left)
- Color tone: 0 (middle)

Notes: This is the setting Jeremy Ian Thomas recommends for those experienced in postproduction color grading, but others argue you may lose natural skin tones, so be sure to test before committing to a particular picture style.

Picture Style: ExtraFlat (see Figure 4.9)

- Sharpness: 2 (two clicks from the left)
- Contrast: −4 (all the way to the left)
- Saturation: −4 (all the way to the left)
- Color tone: +2 (two clicks from the right)

Notes: As you can see, the image is washed out, but some colorists say that using these kinds of settings is the best way to do serious color grading. If you compare both the SuperFlat and ExtraFlat images to the one in Neutral, you can see the black in the car and the pupils of the model's eyes crushed, but the flat settings lower the contrast (blacks not crushed) and provide two stops of latitude out of the shadows.

FIGURE 4.8
User-Defined: SuperFlat. Zeiss
100 mm, f/3.5.
(Photo by Kurt Lancaster.)

FIGURE 4.9
Use-Defined: ExtraFlat. Zeiss
100 mm, f/3.5.
(Photo by Kurt Lancaster.)

ExtraFlat was designed by Eugenia Loli when she wasn't fully satisfied with the SuperFlat setting, claiming that it was too saturated. She took the Neutral setting as her base, and "it's a tiny bit less contrasty, but a lot less saturated, and it doesn't have the 'red face' attribute of the video look" (Loli, E. (2010, January 25). Flatting the flat look. Eugenia.gnomefiles.org. <http://eugenia.gnomefiles.org/2010/01/25/flatting-the-flat-look/>, accessed May 19, 2010).

The ExtraFlat file can be downloaded from <http://eugenia.gnomefiles.org/images2/ExtraFlat.zip>. Steps to install downloaded custom picture styles are covered on page 77; see steps 1–5 and 11–15 of "Picture Styles—Step by Step."

As can be seen in all the picture style photos of the model, Lillie Laraque, the Canon 5D Mark II biases the reds. ExtraFlat is least impacted by this bias. This issue can be corrected in postproduction or altered in the camera's color correction setup feature, which is covered later in the chapter.

Embracing 8-Bit Color Compression

Shane Hurlbut, ASC

With the 5D Mark II, I embrace the compression and that adds to my cocktail of making it look like film.[4] So with 8-bit compressed color, treat it like reversal film stock[5]— you have to get it close [to make it work right]. You cannot take an image that you forgot to adjust your color temp, and it comes in blue and want to turn it white. Well, you can get it there, but it's going to feel unnatural. Treat the image like you are putting the latent image that will have no color correction possibilities onto that CF card. And that has been my recipe. ... I take the camera and turn it into a digital imaging technician. The camera becomes the DIT. So in my picture styles, I have a picture style that I match to my lighting. That's the look of the movie. So if we put the picture style up and if it's day exteriors, we roll with that picture style and we see where it is and then I slide over to what we call SEAL raw [shooting in a flatter mode]. And SEAL raw was a picture style that I basically went into the computer and bent the [color and contrast] curves so that I could suppress the highlights a little bit so they didn't blow so much, and give me a little more latitude in the blacks. So we dial in our exposure and match lighting with the picture style that will be the latent image of the movie, then ... right before we rolled, we slid it down and punched the select button and rolled on SEAL raw. It would give me a little more color correction ability in the under- and the over-exposed areas. Since the film, *Act of Valor* (2012), I have altered this approach as I navigate without an owner's manual. I use an HP 2480 Dreamcolor ZX Lighting monitor with a rec. 709 function LUT [Lookup Table]. Now, I keep a flat picture style on the camera and don't have to switch back and forth. (Red center #056. <http://media.fxguide.com/redcentre/redcentre-056.mp3>, accessed 24 March, 2010)

Adjusting the RED Camera (Scarlet, Epic) with Mysterium-X Sensor

Jim Mathers, a cinematographer and president of the Digital Cinema Society, discusses what he does when adjusting the settings on his RED camera with the Mysterium-X sensor. RED is a camera designed to be shot in a flat mode with the assumption that all the shots will be color-graded in post (and therefore needs to be color-graded in post before you can tell what it looks like):

> The in-camera metering has been steadily improving with each firmware update, but with the new sensor and the latest firmware build, which supports "FLUT™", (Floating-Point Lookup Table,) and REDcolor, the new Color Science for Mysterium-X, it is very well dialed in. There are really more exposure guides than anyone should ever need including False Color, Stop Lights, Zebras, Histogram, Goal Posts, Barber Pole, RAW Check, and... I honestly don't use these in-camera tools too much, or even know what they all do.

---

[4] Hurlbut knows that film is closer to a 20-bit compression. However, he feels if he embraces the limitations of the 8-bit color space of the Canon DSLRs—instead of forcing it to do what it can't—he can work around those limitations and attain a film look that works for him.

[5] In other words, worry about blowing out the highlights, so be sure to expose for the highlights.

What I like to do instead is to record a shot, then quickly load it into REDCINE-X™. This is a free application, downloadable to those registered at RED.com. It provides very sophisticated color analysis software allowing you to view the image in a variety of color spaces and several Gamma Spaces, even custom. As with RED Alert, you can adjust color, contrast, saturation, and adjust the gamma curve with a number of different interfaces, readjusting the settings you had loaded in as Metadata when you shot. You can even White Balance in post by dragging the cursor to whatever you might want to reference as white in your picture on the viewer. To top it off, you can download these settings back into the camera for better on-set calibration, which should be a great help in matching multiple cameras.

There's a lot to play within the new REDCINE-X™, and I found just going through

it to be a very educational exercise in color management. Not that I would think myself competent to grade a movie, but it gives me a glimpse into the kinds of tools available to the trained Colorist, and I think it will help me communicate the next time I'm supervising a color timing session. In this case, it is all about giving me the confidence to make quick decisions on the set as the sun is going down, in and out of clouds, or for whatever reason I am, as usual, rushed.

(*Digital Cinema Society Newsletter*, March 26, 2010 #6.2)

Note: For those not using a RED and needing a sophisticated production tool to communicate with postproduction, take a look at Gamma and Density's DcP software at <http://3cp.gammadensity.com/index-2-prod-3cP.html>. You can download a demo version and test it to see if it meets your needs.

USING TECHNICOLOR'S CINESTYLE IN *GRAND CANYON WINTER*

Video at: http://vimeo.com/33850967 working in collaboration with Canon, Technicolor scientists spent 12 months developing a picture style designed for filmmakers planning to engage in postproduction color correction—the process of not only fixing color in post—but for digging out the widest possible exposure range in Canon DSLR cameras. According to Technicolor, CineStyle "optimizes the dynamic range in the image by leveraging the capabilities of the Canon imaging chipset" (<http://www.technicolor.com/en/hi/cinema/filmmaking/digital-printer-lights/cinestyle>). It does this by using a log color space rather than linear. Linear provides for an equal distribution of data bit information; logarithmic information allows for bits to be distributed into the darks and highlights in order to provide more detail in these areas. Qvo-Labs claims that the log 8-bit color space (found in Canon DSLR's video mode) can reach a "close equivalent" of 12 bits! (See Qvo-Labs detailed explanation: <http://www.qvolabs.com/Digital_Images_ColorSpace_Log_vs_Linear.html>).

Shane Hurlbut agrees. With the new "color science behind" the CineStyle, Hurlbut says he is "finding much cleaner results in the post color correction process." (<http://www.hurlbutvisuals.com/blog/2011/05/08/technicolors-new-picture-style-cine-style/>).

I tested Technicolor's CineStyle in the Grand Canyon during the winter—the snow and canyon walls providing a high contrast range. By shooting after

FIGURE 4.10
Setting up a push-in shot at the Grand Canyon with the Canon 5D Mark II and the Kessler Crane Pocket Dolly, Manfrotto 501HDV head, and Cullman tripod.
(Photo by Stephanie Petrie. Used with permission.)

What was used (see Figure 4.10):
Camera: Canon 5D Mark II
ISO: 160
Shutter: 1/40
Lens: Zeiss Contax 50 mm f/1.4
Aperture: f/8
Filter: Tiffen HT Ultra Clear (55 mm)
ND filter: Light Craft Workshop ND fader (55 mm)
Support: Tripod, Zacuto Z-Finder Pro, Kessler Crane Pocket Dolly Traveler
Picture Style: Technicolor's CineStyle (<http://www.technicolor.com/en/hi/cinema/filmmaking/digital-printer-lights/cinestyle>)
Editing, color grading, and sound:
Final Cut Pro X
Music: <http://incompetech.com/>

a snowstorm, I attempted to overcome the limitations of the DSLR exposure range by pushing the CineStyle picture style to its limits.

I used Light Craft Workshop's ND variable fader, mounted on my Zeiss Contax 50 mm f/1.4 lens. As discussed in the previous chapter, when you want shallow depth of field and want to maintain an open aperture, then the ND filter is the best tool to use when shooting in daylight. However, I initially realized I may have shot too dark, but I knew with CineStyle I could fix it in post!

In either case, instead of burning in color and exposure (such as with Canon's Faithful picture style, for example), the CineStyle does the opposite—it flattens the look, allowing for the widest possible exposure range during post. It looks gray.

For this project, I also wanted to bring motion to the shots. Cinematic motion is like poetry in the film world, so I used my Kessler Crane Pocket Dolly Traveler mounted to a Manfrotto 501HDV head (and Cullman carbon fiber sticks).

Once the footage was shot, I dumped the footage onto my MacBook Pro (quad core with 8 GB of RAM) and external G-Tech mini hard drive (FireWire 800, 7200 rpm, 750 GB).

However, unlike shooting with one of Canon's Picture Styles, where you do not need to do any work in post, the CineStyle *requires* you to do postproduction work, otherwise the image looks washed out and flat. It holds extra data in the bit-space, but you won't see it until you go into postproduction. (See Figure 4.11.)

FIGURE 4.11
A view of the Grand Canyon using Technicolor's CineStyle. Notice how flat, washed out, and grey the image looks. CineStyle requires that you dig out the color and exposure information in postproduction.
(Still from Grand Canyon Winter *by Kurt Lancaster.)*

After applying exposure correction in Final Cut Pro X, the image reveals rich reds and blues as well as details in the highlight area of the snow (see Figure 4.12).

FIGURE 4.12
After post, the Grand Canyon is revealed with bold colors and a large dynamic range (notice the details captured in the snow).
(Still from Grand Canyon Winter *by Kurt Lancaster.)*

I attained this look by adjusting the highlights, midtones, and shadow levels using the color correction tools in Final Cut Pro X. (See Figure 4.13.) Above the line increases the value, while moving the circle below the line decreases values. I adjust the midtones down to help remove the wash in the CineStyle image, making the overall image darker, and increased the highlights to make the image brighter.

FIGURE 4.13
The adjustment tools in Final Cut X provide the tools needed to remove the flat washout look of CineStyle. It digs out the data for the high dynamic range of the image.
(Still from Grand Canyon Winter *by Kurt Lancaster.)*

If you do not want to adjust the correction manually, Pomfort (<http://pomfort. com/plugins/dslrlog2video-tryandbuy.html>) sells an S-curve look up table (LUT), a plugin for Final Cut Pro (7 and X), which allows you to drag and drop the plugin on your footage, applying the correction automatically. (See Figure 4.14.) (It currently retails at $29, so it may be worth the investment.) I noticed with some tests that you still may want to tweak the image, even after applying the effect.

FIGURE 4.14
The DSLRLog2Video plugin for Final Cut Pro X from Pomfort. Just drag and drop the icon onto the image and the effect is applied instantaneously. Notice the shadows are dark, so additional tweaking may still be required after applying the effect.
(Still from Grand Canyon Winter *by Kurt Lancaster.)*

Technicolor's CineStyle may be the strongest tool Canon DSLR shooters have at their disposal when attempting to shape a cinematic look to their films. It helps set up a large dynamic range and when used with a filmic sense of color grading in post, it provides a lot of potential in crafting a film-like look.

PRODUCTION COLOR CORRECTION

Shane Hurlbut, ASC, quickly embraced the Canon 5D Mark II as a cinema camera—but with limitations. He discovered that the 8-bit color space did not give him the postproduction latitude he was accustomed to in film:

Our solution was to go back to the un-compressed Cineform or Adobe CS5 4:4:4 files and start anew.[6] This worked very well and it seemed to give us much more range. I also realized too late that this camera needs light. If you don't feed it enough light, the 8-bit compressed color space quickly goes to 4- and then to 2-bit color space.[7] You can always create contrast by stretching the image by pushing the whites and pulling your blacks down. Underexposure is a powerful tool with this camera, but the whole image cannot be underexposed. It will result in noise, fall apart quickly in color correction and just look muddy.

(Hurlbut, S. (March 30, 2010,). Color Correction: Put Your Best Foot Forward. *Hurlblog* <http://hurlbutvisuals.com/blog/2010/03/30/color-correction-put-your-best-foot-forward>)

Essentially, Hurlbut realized that the H.264 codec Canon uses doesn't have much wiggle room in post with color correction. Although it can be edited natively with some software (including Final Cut Pro), it is not the way to go because it's being used as an origination codec, not a postproduction one. DSLR footage must be up-rezzed to a 4:4:4 or 4:2:2 color space. One of the ways to work around the codec in-camera, Hurlbut suggests, is to try to attain the look with Canon's Picture Style Editor, modifying a RAW still image and then save it as a look you can upload into the camera (see Figure 4.15).

In addition to engaging such user-defined picture styles as SuperFlat, ExtraFlat, or Technicolor's CineStyle, one of the key features of the Canon DSLR revolves around the custom picture style, which allows you to take a RAW photo and set *that* as your user-defined picture style. Only use this process if you have a strong technical mastery over crafting your image and you have a calibrated monitor. I recommend that you shoot with Technicolor's PictureStyle for projects using postproduction color correction. But for those of you wanting to experiment with the look of your film projects, follow these steps:

---

[6] Chapter 6, on postproduction, covers the Cineform codec for decompressing the movie files.
[7] This occurs when a poor lighting and/or wrong ISO setting is used.

FIGURE 4.15
The picture style for *The Last 3 Minutes* was shot in modified neutral with a −4 on Contrast and −2 on Saturation.
(Still from The Last 3 Minutes *©2010 Hurlbut Visuals. Used with permission.)*

PICTURE STYLE—STEP BY STEP

1. Take a RAW picture.[8]
2. Plug the camera into the computer and turn it on.
3. Open up EOS Utility (install from the provided EOS Digital Solution Disk that comes with the camera); it looks like the image in Figure 4.16.

FIGURE 4.16
Canon's software for computer control of the camera.

---

[8] One DSLR shooter notes how he takes a different picture for each ISO and color temperature setting; he created three picture profiles taking into consideration different color temps: Tungsten (indoor), daylight shade, and normal daylight (Tico 2010). <http://hurlbutvisuals.com/blog/2010/03/30/color-correction-put-your-best-foot-forward/>.

4. Click on the Accessories button (there are two: Control Camera and Accessories), which takes you to the window shown in Figure 4.17.

FIGURE 4.17
Window to the Picture Style Editor.

5. Open the Picture Style Editor. If you're installing a picture style you've downloaded, such as ExtraFlat, go to step 11.
6. Open the folder containing the RAW image you want to reference and drag and drop it to the window shown in Figure 4.18.

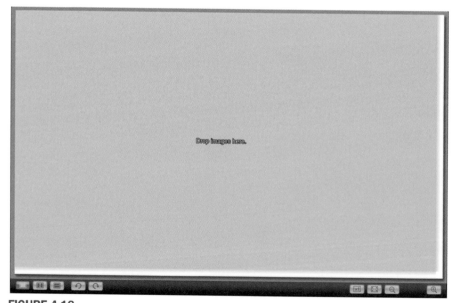

FIGURE 4.18
The empty screen where you can drag an image for picture style manipulation.

7. Click on the second button from the bottom left (the image with two little windows), and you get two images: one is the original, and the second is the one you'll manipulate (see Figure 4.19).

FIGURE 4.19
A two-up image for picture style manipulation. On the left is the untouched RAW image, while the right image shows the changes you can make in the far-right window.

8. The diagonal line in the lower-right grid represents a gamma curve. Adjusting this allows you to shape the look of your picture style. Click on the line and drag the mouse to adjust the image.

9. Dragging a point on the lower part of the line to the left will expand the space in the blacks, providing a bit more dynamic range (see Figure 4.20). Dragging it to the right will crush the blacks. Shane Hurlbut, ASC, recommends just a slight curve to the left to open up the blacks a bit. As you adjust the setting, the input/output will receive a number value. High values—the brights—should be lessened; you can do so by creating a node near the top of the line and then dragging it slightly to the right.

10. The middle of the line allows you to adjust the midrange values. The more you bend the curves, the more extreme the image, so slight adjustments are recommended. Essentially, you're stretching the blacks and whites and making them flat, which is the opposite of the goal in post—where you want to deepen the blacks and slowly roll off the whites. Experimentation is the best school, when it comes to shaping picture profiles! Test it out before going into production.

11. After you've made the adjustment to your taste, getting the look as close as possible to the final look you desire, save the file. If you're doing a

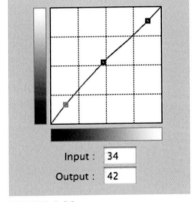

FIGURE 4.20
Click on the gamma curve line to make changes to the image in the picture style window.

professional-style shoot, you'll want two files: one reflecting the final look you want as a lookup table, and the other you'll want to create as a flat look, which is the best way to engage color grading in post. If you're not planning to do much post work, such as when you're shooting a journalism piece needing a fast turnaround, get the look you want as close as possible. This is the new picture style that you'll upload to the camera.

12. Go to EOS Utilities and click on the Camera settings/Remote shooting menu (see Figure 4.21). The camera must be plugged into the computer and turned on for these menu items to appear.

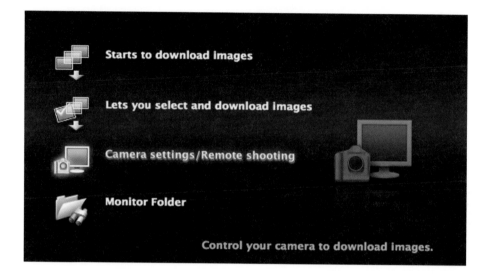

FIGURE 4.21
Main menu.

13. You should see a window with a control panel to your camera, which includes battery life, f-stop settings, color temperature, shutter speed, and what picture style you're currently on, among other features (see Figure 4.22). Look at the Picture Style section and click on User Def. 1 (there are three, and you can choose any one of them).

14. You can click on the picture style and adjust the detail settings, white balance shift, and so forth (see Figure 4.23). Click on Register User Defined style.[9]

15. This will take you to a window where you can select from a drop-down menu or open a folder. In this case, open the folder and select the picture file you created from the adjusted RAW image in Picture Style Editor (see Figure 4.24). *Note: This is the step you use if you're downloading an existing picture style, such as ExtraFlat.*

16. After you've selected your picture style file, your window will show the file. It includes the adjustments made in the picture detail shown in Figure 4.25.

---

[9] Notice the Live View shoot … button. Clicking on it will allow you to see your camera's image through your laptop. If you're in the field and want to use your laptop as a field monitor, this feature allows you to do so.

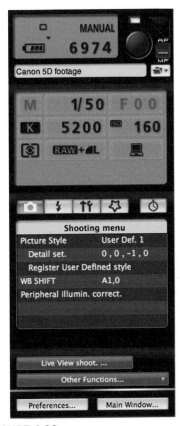

FIGURE 4.22
The control panel to the 5D Mark II camera. It not only provides the current settings of the camera, but allows you to import picture styles.

FIGURE 4.23
The data for the picture style as shown in the control panel window.

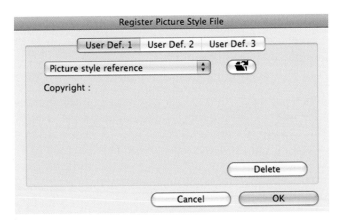

FIGURE 4.24
Three user-defined styles can be assigned. Click the folder button to upload your particular picture style for each.

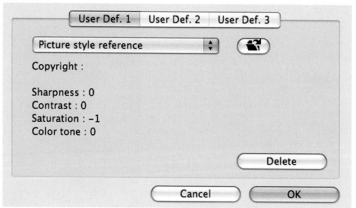

FIGURE 4.25
After you upload the picture style, the window will provide an overview of the settings in-camera.

The picture style has been set and saved into your camera. Anytime you choose this user-defined style, you'll be shooting in the mode you shaped through the Picture Style Editor. Just as a cinematographer will test film stock before shooting, you should test it and experiment with others before shooting. Use a flat mode when shooting if you're planning to do any color grading in post, and use the lookup table as your film look reference point. The best test is to put it through the decompression and editing workflow and export it onto a large screen and view it. You should be making these picture style edits only with a calibrated monitor in order to ensure accuracy, which is imperative if you're transferring the footage to film. And taking the advice of the film-out company you're using is a must when you're planning to screen the end result on film.

COLOR BALANCE

Having used 15 different 5D Mark IIs on the shoot of the Navy SEALS movie, *Act of Valor* (2012), Hurlbut says he noticed different biases in the sensors; some have a slight cast of yellow or magenta. Bernardo Uzeda, the director and postproduction person on the Brazilian short *Casulo* (featured in Chapter 8), notes how the 5D Mark II used on the shoot was "very sensitive to the color red" and he removed "red from almost 100% of the shots" in postproduction.

I teach students to shoot a white or gray card image in the lighting conditions they're shooting under (making sure to dial in the proper color temperature) and be sure the image is truly white (or grey). If there's a slight color cast, then the color balance of the camera may be adjusted manually by clicking on the Menu button on the camera and going into the white balance shift/white balance bracketing (WB SHIFT/BKT) menu located under tab 2 (Shooting 2 submenu of the main menu; see Figure 4.26).

After you select the WB SHIFT/BKT submenu, you will be taken to the color correction window (see Figure 4.27).

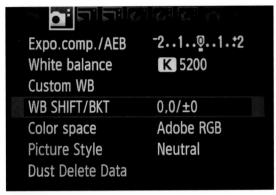

FIGURE 4.26
The list of submenu items under tab 2 of the main menu in the Canon 5D Mark II.
(Image courtesy of Canon.)

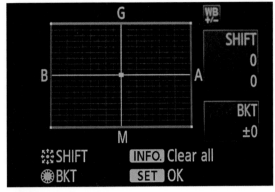

FIGURE 4.27
The white balance shift window. B = blue, G = green, A = amber, M = magenta. Move the camera's toggle switch to adjust the parameters.
(Image courtesy of Canon.)

By making adjustments with the toggle, you can remove the color cast. Use the opposite color for the one you want to alter. If it's reddish, move the point toward the green, for example. You can also use this tool to add color to a scene if you are trying to attain that look. Again, test it first in the field.

The most important point revolves around the fact that an 8-bit color depth is "thin," to use the words of Hdi RAWworks colorist Jeremy Ian Thomas, especially in a Canon 5D Mark II. And as Hurlbut explains, the compressed H.264 codec doesn't help because there's very little room to stretch the look of the image in post. Therefore, attain your look as close as possible to the final product. An additional note, Thomas explains that, as a colorist, he prefers the Canon 7D because the pixels are more dense—not stretched as thin as the 5D—and it gives him a little bit more play in post. Shooting a color-true chart might also be useful when wanting to get your color temperature right (look up "DSC color chart" on the Web), but they can be pricey, around $200.

To sum up, Jared Abrams of WideOpenCamera.com, discusses the importance of planning the look of the film before you shoot:

> You are building a race car, you are priming it and these guys get to paint it and boy wouldn't it be a bummer if they painted it day glow orange on you? Neil Smith at Hdi RAWworks is really passionate about—and I agree with him totally—talking to your colorist; talk to your post people first before you ever shoot with the camera. Talk to someone about the post processing and the color so when you shoot you can favor what they need to make the best product.

This chapter gave you an overview of what picture styles look like and how to engage picture styles to shape the look of your film before shooting it; it also covered the ability to shape the color correction of Canon DSLRs in-camera. The next chapter covers one of the *most* important tools in attaining a film look—recording quality audio—because no matter how good your look is, if the audio is bad, the audience will not be able to see how good it looks. Therefore, a clean audio recording is essential in achieving the potential cinematic quality of your project. Without it, you have less than half a film. Audio is not an afterthought, because good audio can make your film shine more than any other tool.

CHAPTER 5

Recording Quality Audio with DSLRs: Yes, It's Possible!

RECORD SOUND LIKE A FILMMAKER

The cinema law of sound: No one can watch a film if the audio sounds bad. No matter how good the image, poor audio quality will block your viewers from ever appreciating the image. Do not *ever* skimp on sound. It is the most important element in scenes with dialog. In fact, you can present a fairly poor image and if the audio is spot on, people will enjoy the movie—more so than good images accompanied by bad sound. Bad sound is a dead giveaway that the film was made by an amateur.

With DSLR cameras, it's pretty easy to get bad sound. But with some basic knowledge and the proper tools, the DSLR shooter can record great audio. Most of the large sensor video cameras contain XLR inputs, where filmmakers can plug in audio with professional connections—just don't use the built-in microphones of any video camera or DSLR. Dialog should never be recorded with the built-in camera mics—ever. Jared Abrams (WideOpenCamera.com), says he likes the fact that DSLRs make you go "back to basics" of filmmaking:

> The way they started motion picture was one frame at a time. And eventually they just strung 'em together until it looked like something they were used to and liked, and off we went. The DSLR cameras are doing just the same thing. It's a great sync-sound camera. If you treat it like that, then you'll get the most out of it. If you run separate sound, you will get better sound. And the fact that they didn't jam all this audio into it just makes it a more potent camera. That's one of the bad things about standard little video cameras is that they're trying to jam all this audio technology into it.
>
> **(Interview with author, March 2010.)**

Whether you're shooting with a DSLR or a large sensor video camera with XLR inputs[1] the best sound will always come from an external recorder with a field mixer. This is what professional filmmakers do anyway. And DSLRs, when treated like a film camera needing external audio, allows the camera to be excellent at recording video. Because DSLR manufacturers decided to deliver a strong picture over strong audio—and there's a compromise on space—DSLR shooters must shoot like filmmakers when recording sound. Ideally, recording sound separately, or at the very least, disabling the automatic gain control (AGC) in the camera, getting the proper microphones, and connecting the mic to a professional audio adapter (containing a preamp with limiters) are essential in getting the best possible sound.

This chapter defines sound quality, provides terminology for different microphone types, the different audio gear you can get, how to use Magic Lantern to get in-camera monitoring of audio on some Canon DSLRs, and a case-study on capturing "run-and-gun" audio with a 5D Mark II.

> DSLR shooters must shoot like filmmakers when recording sound.

The following are some basics you, as the filmmaker, should consider when recording audio for your projects:

1. What is the *sound quality* of the space you're recording, whether indoors or outdoors?
2. What *type of microphone* will you use, such as a shotgun mic or a lavaliere? Or are you stuck with just an onboard mic? The choice will determine your pickup pattern (what area of sound the mic will favor when recording).
3. Will you use a *condenser* or *dynamic* mic? Will it be powered through its own battery or from the camera's power, providing "phantom" power? (Most DSLRs don't provide phantom.)
4. Will you have *high impedance* or *low impedance*—minijack input or XLR input? A high impedance mic can pick up radio interference.
5. Can you *disable automatic gain control* of your audio and manually control the sound?
6. What is the *compression* of your audio recording?
7. Where will you *place* the microphone? Will it be a camera-mounted mic, or will you use a boom pole or pistol grip? Microphones mounted on a camera must be close to the subject in order to get a clean signal.

---

[1] XLR inputs are not the savior of good audio! Some argue against using DSLRs because they lack XLR inputs—I've taught some form of video production for over 12 years; most of that time was dedicated to using prosumer video cameras containing XLR inputs, but I would still get bad audio from some students. And I have some students now who will record with a Zoom H4n, and they'll still get bad recordings—not because they're using a DSLR, but because if you do not know now to place a mic properly or set levels correctly it doesn't matter if the camera contains XLR inputs or not—a bad mic placement will result in poor audio and improper levels.

8. Will you use an *external audio recorder* or just record it to the camera (or both)? Most external audio recorders provide phantom power, but it eats up the batteries fast.

The answers to these questions will determine your audio quality. This chapter covers these topics so you can be more informed in your choices as you shoot and know the impact of compromises. You should test through postproduction and into a final export of your project to understand what your final field audio recording will sound like.

Sound Quality

Just as the cinematographer must be aware of the quality and source of light in a scene, filmmakers need to be aware of the ambient room quality. Is it hard or soft? Hard walls and hard floors will reverb your audio, providing micro-echoes of sound in the space. Test the sound quality by yelling in the space. If you hear an echo, reverb will be abundant and the audio may sound a bit tinny. A room with carpeting, furniture, and so forth will absorb the sound and break up the audio wavelengths, so the reverb will be minimized. Outdoors (other than an alley, for example) will likely provide a soft sound quality. A windy day will cause audio impacts, pretty much ruining the recording. Using a windscreen will minimize this damage—not the foam windscreen that usually comes with the mic, but a large, thick, furry screen covering a sound blimp for wind production (such as the one depicted in Figure 5.8).

In addition, the filmmaker must decide if the subjects should sound close or far away. In most cases, their voices should sound as though they're close, so the microphone must be brought in close (less than three feet or closer). If distance needs to be conveyed, then pull the microphone back so it sounds as though someone is talking across the room, for example.

In addition, many DSLR cameras utilize automatic gain control, which means the camera will adjust the levels of the audio coming into the recording, depending on how much sound is hitting the mic. A lot of sound will lower the input, whereas soft sounds will force the camera to increase the levels, typically causing unwanted hiss. In either case, the AGC will result in *bad* sound by recording uneven audio levels and adding extra noise when the levels are low and the AGC increases to compensate. In most cases, you want to turn off the AGC, which is really not an option for most DSLR cameras. The Canon 5D Mark II and III, Canon 60D, and the Rebel T3i allow for manual control of the audio. BeachTek and juicedLink are two companies that provide devices to disable the AGC of cameras and allow you to input XLR microphones (more about them later in the chapter). These devices trick the camera so that it thinks all the audio is even, allowing manual control of the audio. In addition, the firmware hack Magic Lantern will remove AGC as well (but not in the Rebel T3i or 7D).

Furthermore, audio is recorded at different qualities. A 44.1 kHz, 16-bit recording is lower quality than a 48 kHz, 24-bit recording. The first number refers to the sampling rate—the amount of times per second the audio is sampled

(44,100/second), and the second number refers to the amount of information recorded per sample (16 or 24). If you're using an external recorder, you have the option of setting different compression schemes. Just make sure you set the same compression as the camera so you can sync them up in post. Do not use compressed mp3 recording—no matter how high the bit rate. Keep your audio data as raw as possible!

Also, when recording audio, such as dialog, be sure to record room tone in every space you record. Have everyone on set be quiet and record blank audio for at least a minute. This will capture the ambient sound you will need in editing in order to fill in gaps between takes or to even out the sound quality from different takes.

Checklist for Sound Quality

1. Are you indoors or outdoors?
2. What is the surface quality of the environment? Will the sound reverb, or is it absorbed in the environment? If you're getting a lot of reverb, get the microphone in really close.
3. Do you want your subject to sound close?
4. Do you want your subject to sound far away?
5. Can you turn off the automatic gain control? If not, then use an audio adapter (or Magic Lantern on some Canon DSLRs) that turns it off or use an external digital audio recorder.
6. What is your compression value? (You don't need this unless you're using an external device.)

The following sections provide an overview of some of the equipment you may think about using on your shoots. They include a justification of what works well and why. Some of this information may be a review for experienced filmmakers, so feel free to skip over it. If you're relatively new to filmmaking, the information may be useful, especially if you're trying to get better sound for your projects. The final section of the chapter will walk you through two audio workflow setups covering the recording of an external onboard mic and an external digital recorder with the intention of syncing your audio (covered in Chapter 6 on postproduction workflow).

Microphone Types

Microphone types sound differently; they will convey distinctive audio qualities depending on the space you're in. The major mic types include lavalieres (lavs), omnidirectionals (omnis), cardioids, and shotguns. They will never sound the same.

- Lavs are needed for wide shots with dialog (we'll see the boom pole with a shotgun mic in a wide shot).

- Cardioids are for use indoors.
- Shotguns are for outdoor medium and close-up shots.

Cardioids provide the best sound recording but pick up too much noise out-side. Because shotgun mics have the rear lobe pickup pattern, they'll pick up reflections of sound off the ceiling and wall, resulting in interference when shooting indoors. Lavs, although useful for picking up dialog in a wide shot, don't sound as good and need to be postprocessed to bring back the warmth of a person's voice. For run-and-gun journalists and documentary filmmakers, the shotgun is the best choice if you can choose only one mic.

Many of these mics include space for a battery, but you will want to use phan-tom power if available because it will increase the quality during recording, although it will reduce the battery life of your recorder. The voltage allows the signal to be picked up when sound waves hit the front plate, changing the value of the air quality against a capacitor and turning it into an electric signal. On the other hand, dynamic microphones—the ones you see reporters use on television news—are more rugged and do not require any external power. But the sound quality is not as good as condenser microphones.

Shotgun microphones are unidirectional, oftentimes with a cardioid or super-cardioid pickup pattern. A cardioid pattern allows you to record sounds from the direction the microphone is pointed (see Figure 5.1), whereas a supercar-dioid—found in shotgun mics—does the same thing but also picks up some sound from the rear (see Figure 5.2).

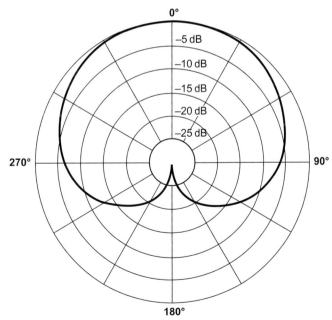

FIGURE 5.1
Cardioid pickup pattern. (The Microphone, your voice's Gateway to the World. *Voiceover4us.com.* <http://www.voiceover4us.com/blog/2008/07/15/14/>, accessed February 2,2010.)

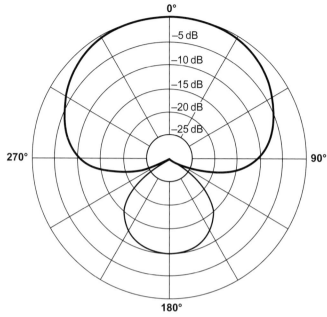

0°

−5 dB

−10 dB

−15 dB

−20 dB

−25 dB

270°

90°

180°

FIGURE 5.2
Super cardioid pickup pattern. Typically found in shotgun mics. (The Microphone, your voice's Gateway to the World. *Voiceover4us.com.* <http://www.voiceover4us.com/blog/2008/07/15/14/>, accessed February 2, 2010.)

FIGURE 5.3
Rode VideoMic Pro with foam cover. This mic includes a built-in shock mount to reduce noise from movement. The foam windscreen is not useful against wind; you'll need a wind muff that's designed for this mic. The frequency response of this mic ranges from 40 Hz to 20 kHz. This mic uses a minijack connector; it's a high impedance mic but can connect directly to the DSLR's microphone jack without any kind of adapter. This minijack mic could be plugged directly into an external audio recorder. You may want to tape the minijack plug so that there's less of a chance of having the cord accidentally being pulled during a recording.
(Image courtesy of Rode.)

One of the popular mics that can be attached to the DSLR's accessory shoe is the Rode VideoMic Pro (see Figure 5.3), a light shotgun mic that attaches on top of the DSLR (see Figure 5.4 for a polar pickup pattern chart for this mic). If you're traveling light and shooting a news piece, documentary, or a wedding solo (without anyone helping out with sound), then this is probably one of the most useful mics you can get for your DSLR. It will not be as good as a shotgun mic with an XLR adapter, but it will provide usable sound for your production.

The Rode VideoMic Pro will provide usable sound for run-and-gun style documentary and journalism work, but it's recommended that it be used to record decent reference audio and as a backup source in case your audio recorder fails. It is better to use a higher-end mic with an XLR adapter, especially if you're submitting for broadcast or to a film festival, where audio really matters.

If you're shooting solo and going for speed, attaching an on-camera mic, such as the Rode VideoMic Pro, is a great choice. When you're talking to someone, be sure that person is close, no more than three feet away, if you want to capture as clean a sound as possible. This may work great for news and documentary. However, when shooting short fiction pieces and commercials, you will want wider shots and still pick up clean audio. But because the performers are more than a few feet away (even five feet is too far), you'll need to run longer cable. Be aware that microphones with minijack plugs (the standard tip-ring-sleeve, or TRS, connectors) are high impedance using unbalanced cables and the signal will weaken over distance, and these mics are prone to picking up noise and interference (such as a radio station). It's best to use a balanced cable (XLR).

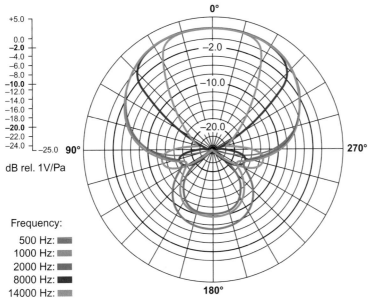

FIGURE 5.4
Rode VideoMic Pro's polar pickup pattern measured in frequency response. The Hertz refers to the wavelength. The lower number is low-frequency sounds such as rumbles and bass. The higher frequency expresses higher tones. A human voice can range from 80 Hz to 1100 Hz.
(Image courtesy of Rode.)

The Rode NTG-2 shotgun mic is a decent dialog microphone, most useful for outdoor shots or indoors if sound reflection is minimal (see Figure 5.5), and if you're shooting solo, attach this mic to a DSLR rig along with an XLR adapter that provides phantom power, and you'll get really good sound. If you have a sound person, this type of mic is a great choice when attaching it to an external recorder (such as a Tascam DR-40 or Zoom H4n).

Whatever shotgun mic you end up using, knowing its strengths and weaknesses is important. Note, for example, the frequency response of the Rode VideoMic Pro compared to the Rode NTG-2. The NTG-2 can go as low as 20 Hz, whereas the VideoMic Pro is limited to 40 Hz. Fewer low frequencies will be picked up by the VideoMic Pro. However, often a boom pole sound

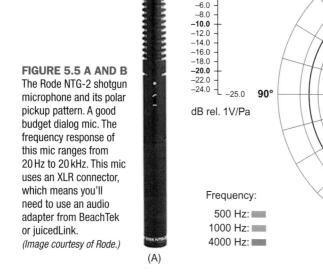

FIGURE 5.5 A AND B
The Rode NTG-2 shotgun microphone and its polar pickup pattern. A good budget dialog mic. The frequency response of this mic ranges from 20 Hz to 20 kHz. This mic uses an XLR connector, which means you'll need to use an audio adapter from BeachTek or juicedLink.
(Image courtesy of Rode.)

(A)

(B)

operator will engage the low-cut filter to minimize boom pole handling, removing the lower frequencies from the shotgun mic.

Shotgun mics provide the best sound in your recording work, but using a shotgun inside a room with a lot of reverb will cause extra audio muddiness.

If, instead, you use a mic with an XLR connector (with balanced cable, which will resist the noise that high-impedance lines will pick up), you will have the advantage of running long cable, and it'll pick up very little to no noise, and the audio quality will stay high. Interference will be minimized. But you will need to hook it up to an XLR adapter if shooting with a DSLR or use an external audio recorder with XLR inputs, because DSLR cameras currently available do not contain XLR inputs (see the "XLR Adapters" section later).

It must be noted that the interference tube in shotgun mics doesn't work well indoors—unless there's a lot of sound absorption material, such as furniture. Sound reflecting off the wall skews the frequency and draws attention to the echo sounds. If all you have is a shotgun mic, typical of run-and-gun style doc shooters, video journalists, and indies, be aware of the space you're in and adjust the direction of the mic, as needed. Holding the mic from below, for example, may minimize sounds bouncing off the walls.

When pointing a shotgun mic at someone, remember that it will pick up sound behind the person, so if she is standing on a sidewalk and you're facing the street with the camera-mic setup, you'll get loud traffic noise. If you have the person turn around so you're facing a storefront, you'll get much cleaner sound. When shooting a documentary in Hood River, Oregon, I interviewed many people on the street asking them about their Sasquatch sightings. The shotgun mic was held close to them, and traffic noise was minimal, despite the number of cars and trucks rumbling by. In addition, holding the mic up in the air (with a boom pole or pistol grip) and pointing down toward your performer's voice will also minimize external sounds because extra noise is minimal when pointing toward the ground.

Most lavaliere mics are omnidirectional, picking up sound from all directions. If you want someone to sound close up and personal, the lav mic, when wired properly, provides good, clean sound. Lavs require a transmitter box that typically hooks to the subject's belt, and a wire attached to the mic is strung up beneath the subject's shirt and hooks onto the shirt collar (see Figure 5.6). An XLR wire connects the transmitter box to the camera's XLR adapter. There are also wireless models, which allow the transmitter to send the audio remotely to a receiver that connects to the XLR adapter.

FIGURE 5.6
Sennheiser's wireless lav G3 microphone system. It's expensive at $600, but the wireless will give you a lot of flexibility on shoots.
(Image courtesy of Rode.)

Built-in mics, no matter the camera, are nearly useless and usually provide poor sound quality. They're useful only for reference audio if you're recording sound externally on a digital recording device. If you must use the onboard mic, make sure it's not windy and make sure your subject is standing less than three feet away.

For DSLR cameras, phantom power is provided only with onboard external XLR adapters or external digital recorders.

Getting the Right Mic and Using a Boom Operator

Filmmaker David Anselmi says that "even a crappy mic sounds better on a boom! A mic with a boom pole and a good boom operator can give you great sound—much, much better than a $1,000 Sennheiser 416 mounted on the camera!"

In addition, Anselmi recommends going for microphones in the $600–$1,000 range. "You may want to do an A/B comparison of a lower-end mic with a high-end mic with excellent audio monitors, so you can hear the difference—you'll never be satisfied with a $250 mic again. Also, for outdoors—especially in heavy wind—a blimp is essential." Words of wisdom as you shop for the right microphone. Testing is always the best rule of thumb. If you're in New York City, B&H Photo has an audio room where you can test microphones (other professional video/audio gear stores will also allow you to test microphones).

Windscreens

Windscreens are absolutely essential when shooting outdoors, even if there's only a light breeze. Wind impacts a microphone's diaphragm hard and can easily damage your audio. The foam covers that come with

FIGURE 5.7
The Rycote Softie offers some protection against wind but is not good for moderate levels of wind.

FIGURE 5.8
Rycote's Miniscreen is a great budget option (~$80) for taking out moderate wind noise on a shotgun microphone.

microphones are really designed to soften the speech of the performer; they're not windscreens and will not hold up to outdoor use even on a light windy day. Rather, using a wind muff or windscreen is the way to go when there is a breeze (see Figure 5.7). They slip over the microphone, and their thick, furry cover breaks up the impact of light breezes. Some models cover the microphone snuggly; others, such as Rycote's Miniscreen, leave a gap between the mic and windscreen, which, from my tests, seems to work better in stronger wind (see Figure 5.8).

XLR Adapters

If you want to get good sound out of a DSLR, utilizing a preamp with XLR connectors is one of the best options if you're not using an external recorder. You'll get a rich and clean signal. This option also allows you to use professional XLR microphones.

Furthermore, using an XLR cable is a must for recording over a distance of a few feet, and because DSLR cameras do not contain XLR inputs, you'll need to use an XLR adapter. JuicedLink and BeachTek are two popular companies that build XLR adapters. The two products I'll describe here also allow for audio monitoring (with headphone inputs), provide phantom power for microphones, and subvert the automatic gain control of the audio in-camera. As noted before, most, if not all, DSLR cameras use AGC; the only exceptions as of this writing are the Canon 60D, 5D Mark II and III, Rebel T3i and the 7D.

Be sure the adapter has the proper transformer and circuits; otherwise, the noise resistance natural to the XLR cable will be lost. In addition, the XLR adaptor box contains a mini-jack that plugs into the DSLR's mic input; this input can easily break. Some people hot glue the right angle connector into the minijack and cable-tie the slack to the camera, connecting and disconnecting the cable from the adapter box.

BEACHTEK DXA-SLR XLR ADAPTER

BeachTek's DXA-SLR model includes a microphone preamp (15 dB) to help provide a clean signal for your microphone (see Figure 5.9). It's designed so you can access the battery of the Canon 5D Mark II. It also has 48 volts of phantom power, which is an added bonus for powering your mics. It doesn't have LED meters for monitoring audio input levels, but it uses a single LED to indicate red when audio clips.

JUICEDLINK'S PREAMP DT454

JuicedLink's preamp DT454 provides clean audio with the circuitry of its preamp—a product designed for video cameras needing XLR adapters (see Figure 5.10). It overrides the automatic gain control of DSLR cameras with an AGC disabler not needed for the Canon 5D, 60D, and Rebel T3i. It allows you to use up to two XLR mics, as well as two minijack unbalanced mics (useful for those who own Rode's VideoMic Pro but want a clean connection and clean sound). It also includes LED level meters, a headphone jack (a must-have!), as well as 48V and 12V of phantom power.

Pistol Grip and Boom Pole

Pistol grips and boom poles are basic tools if you're working with a crew. If you're running and gunning, then stick with your onboard external microphone, but if you have at least one other person helping out on the shoot, use a boom pole to bring your mic in close to your subject. A pistol grip provides a similar tool for medium and close-up shots (see Figure 5.11). I've sat in a chair during an interview and handheld the mic with a pistol grip, just out of frame, and received excellent quality sound because I can place the mic a foot or two closer to the subject than just placing it on-camera. In this kind of setup, I put the camera on a tripod, use an external audio recorder, and sit beside the camera so I can monitor the image during the interview. When using a boom pole, be sure to strap the cord to the pole, so the wire doesn't hit the pole, creating additional noise.

FIGURE 5.9
BeachTek's DXA-SLR model.
(Image courtesy of BeachTek.)

FIGURE 5.10
JuicedLink's preamp DT454.
(Image courtesy of JuicedLink

FIGURE 5.11
A Rycote pistol grip. Great for getting a mic in close when you have tighter shots. The device is designed to minimize noise when holding a shotgun microphone.
(Image courtesy of Rycote.)

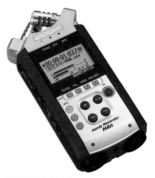

FIGURE 5.12
Zoom H4n audio
recorder.
(Image courtesy of Tascam.)

FIGURE 5.13
Tascam DR-40 audio
recorder.
*(Image courtesy of
Tascam.)*

External Recorders

If you want to get good clean audio with DSLR or large sensor video cameras, the Zoom H4n (~$300) (see Figure 5.12) and Tascam DR-40 (~$200) (see Figure 5.13) are two possible choices for you to record sound separately, while getting a professionally clean recording with XLR mics. For a bit more money, Tascam's DR-100mkii (~$330) is their update for their quality DR-100 model. They record digitally onto an SDHC card.

Essentially, these recorders allow you to hook up a professional microphone to their XLR inputs, so you'll get the clean audio. There are also a variety of settings that can be chosen, but be sure to pick a non-MP3 compressed format. Use 44.1 kHz, 16-bit or 48 kHz, 24-bit (or the one that matches the audio compression of the camera—if it's a different rate, you may get material out of sync). You will still record audio on the camera's microphone and use it as a reference, and replace it with the clean audio after you've synced it up using a lip sync software, such DualEyes, a standalone application for PC or Mac. (Final Cut Pro X has a synchronization feature built into the software.) As a back-up (in case you have to do a manual sync) record a slapping of hands or use a slate at the beginning of the take, and make sure everything's recording; it's sometimes too easy to forget to turn on the external recorder!

Use the Rode VideoMic Pro connected to the DSLR's hotshoe as your reference and backup sound (or hook up a shotgun mic to your video camera; then bring in the XLR mic as close as possible. You could consider putting the device on a small tripod. If you're using only a minijack microphone, you may want to consider getting the Marantz PMD620 audio recorder. It doesn't have XLR inputs, but it'll give you a clean recording—much better than the on-camera mic.

If you do not want to deal with an external recorder and you want the best possible sound out of *any* video camera or DSLR, you may want to consider a more expensive option (~$750): Sound Devices MixPre-D (see Figure 5.14). It's a portable field mixer and mic preamp that contains unclippable limiters, so, if set properly, it will not blow out any sound. It's made of metal, so the rugged device will hold up to some impact abuse. If you're utilizing this with a DSLR, the MixPre-D includes a locking connector to the DSLR, feeding the field mixer's clean audio to the camera. The chief advantage is the ability to use XLR microphones, but you can also monitor audio, engage phantom power for mics, adjust the levels, and view an LED level meter. Hooking this up to an audio recorder (such as the Tascam DR-40) will provide *pristine* sound.

Without such limiters found in the MixPre-D, you'll want to record your audio at 212 dBu or 220 dBu to minimize the risk of clipping audio if a subject or performer gets too loud. However, the audio levels will be low and will have to be boosted in post (usually the normalization gain). When you're boosting, the audio will usually result in increased noise, so you may need to use a noise reduction plug-in for the software. With an optional plate, this device can be attached to the tripod connector of the camera.

External Microphone Audio Recorder

The Rode VideoMic H D (see Fig 5.15) contains not only a modified NTG-3 condenser shotgun microphone and a metal casing mini-blimp (for wind protection), but also a built-in audio recorder—all of which mounts on the shoe adapter of the camera. In addition, it also includes a mini-jack microphone input, a line input, a headphone jack (most DSLRs don't include them) with a headphone amplifier, a level meter, among other features.

Headphones

You *need* to monitor the audio when shooting. The problem with most, if not all, DSLRs is their lack of a headphone jack—thus, the importance of getting an XLR adapter with a headphone input or using an external digital audio recorder. Monitoring sound will allow you to know when something's not working right. Unfortunately, without a headphone jack on the DSLR and monitoring only through the XLR adapter, you don't know if something is going bad with the sound in-camera. This is another reason why using external recorders for DSLRs is important.

With that said, there are headphones designed to sound pretty, and then there are headphones designed to sound accurate: monitor headphones. You want the headphones that sound accurate. One of the best websites detailing unbiased ratings and sales of headphones is <http://headphone.com>. For studio use—mics that will sound accurate—this site recommends four models for ~$100 and under (two of which are at ~$60): Beyerdynamic DT2325 (~$60) and Shure SRH240 (~$60 see Figure 5.15); and Sennheiser HD 280Pro and Shure SRH440 (at ~$100). Go to their site and scroll down to "Headphones for Studio Use": <http://www.headphone.com/selection-guide/dj-and-studio.php>. Sony also makes a monitoring headphone that is good for field production: the MDR-7506 (~$90).

Getting the right headphones—within the parameter of making sure they're designed for monitoring sound (studio and/or field production)—is essential. But once you have the choice paired down to headphones that are designed for accurate monitoring, the ones you purchase should be those that are comfortable for you to wear.

Magic Lantern for Canon DSLRs

The Magic Lantern firmware hack (instructions and software located here: <http://magiclantern.wikia.com/wiki/Unified>) that temporarily updates the camera's firmware booted from the camera's memory card, adding such video camera features as audio meters, headphone monitoring, spot meter,

FIGURE 5.14
Sound Devices MixPre-D is a powerful preamp for adding quality audio to your recordings. Clean and quiet preamps with unclippable limiters make this one of the most powerful tools in your audio arsenal. It includes a DSLR feature that allows you to input this device directly to the camera's unbalanced (high impedance) microphone input.

FIGURE 5.15
Rode's VideoMic H D contains not only a high-end microphone based on their NTG-3 mic, but an audio recorder, as well as a headphone jack, useful for DSLR shooters.
(Image courtesy of Rode.)

histogram, among other functions on most Canon DSLRs. It is free, but it does not work on the 7D and the audio capabilities don't work on the Rebel T3i 600D, but it works with the Canon 5D Mark II, 600D, and Rebel T2i (550D). Installing Magic Lantern does *void* your warranty, and it is not supported by Canon, and this author only recommends it for experienced shooters (he and Focal Press make no warranties or guarantees for your camera). You proceed at your own risk.

Magic Lantern includes disabling of the automatic gain control (AGC) for audio (useful for those shooting with a Rebel T2i 550D—which is absolutely key when you want to even attempt to get usable audio in your footage. Furthermore, it puts the audio bars on the LCD screen so you can see what the audio is doing. Sescom makes a cable that plugs into the AV port of the camera and converts it to a headphones jack. (The Rebel T2i/550D and 60D cable is located here: <http://www.sescom.com/product.asp?item=DSLR-550D-HOCF>; the 5D Mark II cable is located here: <http://www.sescom.com/product.asp?item=DSLR-5DMKII-HOCF>.)

Furthermore, it contains a focus assist tool that lights up the focus plane with blue pixels, so you don't have to wonder if you're close on the focus—you know you're there (the feature doesn't work well in low light, however). You can even dial in color temperature on the Rebel T2i (550D), which is a feature already in most of the other Canon cameras.

I have installed it on a Rebel T2i, a 60D, and my personal 5D Mark II and never had a problem with it. Another feature includes the focal length of a zoom lens, as well as the focal plane distance, so focus can be pulled more precisely and helps with marking tape. (See Figure 5.16.)

FIGURE 5.16
Magic Lantern Unified on a Canon 60D. Along the top, we can see the audio meters that change color (green for within the zone, yellow getting hot, red for clipping). It shows the remaining space on the memory card (11.8 GB). The spot meter in the center places the exposure at 34%. While the histogram hovers above center to the right. Along the bottom can be seen the size of the lens and the f-stop setting (50 mm at f/1.8), the shutter speed 1/41, the ISO (400), and the color temperature preset (Sunny). *(Photo by Kurt Lancaster.)*

The installation instructions are located here:

<http://magiclantern.wikia.com/wiki/Unified/install>.

The user guide instructions is located here:

<http://magiclantern.wikia.com/wiki/Unified/UserGuide>.

Here's my short guide for installation (again, I take no responsibility for failed installs and damage to your camera. Proceed at your own risk.):

1. Be sure the camera has the latest firmware release (as of this writing, it's 1.0.9 for the Rebel T2i (550D). Be sure to read the site's latest updates (in some cases, you may need to roll back a Canon update in order to have Magic Lantern work). If not, then go to Canon's website and scroll to the bottom of this page and hit "I agree": <http://web.canon.jp/imaging/ eosd/firm-e/eosdigital7/firmware.html>. You'll be taken to another page where you can download the firmware. Place the file on your memory card and put it back into the camera. Put the camera in manual mode, then index finger dial over to the third toolbar menu. Go to firmware and click on it to update. Be sure your battery is fully charged. (A battery dying during the install can be very bad.)

2. After updating, plug in your camera's memory card to your computer and delete Canon's 1.0.9 firmware from the card.

3. Download the firmware from this page: (as of this writing, the latest version is dated December 22, 2011), <http://magiclantern.wikia.com/wiki/ Release_2011Dec22%20and%20unzip%20it.>

4. Copy all of the Magic Lantern files to the card (don't place it in any folders).

5. Put the memory card back into the camera.

6. Update the Magic Lantern firmware as if you're doing step 1: Put the camera in manual mode on the top dial and dial over to the third toolbar menu. Go to firmware and click on it to update. It'll tell you when it has updated successfully.

7. Pull out the battery for about 10 seconds and turn the camera off.

8. Dial the camera to video mode. Turn on the camera and hit the delete button to bring up the menu.

9. The camera will use Magic Lantern with this card. If you want to use it on other cards, then you will need to install the same files. If you format that card, you'll be given the option to keep Magic Lantern on the card, otherwise you'll have to reinstall it.

10. Read the User's Guide to see what each function does.

My Magic Lantern menu settings (default unless otherwise noted; read the manual for an explanation of the all the settings):

Audio
Audio Gain: This is where you adjust the levels. Mine is currently at 23 dB.
Input Source: You can adjust to include external and internal at the same or choose "external stereo" (which is what I normally do).
Output volume: Sets headphone levels. I've set mine to the maximum of 6 dB.
Audio Meters: ON.

LiveV (I keep everything off, except the following:) Global Draw: ON Focus Peak: D1xy, 1.0, local (Aside from the audio settings, this is the key reason I use Magic Lantern--the ability to know where you are in focus.)
Spotmeter: Percent, AFF
Waveform: Small (sometimes I'll use this over the histogram).

Movie
Movie Restart: ON (When the camera hits the 4GB file size limit around 12 minutes, instead of the recording shutting off, it'll turn itself back on, so you'll only lose about a second.)

I don't adjust any of the other menu settings.

Magic Lantern Case Study—Occupy Wall Street with the Canon 5D Mark II

When shooting on the run, it's important to travel light. I was in New York City on other business in October 2011, when I decided stop on by Zuccotti Park and observe Occupy Wall Street. I brought my Canon 5D Mark II with two Zeiss Contax 50 mm f/1.4 and 35 mm f/2.8 lenses with a Lightcraft ND fader, a Sennheiser ME62/K6 omni-directional condenser microphone (it is a great dialogue mic and short), a Lightwave windscreen, a special XLR to minijack connector (made by ETS), a Sescom AV headphone cable, and headphones. I had one spare battery and two 16 GB memory cards. (See video at: <http://vimeo.com/30500114>.)

Pulling out my gear, I noticed many others using larger video cameras, but with my low-profile setup, I had easy access to many different subjects. I handheld all of the shots (with no rig attached to the camera). I kept the camera close to the subjects (in most cases three feet or less) so as to get their audio clear on my mic as possible (see Figure 5.17). Although I wished I had brought along my shotgun mic, I couldn't find the right windscreen, so I kept with the low profile mic, because I had a windscreen, and I felt that was more important than getting the directional sound of a shotgun mic.

I attached the Sennheiser mic to the shoe mount using a shockmount, and plugged it directly into the mic input of the 5D using the new XLR to minijack camera balun (the ETS PA910) series, providing a low to high impedance connection to the camera. (See Figure 5.18.) In other words,

FIGURE 5.17
By keeping the camera close to the subject (2.5'-3') at Occupy Wall Street in New York City, I was able to record decent audio with a Sennheiser ME62/K6 attached to a 5D Mark II with a shockmount and a XLR to minijack step down cable. Lens: Zeiss Contax 50 mm f/1.4. The open aperture provided a nice shallow depth of field for the interview shots, which allows for the audience to focus on what the subject is saying, while the wider lens was used for deep focus scenic shots. (Lancaster, K. and Sotosky, S. (2011). *Occupy Wall Street—New York City*. Vimeo. com. <http://vimeo.com/30500114>).
(©2011 Kurt Lancaster)

in a pinch, it'll provide decent audio when you don't have a separate digital audio recorder on hand (such as the Tascam DR-40). However, I would not have done the shoot without using Magic Lantern, so I could see audio meters while recording and monitoring the audio by plugging into the AV port of the 5D. Indeed, I adjusted the audio several times based on the levels I watched.

I shot the project handheld with no strap, no DSLR rig. The omnidirectional aspect of the ME62 picked up a lot of side and background noise, but it ended up adding to the atmosphere of the piece. Furthermore, I stood close to the subject, so the microphone was less then three feet away. I shifted my head to the left, while hand-holding the camera, so the subject being interviewed would look at me and not the camera. The project was edited by my friend, Stacey Sotosky.

This was my test whether the step-down cable with a high quality mic could record usable audio. It did. At the same time, Magic Lantern's capabilities for audio monitoring allowed me to treat the project as if I were using a video camera—but with the benefits of the cinematic quality of a Canon 5D Mark II.

FIGURE 5.18
Light run and gun setup for Occupy Wall Street. The setup included a Canon 5D Mark II and a Zeiss Contax 50 mm f/1.4 lens along with a shockmount holding a Sennheiser microphone attached to the camera, and the ETS step down cable (XLR to minijack), as well as a headphone adapter by Sescom providing the ability to use headphones when Magic Lantern is installed. *(Photo by Kurt Lancaster.)*

Checklist for External Onboard Minijack Mic

1. Choose your microphone (such as the Rode VideoMic Pro or a shotgun mic with an XLR to minijack step-down cable if shooting with a DSLR), attach it to the accessory shoe plate, and plug the mic directly to the microphone jack of the camera.
2. Turn on the mic (be sure you put a fresh battery into the microphone).
3. If possible, turn off the AGC and set the audio input levels of the camera at 212 dBu to minimize clipped audio (keep the levels under −6 on the meter).
4. Keep your subject no more than a few feet away or so; this will provide the strongest audio signal.
5. Monitor with headphones and adjust levels as needed. If you're shooting with a DSLR with no audio monitoring capabilities, consider installing Magic Lantern.
6. Input your files normally. The audio is recorded simultaneously with the video.

Checklist for External XLR Mic with XLR Adapter

1. Choose your microphone (such as an XLR shotgun mic).
2. Attach the XLR adapter and connect the XLR's minijack plug into the camera's minijack microphone input. (Make sure you put fresh batteries into the adapter.)
3. Plug the mic's XLR cable into input 1 of the XLR adapter.

4. If the camera has automatic gain control (most DSLR cameras do, but read the manual to find out), turn on the XLR adapter's AGC disabler.

5. Use either a boom pole or pistol grip, or mount it to the camera with a shock-mount with an accessory shoe adapter. Plug the mic to the microphone input of the XLR adapter.

6. Turn on the phantom power (it'll be either 48 V or 12 V). If you have a 12 V option, you may want to use this to save battery life, but be sure the mic you choose can utilize 12 V of phantom power.

7. Plug in your headphones.

8. Set the max levels of your audio to 212 dBu (−6 on the meter) to help prevent clipping if a performer or subject gets too loud. This will give you 12 decibels of headroom.

9. Keep your microphone less than three feet away from the performer.

10. The audio is recorded simultaneously with the video, so no additional steps are needed when you export your files from the camera to the computer.

Checklist for External Recorders (Tascam DR-40)

1. Do two recordings: one on-camera for reference and backup and the other externally. Choose your microphone type and follow the previous checklist for mini-jack on-camera recording. For DSLR shooters, don't worry about an external XLR adapter because that just complicates the workflow. You could just use the camera's mic, but if you hook up a Rode VideoMic Pro, for example, you'll get usable sound, so if something did go wrong in the external recording, you'll have a backup.

2. Most audio recorders contain a tripod screw hole, so you can mount the recorder onto its own tripod, if desired, or mount it to a DSLR rig.

3. Put fresh batteries into the recorder.

4. Choose your microphone for the digital audio recorder (XLR shotgun, XLR lav, or both—using the two different inputs) and hook it up to a boom pole, pistol grip, or tripod. Make sure it's no more than three feet away.

5. Attach the XLR cable to the mic and the input of the audio recorder (if you're using two mics, plug both into the recorder).

6. Set your audio recorder's audio compression scheme; be sure it matches the camera's recording capabilities (it'll most likely be 44.1 kHz, 16-bit or 48 kHz, 24-bit). Some recorders can do 96-bit, which will give you an even better recording to work with in post. Just be sure the kilohertz (44.1 kHz or 48 kHz) matches the camera setting.

7. Unless you're using a field mixer with limiters (such as the MixPre), set the max levels of your audio to 212 dBu (keep the levels below −6 on the meter) to help prevent clipping if a performer or subject gets too loud. This will give you 12 decibels of headroom.

8. Turn on the phantom power (it'll be either 48 V or 12 V). If you have a 12 V option, you may want to use this to save battery life, but be sure your mic can utilize 12 V of power. Otherwise, just stick with 48 V.

9. Plug in your headphones. There's a separate volume control for the headphones, but what you're hearing isn't exactly what you're actually recording!

10. Press Record on the digital audio recorder. The first time you press the Record button, it'll flash red and provide an audio level signal so you can test your levels before actually recording.

11. Set your levels by doing an audio test.

12. Press the Record button a second time to start recording. Double-check the timelapse clock to see if it's ticking; this will assure you that you're recording the audio!

13. Start recording on the camera.

14. Clap your hands or use a slate.

15. Begin the scene.

16. When the scene is completed, press the Stop button. (If you press the Pause button, you will keep one file if you press the Stop, then each time you record, a new file will be created—which is useful when recording multiple takes of video.)

17. Take note of the file number on the audio recorder, so you can match it to the right take on the camera.

18. Export the camera's video-audio footage into your computer. This will need to be processed (see the Chapter 6 on postproduction workflow). When you process it, keep the audio in its native format (44.1 kHz or 48 kHz). This audio will be your synced reference audio.

19. Export the audio from the audio recorder. You'll use this audio to replace the camera audio after you've synced it using the synchronization feature of Final Cut Pro X or DualEyes (see Chapter 6), or if you do it manually.

This chapter should have provided you with the tools to get the quality sound you need for your film projects. The next chapter covers the final toolkit for the filmmaker: postproduction workflow for audio and video.

DSLR Postproduction Workflow and Techniques

WHICH SOFTWARE TO USE?

Unless you're working for a client that requests a project to be edited on specific software, the choice is up to you, and that will depend upon the type of interface you like, the performance of the software engine, and the type of computer you choose to use. In many respects, a lot of student filmmakers—especially multimedia journalism students—have to tackle a large learning curve before mastering such complex software.

Avid Media Composer (version 6 as of this writing) is the industry standard, but at ~$2400 it's out of many low budget filmmakers' and video journalists' budget (a student price of about $300 is a different story!)—and it can be used on a PC or Mac. It's a complex piece of software and not intuitive to learn.

Apple's Final Cut Pro became an industry standard for the indie filmmaker and with its full studio suite, a lot of pros became attracted to the Mac-based software. However, it was originally designed by Macromedia and never had the intuitive design feel of an Apple product—and with its long pre-render times it was clunky to use and required patience to master. It also never engaged the 64-bit hardware architecture of Apple's computers. But with the release of Final Cut X, Apple threw out the Macromedia engine and rebuilt it from scratch, engaging a more intuitive software design, placing renders in the background, and utilizing Apple's 64-bit architecture and multiple CPU cores. At its initial launch, however, it lacked many of the features professionals were used to in its earlier manifestations, so they either stuck with version 7 or jumped ship and switched to Avid or Adobe Premiere Pro. Since Final Cut 7 is outdated, it will not be covered in this book (see the first edition of *DSLR Cinema* for that workflow).

This chapter will examine the workflow for Final Cut Pro X and Adobe Premiere Pro for a DSLR workflow. The workflow for other large sensor cameras will be similar and may require adjusting the types of settings you use.

(However, this book will not teach you how to edit, since there are numerous books, manuals, and video tutorials for beginning filmmakers to learn software.) The first step before editing is to transcode the footage.

TRANSCODING FOOTAGE

Most HDSLR cameras shoot in some form of the H.264 codec, which is essentially a finishing or output mode designed for the Web and Blu-ray DVDs. It is *not* designed to be edited. Why is this codec used then? Because it's what allows HD to be a viable form—putting a lot of data onto a memory card. When these cameras begin to shoot RAW, there will be a lot more data space needed. The d16 Digital Bolex camera shoots 2K RAW, and may be an option for indie film shooters—because it shoots raw, you'll only get 8–10 minutes on a 32 GB card!

Both Premiere 5 (and higher) and Final Cut X will allow you to edit H.264 files natively, but it is highly recommended that you transcode to Apple ProRes 422 when using Final Cut—and professional editors would agree. On the other hand, Premiere 5 utilizes a software engine where the native files work without needing to transcode—professional filmmakers, such as Shane Hurlbut, ASC utilize this approach. However, if you're using software other than Final Cut X or Premiere Pro, you may need to transcode your footage using an external application, such as the freeware, MPEG Streamclip or Cinemform's NeoScene (a high end professional transcoding software, running at $129, as of this writing). Take your footage through the workflow and test out various options.

In most cases, a transcoded file will provide much more "headroom" in post and allow for a smoother workflow when you're editing. The transcoding process, whether you're using Squared 5's MPEG Streamclip, Cineform's codec, Rarevision's 5DtoRGB, or Final Cut's ProRes, will expand the footage to a 4:4:4 or 4:2:2 color space (see Appendix 4 on chrominance and luminance compression).

This section includes a step-by-step guide in converting your DSLR footage using Squared 5's MPEG Streamclip (freeware for both Mac and PC), Cineform's NeoScene (which can be used for Apple and PC computers), and Final Cut Pro X's settings for transcoding to Apple ProRes 422. You may choose to use MPEG Streamclip or NeoScene for Premiere Pro, but it is not needed—test out the workflow to see what works best for you. Later in the chapter, I will also provide the workflow necessary to convert external audio recording (such as with the Tascam DR-40 or Zoom H4n) using DualEyes syncing software, as well as with Final Cut X's easy to use sync feature. Lastly, it covers some of the basics of color grading with Magic Bullet, a powerful tool for filmmakers to put the final touches on their project in crafting a film look.

Another software for transcoding footage is Rarevision's 5DtoRGB (http://rarevision.com/5dtorgb/). The "Lite" version is available for free on Apple's App Store. The advanced version allowing for batch processing costs about $50.

Deinterlace Your Video

Most DSLRs, such as the Canons, shoot in 1080p, progressively scanned. A few may shoot in 1080i (interlaced mode, such as Panasonic's GH1). Deinterlacing a digital movie if shot in 1080i is one of the key tools a cinematographer must utilize to avoid the video look. It is far, far better to get a camera that shoots progressive scan. If you need to deinterlace, use Magic Bullet Frames.

GETTING FILES INTO THE COMPUTER

One of the benefits of DSLRs is their tapeless recording. Cameras such as the Canon 5D Mark II and 7D record on Compact Flash, whereas the Rebel T2i (550D), T3i (600D), 60D, and Panasonic's GH1 and GH2 record on the smaller-sized SDHC cards (which are about half the price). It's not practical to buy dozens of memory cards and keep them as permanent archive media (unless you have the money!).

1. Drag and drop files onto the computer (and I recommend at least two other hard drives: one as a backup; the other as an archive).[1]
2. If you're editing on Final Cut X, you may choose to copy files to the "event folder" on import and it'll back up the original files as well as transcode them into ProRes 422.

SQUARED 5 MPEG STREAMCLIP WORKFLOW

To use Squared 5's MPEG Streamclip freeware, follow these steps:

1. Download and install MPEG Streamclip from <http://www.squared5.com/>.
2. If you're converting one file at a time, go to File→Open and search for the files you want to decompress. However, if you're doing more than one file, then batch process the files. Go to List—Batch List (see Figure 6.1a), then click the button, Add Files (see Figure 6.1b)—while Canon's 5D Mark III uses both.
3. Your file appears in the main window. You may set in and out points (I and O) if you need to convert only a section of the clip. Choose File→Export and select Export to QuickTime (see Figure 6.2) or another format if desired.

---

[1] Don't use a hard drive as a long-term archive solution. Use it as a backup throughout production and postproduction. If you know you no longer need the footage, then you're good. However, if you're working for a client or you work at a production company, keeping an archive is essential—and making hard drive backups is not recommended as the best solution for long-term archival purposes. Rather, going with an Enterprise Tape solution (LTO-4 800GB tapes) with an archival drive will cost about $7,000, which is a much wiser choice, and if you have a client needing archive material, that price is a lot cheaper than having to go back in the field and get new footage.

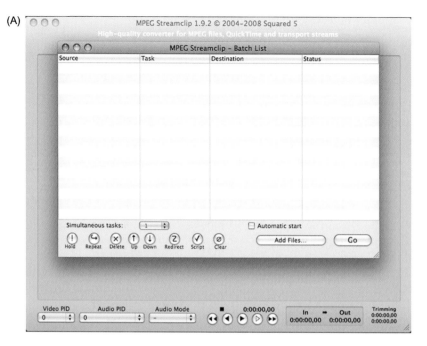

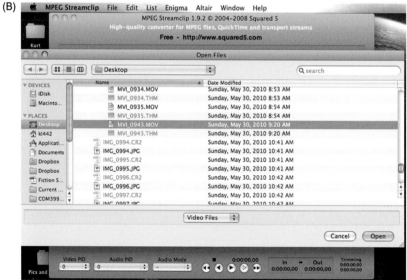

FIGURE 6.1
Open the files you need to convert using MPEG Streamclip.

FIGURE 6.2
Select the export type you need (typically QuickTime for Mac users); in this case, I chose Export to QuickTime

4. The Exporter window (for Mac) defaults to Apple Motion JPEG A and places the quality of your clip at 50% and with interlacing (see Figure 6.3). You will need to change these parameters. Slide the quality to 100%. Deselect Interlaced Scaling (if your footage was shot progressive, which the Canon HDSLRs do). The Frame size should default to the original footage size (in this case, 1920×1080).

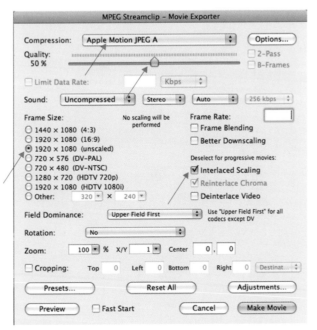

FIGURE 6.3
You will need to change the default settings to make your footage look as good as possible: Deselect Interlaced Scaling (for progressive cameras, such as the Canon), slide Quality to 100%, and change Apple Motion JPEG compression.

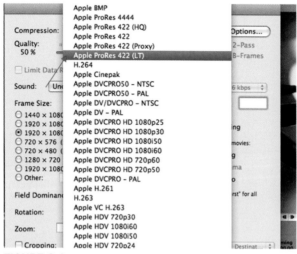

FIGURE 6.4
You can choose from a variety of codecs when exporting with MPEG Streamclip. Apple ProRes is the standard for Final Cut Pro users.

5. For Mac users, select Apple ProRes 422 for a fast render (see Figure 6.4). Higher-quality renders should be used for work exporting to film (ProRes 4444). Philip Bloom uses 422 for web-produced work, and it works just fine. Use 4444 if you're going to film-out or full-screen project—but it will increase your file size a lot, so be sure to have enough hard drive space. PC users should test what best works for them. A test I did of an AVI file failed to import the video track in Vegas Pro (only audio came in).

6. After completing the Compression format selection (Apple ProRes 422 (LT)), placing the Quality to 100%, and removing Interlaced Scaling (see Figure 6.5), click on the Make Movie button.

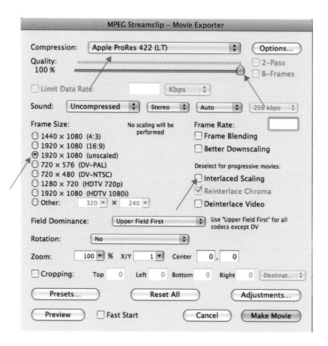

FIGURE 6.5
The screen as it appears when ready to convert the file.

7. After you click Make Movie, the file is encoded into a file size about twice the original (when using Apple ProRes 422; see Figure 6.6). You may choose the LT version which has a much faster rate than files used by Apple's transcoding process in Final Cut 7 and is faster than CineForm's NeoScene. Because of its faster speed, I recommend that video journalists use MPEG Streamclip when working on tight deadlines.

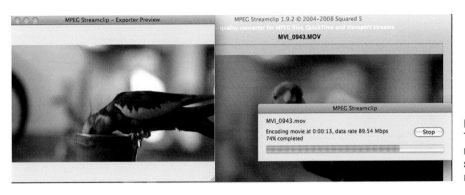

FIGURE 6.6
The file transcodes, nearly doubling the file size in LT mode after the render is completed.

CINEFORM NEOSCENE WORKFLOW

The Cineform Neo Scene Workflow software is available for about $130 and will convert your files into a form that can be edited in just about any software you choose to use. The software can be installed on a PC or Mac. When transcoding, follow these steps:

1. Open Cineform Neo Scene and select a destination folder for converted videos (see Figure 6.7).

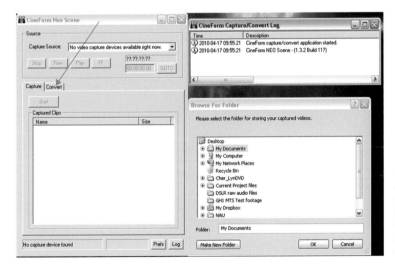

FIGURE 6.7
As soon as you open Cineform's NeoScene on a PC, it will ask for a destination folder. Select it and then choose the Convert tab.

2. Import your files and click on the Convert tab. You may use the Capture window which appears when you plug in a camera, but this is not recommended. Rather, copy your folder and/or files over to the computer and copy them again onto at least one other external drive as a backup (having two backups is even better).
3. Click on Select Files or Select Folder and browse to the folder containing the files and select them (see Figure 6.8). Click on Open to bring them into the SourceClips window (see Figure 6.9).

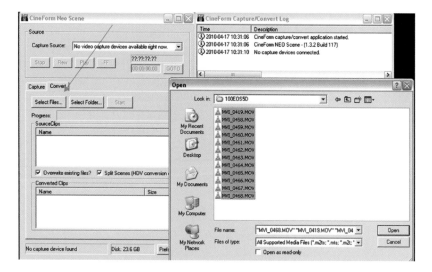

FIGURE 6.8
Select files or folders and import the files needing conversion.

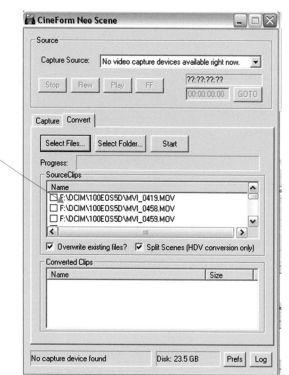

FIGURE 6.9
Files are imported into the SourceClips window.

4. Click on the Prefs button for preferences. Choose the following (see Figure 6.10):
   - Automatically convert to CineForm Intermediate.
   - Split file on scene changes.

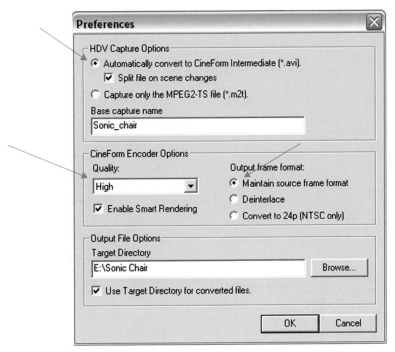

- CineForm Encoder Quality High.
- Output Frame Format: Maintain the source frame format (you could also choose Convert to 24p if you didn't shoot 24p natively). Select Deinterlace if your footage was shot 1080i (it's highly recommended that you use Magic Bullet Frames for deinterlacing, however).
- Target Directory: Choose the folder where you want your converted files to be placed.

5. Click OK.
6. Click the Start button. As the files are converted, they'll appear in the Converted Clips window (see Figure 6.11). If you click the Log button, you can see the conversion status of each file (see Figure 6.12). In addition, the files are checked off in the SourceClips window as they are completed.

The converted files will appear in the destination folder you chose, and you can now import them into your computer's editing software.

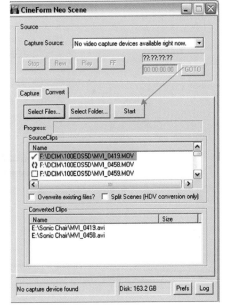

FIGURE 6.11
After you click the Start button, the files are automatically converted and appear in the Converted Clips window.

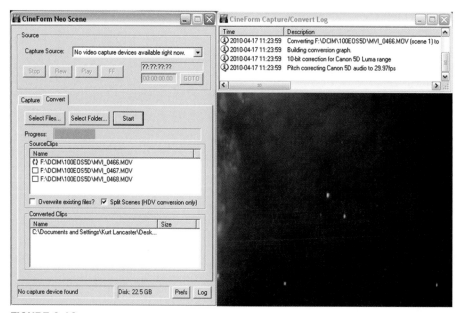

FIGURE 6.12
As the files are converted, the Log window (which opens when you click the Log button) shows the progress of each file being converted.

In Praise of Dissent: Adobe CS5 Paves The Way by Shane Hurlbut, ASC

Dissent: Voicing opinions that conflict with those that are commonly accepted or officially espoused.

When my Elite Team and I started blazing this trail, we had already become dissenters. We embraced a technology that in Hollywood was a joke, a fad, not viable. This is one of the great paradoxes of the human condition. On one hand the movie industry is built upon the ability of diverse groups of people to conform to common sets of rules and principles. Yet, there is an enormous benefit that awaits when somebody or a group is brave enough to disrupt this coveted social harmony and challenge prevailing convention. That is what all of you are, dissenters. Now that we all know who we are, why fall for conformity? Why not continue the dissent?

If you had a choice of an editing system on a system that was designed for your Canon camera's color space and codec or one that wasn't, which one would you choose?

Personally I would pick the one that was designed for the camera, because to me that means faster, better, more latitude, more options, it just makes sense.

The first time I saw our *Act of Valor* footage loaded into CS5, I was hooked as a cinematographer. The range, dimension, the filmic quality was so apparent. I went to Jacob Rosenberg who is the head of Bandito Brothers Post and asked him why this looks so different. He said two things: backward engineering and understanding the platform.

This is why CS5 is so special. Adobe went to Canon and asked them to open up their color space to them so that they could do their best to understand it and to expand it. They worked together to find a cocktail to increase depth, dimension in this limited 8 bit compressed color space. The next was to the camera's codec. They designed Premiere Pro specifically to deal with the h.264 codec. How many times has this codec failed in Final Cut Pro 7?

How about an editing system that requires no converting? You can input directly from the CF cards if you would like. This is huge. We all know how long it takes to convert. Adobe is investing in their software as they see this as the future. Everything is shrinking to your desktop. Save time, edit faster, expanded organic looking 4:2:2 color space, filmic looking blacks, no conversion, REAL TIME editing without the barber shop blue scroll. WOW!!!

When we talked about doing the Hurlbut Visuals HDSLR Bootcamp and giving the students the ability to color correct their edited footage on a 25′ screen by the end of the day, CS5 and Premiere Pro was the only viable option. When I started to use it, I quickly understood the power of this amazing tool. Be a dissenter, go against the grain, go the distance, expand your creativity.

Hurlbut, S, (2010, Dec. 2) Hurlblog. <http://www.hurlbutvisuals. com/blog/2010/12/in-praise-of-dissent-adobe-cs5-paves-the-way/>.

PREMIERE PRO WORKFLOW

The strengths of using Premiere Pro for DSLR shooters cannot be under-estimated when Shane Hurlbut, ASC—one of the top leaders in the DSLR filmmaking movement—recommends it in his workflow. Vincent Laforet—one of the first to adopt DSLRs in his shoots—also recommends it.

1. Setup: Create new project (Figure 6.13). I set my scratch disks to the folder on my external hard drive and the location of the project.

FIGURE 6.13
Adobe Premiere Pro New Project window.

2. Select Sequence Presets for the project's sequence (Figure 6.14). Choose the Digital SLR folder and select the proper format and frame rate (such as DSLR 1080p24).

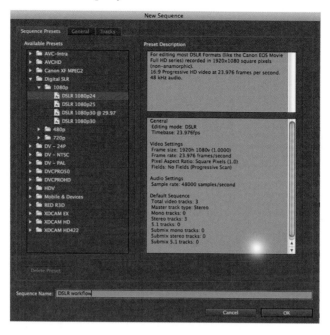

FIGURE 6.14
Select the correct format and frame rate from the folder of the New Sequence window.

3. Go to the "General" tab of the New Sequence window and make sure your settings are accurate (Editing Mode: DSLR Audio Sample Rate, and so forth)—Figure 6.15.

FIGURE 6.15
The General tab of New Sequence provides an overview of the sequences settings.

4. With your project properties setup you can select your files by choosing the hard drive and folder in the lower left Media Browser window, then double-click the file to bring it up to the preview window, setting your in and out points, and dragging it to the timeline to edit (Figure 6.16.). No transcoding needed. The files can be edited natively.

FIGURE 6.16
The editing layout window of Adobe Premiere 5. The media files can be found in the lower left under Media Browser, where you can then select files for preview and editing.

APPLE FINAL CUT PRO WORKFLOW

A lot of controversy occurred when Apple decided reset the design and parameters of Final Cut Pro X. However, after having taught with the software for a year at Northern Arizona University to beginning film production and multimedia journalism students, I actually find it easy to teach and learn. I've also edited a series of videos for the National Park Service and Northern Arizona University's marketing department using this software and find it a pleasure to edit with as well as attaining features (such as color grading and audio mixing) that are easy to use and powerful enough for professional work. It is a breakthrough in editing styles, and as Apple updates newer versions of it—bringing in the features professional editors need for their projects—it is likely to receive wider adoption. Fundamentally, it removes some of the clunkiness found in its earlier iterations (it renders effects in the background so you can edit at the same time), and it provides a sleek and mostly intuitive interface, using a non-destructive "magnetic" timeline.

1. Create a new event

Final Cut X names folders as events. You can move files in between folders (events) and access multiple files in a variety of events for you project. If the project is small, I'll create one event and import all of my media into it. Right click on the hard drive icon where you want to create your event folder (Figure 6.17).

FIGURE 6.17
Right click on the hard drive and choose "New Event" to create an event folder in Final Cut Pro.

2. Import media files

Browse your hard drive (or the memory card containing the original media files) and select the files you want to import. There are several menu events to choose (Figure 6.18).

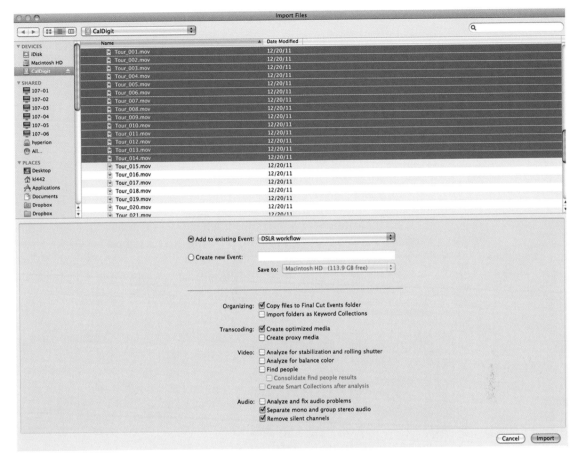

FIGURE 6.18
Browse the hard drive or the memory card to choose the files you want to import. Follow the steps below for choosing the different menu options.

- You may "Add to existing Event", if you've already created the folder or choose "Create new Event" if you want to create a new folder for these files (choose the hard drive you want to "Save to:" from the drop down menu).
- Organizing: Choose "Copy files to Final Cut Events folder" if you want a copy of the original files placed within Final Cut's folder structure. If you've already organized them and placed the original files where you want them, then you do not need to choose this option. The "Import files as Keyword Collections" is useful for large projects where you've already named each file. Do not choose this option if you're just keeping the original numbered file name from the camera.
- Transcoding: For smaller projects, choose "Create optimized media"—this will convert your footage to Apple ProRes 422, which is the recommended setting for editing footage that is not being transferred to film. Choose "Create proxy media" if you're editing a large project (such as a

feature length film), as your computer performance may be too slow to handle it all.

- Video: Ignore these options. If you need any of these functions, they can be chosen later.
- Audio: When using external recorders, it's useful to check off "Separate mono and group stereo audio" and "Remove silent channels".

3. Create a new project

Open Final Cut X and select New Project (name the project)—Final Cut will keep (and show) your entire media library for all of your projects, so naming them and storing your footage in organized folders is essential and wise, but use the structure within Final Cut X. If you start renaming folders and moving files outside the software, you'll run into errors.

- Press the + button on the bottom left side of the screen to create a new project. It'll bring up the project settings window (Figure 6.19.) Name the project. Choose the Default Event the project will reference (when you drag and drop a file from your desktop, for example, it'll automatically copy it into the selected Default Event folder).

FIGURE 6.19
Right click on the hard drive and choose "New Event" to create an event folder in Final Cut Pro.

- Video Properties: I choose Custom every time to make sure I have the correct format for my project. In this case, 1080p HD at 1920×1080, with a frame rate of 23.98p.
- The audio defaults to surround sound (which is useful when utilizing a surround sound system), but since most of my projects are for the Web, I choose Custom and set to Stereo at 48 kHz.
- The Render Format is where you choose the project render settings (this can be changed in the project proper-ties, later, if needed). It defaults to ProRes 422, but you may also choose ProRes 4444 (for projects being transferred to film), or select a high quality version of ProRes 422 (HQ), or for an uncom-pressed version, choose Uncompressed 10-bit 4:2:2 (see Figure 6.20).

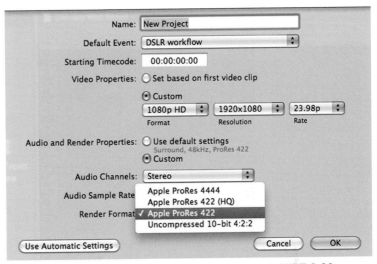

FIGURE 6.20
Drop-down menu for choosing the render settings of your project in Final Cut Pro.

Once you import the files, they will begin to render in the background. You may begin previewing footage, setting in and out points, as well as editing. The shots will eventually get replaced as they become converted to ProRes.

SYNCING AUDIO—FINAL CUT PRO WORKFLOW

Final Cut Pro X includes an audio syncing feature for filmmakers recording on external audio (such as the Zoom H4n or Tascam DR-40). It takes the refer-ence audio from the camera, analyzes the waveform data and matches with the external audio's data, creating a new compound synchronized clip. This feature works easily and I have not run into any issues using it.

1. Choose the proper audio and video clips (Command-click) once on the audio and once on the video, then right-click, Synchronize Clips. The files will process, creating a new compound clip, labeled, "Synchronized Clip" (See Figure 6.21)
2. On the bottom left of the browser window, you can see the Synchronized clip. I review it and place it in the timeline, which is highlighted in yellow.
3. After selecting the Synchronized clip, I select the info panel and choose Audio, then choose the "Channel Configuration," unchecking the clip's audio, while keeping the Tascam audio (from the external recorder). This replaces the noisier reference audio from the camera with the cleaner audio from the external recorder (See Figure 6.22).

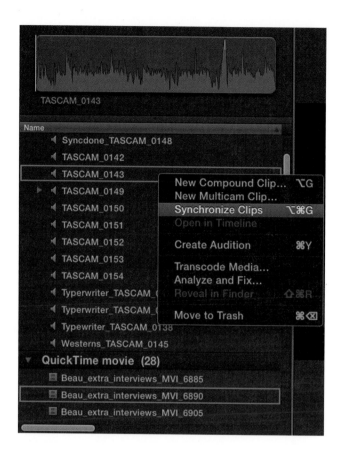

FIGURE 6.21
Right-click on the one proper audio and one correct video file, then right click, choosing Synchronize Clips. This will create a new compound clip.

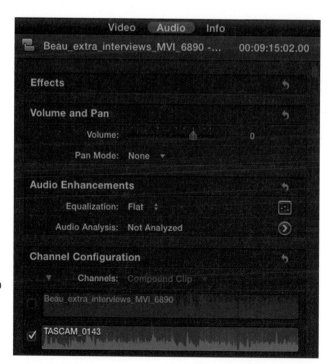

FIGURE 6.22
Change the channel configuration from stereo to dual mono, then de-select the camera's audio and use only the external audio (Tascam, in this case).

SYNCING AUDIO—DUALEYES WORKFLOW

Red Giant Software's DualEyes is a stand-alone software designed to sync external audio files with on-camera audio. If you're not using Final Cut Pro X, this is a good option for syncing your files.

1. Open DuelEyes and select New Project. Select the directory to where you want to save the project (Figure 6.23).

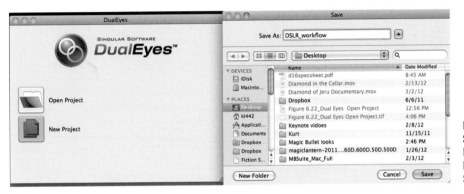

FIGURE 6.23
Singular Software's DualEyes. Choose New Project and select your Save directory.

2. After you've imported your video and audio files, select the files you want to sync. Hit the + icon and choose the files you want to import (Figure 6.24). Click on the – icon to remove files from the list.

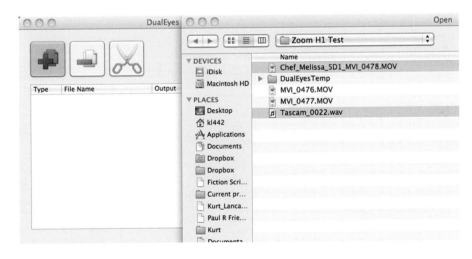

FIGURE 6.24
Hit the + icon and choose the files you want to import.

3. Set the Output Directory—where you want your synced files to appear. Go to File→Set Output Directory. You may choose to place them in the original directory alongside the original or chose a new folder (Figures 6.25 and 6.26).

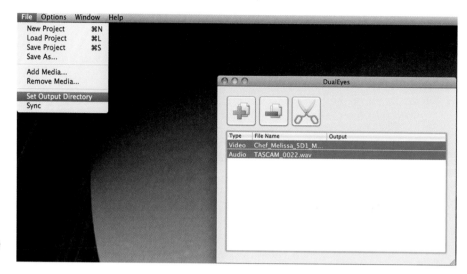

FIGURE 6.25
Go to File→Set Output Directory to place where you synced files will go.

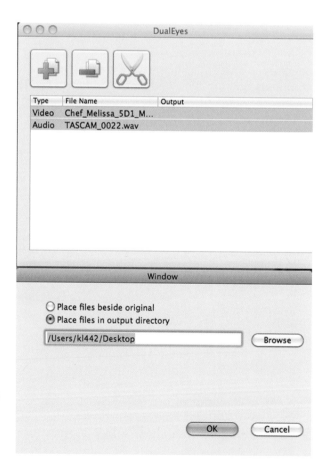

FIGURE 6.26
You can choose to place them in the original directory alongside the original or chose a new folder.

4. Click on the scissor icon and it'll process the files and place them in the folder you chose in 3 (Figure 6.27). It will say, "Extracting Audio."

FIGURE 6.27
Click on the scissor icon and it'll process the files.

5. Import the synced files to your editing software.

Menu options allow you to choose replacement of audio in the .mov files, among other choices.

A recommended alternative to using DualEyes when using a dual-audio recording system setup is one developed by David Anselmi of Practical Mystic Productions (<http://www.practicalmysticproductions.com/>):

1. Separate the audio tracks of the two separate recordings.
2. Pan hard left on the first track and hard right on the other track.
3. Adjust relative volume so both tracks match.
4. Listen on headphones.
5. Nudge one of the audio tracks back and forth, until the flanging—the audio delay between the two—stops. You've just synced the audio!

COLOR CORRECTION WORKFLOW

After you've synced up your audio, edited the piece, mixed proper audio levels, added text (such as lower thirds), your final step in the postproduction work-flow is to color correct your images. Although most professional editing software packages include tools for post production color work, I don't have the space in this book to cover how to use them all. However, I will show the steps of basic color correction and color grading in Final Cut Pro, and then, following this sec-tion, I examine how you can use some of the tools in Red Giant Software's Magic Bullet Looks to create your film look, an easy to use plug-in software.

BASIC STEPS IN COLOR CORRECTION AND COLOR GRADING

A nice overview of color correction and grading can be found at <http://www.hurlbutvisuals.com/blog/2012/01/20/7-tips-for-hd-color-correction-and-dslr-color-correction>. Here, Shane Hurlbut's editor, Vashi Nedomanksy provides some of the major tools and information needed to do fundamental postproduction work in Adobe Premiere. As Vashi defines it:

COLOR CORRECTION is the process where every clip is manually tweaked to get a good exposure and balance of light. Each clip is adjusted to match color temperature to a predefined choice for each scene. This tedious and mechanical process is essential and in its own way, an art form. The use of SCOPES (Waveform, Vectorscope, Parade) is critical to this step and luckily most NLE's and Grading software have them built-in. Without them you are literally flying blind and solely trusting your eyes, which have to adjust to room light ambience, fatigue, funky monitors and other factors constantly. Trust the SCOPES and let them guide you into accurate and creative decision making.

COLOR GRADING is the creative process where decisions are made to further enhance or establish a new visual tone to the project through software including: introducing new color themes, re-lighting within a frame, film stock emulations, color gradients and a slew of other choices. Being that this is purely creative, there is no wrong or right … only what the DP, director and colorist feel is appropriate for the story. It can be subtle and invisible or over-the-top and uber-stylized. Therein lies the challenge … The challenge of choices. The tools available are so numerous, powerful and often free (Davinci Resolve Lite!) that you have no excuse not to explore these options further before you embark on the Grading journey.

Vashi recommends the following steps in the process (not all steps will be used in all situations):

1. Remove artifacts and de-noise.
2. Balance your shots by adjusting blacks/mids/whites, saturation, and white balance.
3. Relight within a shot using power windows or masks.
4. Add gradients, diffusion and other lens filters.
5. Add vignettes.

6. Grade your images.
7. Simulate a film stock of your choice.
8. Resize and sharpen.

(Nedomanksy, V. (January 20, 2012). "7 Tips for HD Color Correction and DSLR Color Correction." Hurlbut Visuals. <http://www.hurlbutvisuals.com/blog/2012/01/20/7-tips-for-hd-color-correction-and-dslr-color-correction/>, accessed March 14, 2012) Used with permission.

As mentioned in Chapter 4, shooting flat (such as with Technicolor's CineStyle) is the best way to go when doing postproduction color correction. It leaves a lot of data that you can dig out using these tools, explained below.

Eyeballing your correction work is important, but more important is to utilize the variety of scopes to make sure what you see is as precise as you can get it. In this example, I've laid out the waveform monitor for luminance, the RGB parade (color values of red, blue, and green), and the vectorscope (showing a diagonal line where the values of the skin tones should fall) (see Figure 6.28). As can be seen in the Luma scope, the highlights are a bit low. Also, the Vectorscope reveals what the eye is telling us—the image is too yellow (notice the vector of the color falls below the diagonal "flesh tone" line, edging towards yellow). And the RGB tells us that there is a lot of red in the image (which is obvious, the tool will allow us to even out the red, green, and blue—unless we want a particular hue to increase in value).

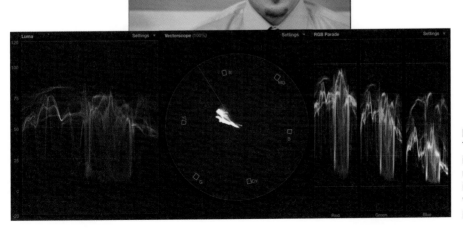

FIGURE 6.28
The uncorrected image in Final Cut Pro with the uncorrected values found in the waveform monitor, vectorscope, and RGB parade.

Here are the basic steps needed and how they work in Final Cut Pro:

1. Adjust the blacks, then the highlights, then the midtones (which correspond to skin tones) (Figure 6.29).

FIGURE 6.29
The image corrected along the luminance. The shadows were adjusted down, making the blacks touch just near 0, and then the highlights were raised 9%, just so there's enough contrast spread—but not so much the images blows out. Finally, the midtones were adjusted −26% in order to compensate for the high level of midtones in the exposure.

2. I next adjust the image to even out as much as possible the reds, greens, and blues using the RGB Parade (Figure 6.30).

FIGURE 6.30
I adjust the midtone wheel, bringing up the blues (+23%) in order to negate some of the yellow. I also bring up the highlights 14% in the blues as well, since these were still coming in too yellow on the subject's face.

3. Lastly, I adjust the Vectorscope, moving the midtone and highlight colors until the spread of color falls on the skin tone line (Figure 6.31).

FIGURE 6.31
I continue to adjust the midtones and highlights until the vector of colors fall along the skin tone line. If the colors reach too far to the edge of the circle, indicating the colors are oversaturated, I can use the Saturation tool to desaturate.

4. All of these steps are not linear. I continually shift among the three scopes, making minor adjustments until I'm happy with the overall look of the image.

No matter which software you use, the steps examined above on color correction and the use of scopes is essential to getting an accurate film-like look for your projects. In the next section, I'll examine Magic Bullet as an additional tool where you can make further adjustments for your film—this takes you to the color grading process by which you shape the look of the film (after it has been color corrected).

Filmmaker Khalid Mohtaseb used Magic Bullet Looks to grade his short, titled *Haiti Earthquake Aftermath Montage* (<http://vimeo.com/9608637>), shot on a Canon 5D Mark II. The two examples in Figures 6.32 and 6.33 show the power of this software in helping to create the film look. Mohtaseb actually uses Photoshop for his first step, "retouching a screenshot from the clip," using that retouched still as a reference point. Then he utilizes Final Cut Pro's three-way color corrector "to shift the mids and shadows to a warmer color tone." Lastly, he fires up Magic Bullet Looks "to fine-tune the exposure and colors. I rarely ever use the Looks presets as they are overused and [I] can get more precise results by building my own" (Mohtaseb, K. (March 25, 2010). Into the Haiti Earthquake Zone—Khalid Mohtaseb Covers the Aftermath on 5DMKII. *DSLR News Shooter.* <http://www.dslrnewsshooter.com/2010/03/25/into-the-haiti-earthquake-zone-khalid-mohtaseb-covers-the-aftermath-on-5dmkii/>, accessed April 19, 2010). He shot in Standard picture style, with some of the shots' contrast pulled all the way down.

FIGURES 6.32 AND 6.33
Cinematographer Khalid Mohtaseb utilizes Magic Bullet Looks to color-grade his film projects. The before image (6.32) is on the left, while the postgrading process (6.33) is on the right.
(© 2010 Khalid Mohtaseb. Used with permission.)

Noise Reduction Software

A lot of video picks up noise—especially at high ISO settings. Noise reduction software is a useful tool that can help offset such noise. One such application can be found at <http://www.neatvideo.com/>. The plug-in is available for After Effects, Premiere, Final Cut, VirtualDub, Sony Vegas, and Pinnacle Studio. A limited functionality demo is available for free. The Pro version, which allows for HD 1920×1080 noise removal, costs just under $100. To see an example of the result of this software, read the case study for *Casulo*, a Brazilian short transferred to 35 mm film, in Chapter 8. For the same price, Red Giant Software sells Magic Bullet Denoiser II at <http://www.redgiantsoftware.com/products/all/denoiser-II/>.

WEBLINK
Video tutorials of Magic Bullet can be found here: <http://www.redgiantsoftware.com/videos/tutorials/#magic-bullet-looks>

COLOR GRADING WITH MAGIC BULLET LOOKS WORKFLOW

Follow these steps for doing basic color grading with Magic Bullet Looks:

1. Once the software is installed (actually a plug-in), open your Final Cut Pro project and click on the effects icon. Scroll down to Magic Bullet Looks (Figure 6.34).

FIGURE 6.34
The Magic Bullet Looks plug-in for Final Cut Pro.

2. Drag and drop the Magic Bullet Looks icon onto the clip you want to color grade. Click on the Edit box in the Look row. (If you're using a trial version of Magic Bullet Looks, a Register button will appear above the Edit box; it's a shortcut that will take you to Red Giant's registration/purchasing page.)

3. You will be taken to the LooksBuilder, or editor, of Magic Bullet Looks. Your clip will appear as a large image in the center of the screen. When you hover the mouse along the left edge of the screen, the Looks window will slide out and you'll see a variety of preset looks from which you can choose. When you hover the mouse along the right edge of the screen, another window containing a variety of tools slide out. These are the tools used to shape a variety of looks from color correction to shaping a graduated exposure.

4. Hover the mouse along the left edge and scan through the dozens of pre-built effects plug-ins—everything from film stock emulation to crime show TV drama (see Figure 6.35). The software engineers have gone through the tools of Magic Bullet Looks and emulated a variety of looks found on television shows, movies, and music videos, among others. You can click on any one of the looks, and you'll see an immediate preview in the center image of the main page. Take the time to experiment to get the one that's closest to the emotional look you want to convey—the one that most closely fits your story.

FIGURE 6.35
Magic Bullet FCP Classic
Stock Emulation table.
Note the variety of tools
the Colorist can use.

5. See Figure 6.36 for the original image. Once you've selected the effect plug-in you desire (I choose No 85 from the Classic Stock Emulation), notice the series of icons along the bottom of the main screen—these were the

FIGURE 6.36
Here's the original image
from Final Cut, before the
effect is applied to it.
(Still from NAU Marketing
video, Chef and Melissa *by
Jay Butler, Kurt Lancaster,
and Jenna Lyter.)*

FIGURE 6.37
Here you can see how the effect of No. 85 shapes the look of the clip I chose in Final Cut. In addition, you can see a series of tools that were used to create that look. Each one can be manipulated further to fine-tune the look you want. The tools used to create the No. 85 look include Contrast, Saturation, Color Ranges, Curves, Warm/Cool, Color Contrast, and Ranged Saturation.
(Still from NAU Marketing video, Chef and Melissa by Jay Butler, Kurt Lancaster, and Jenna Lyter.)

tools (found on the right edge of the screen when you hover the mouse there) used to design the particular look you chose (Figure 6.37). Click on the icon and you can see the specific parameters used for that tool—and you can adjust them to further shape the look.

6. Click on any one of the tools along the bottom row, and you'll see the parameters of the particular tool in the far-right column. For example, Figure 6.38 is a close-up of the Curves tool. Different effects plug-ins will reveal different tools.

FIGURE 6.38
The Curves tool as used in helping to create the "No. 85" effect plug-in. The look can be manipulated further by adjusting the full RGB curve or individual RGB curves. You will be given instant feedback as you adjust them.

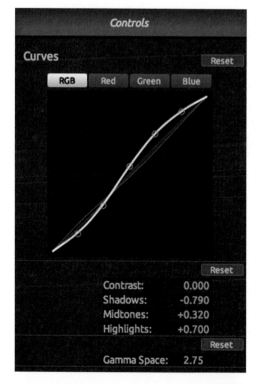

7. Examine the variety of tools and adjust the parameters as needed.

8. If you want to add additional tools to manipulate or simply not use any of the Looks preset plug-ins, hover the mouse along the right edge of the window and you'll be able to see dozens of tools that can be used to shape the look you want from scratch. There are menus for manipulating the look of the Subject, Matte, Lens, Camera, and Post.

9. When you have the look you want, you can save the look by clicking on the Finished button in the bottom-right window, and you'll be taken back to Final Cut with those changes in place for the clip you manipulated.

> **TIP**
> Right click on the clip you just changed and select Copy (or Command C), then go to Edit→Paste Effects on another clip where you want to apply the same effect. You may need to go into the Magic Bullet editor to fine turn it, but all of the changes will be applied.

The variety of tools allow you to manipulate the look of the scene—such as adding a filter that would normally be applied in-camera when shooting, but can be done in post with Magic Bullet. You could spot-meter a section and change the exposure of it. These powerful tools can help change the entire look of your film, but the goal is to adjust it so that it feels right for the story, not to have it stand out and look as though it was color-graded. (See Figures 6.39 and 6.40 for examples for Camera and Lens.)

FIGURE 6.39
The Tools menu for Camera (click on the tab on the bottom of the menu to see the different menu choices). For Camera, such tools include Exposure, Spot Exposure, Graduated Exposure, Negative Bleach Bypass, Contrast, Color Contrast, Shutter Streak, Crush, Color Reversal, Black & White, Saturation, Ranged Saturation, Shoulder, 2-Strip Process, 3-Strip Process, and Warm/Cool.

FIGURE 6.40
The Lens tool pvrovides for postproduction changes in Exposure, Spot Exposure, Grad Exposure, Vignette, Anamorphic Flare, Deflare, Chromatic Aberration, Edge Softness, Swing-Tilt, Lens Distortion, and Haze/Flare.

Using Magic Bullet Looks is a great way to experiment and explore with the film look. In Part II of the book, there are examples of before and after shots of several films, showing how the color grading process worked for those projects. But to just show some of the potential power of this software, the examples shown here in Figures 6.41 through 6.43 reveal how you can change an image through Magic Bullet Looks' color

FIGURE 6.41
The Magic Bullet Looks 3-Way color corrector (called Color Ranges) allows you to adjust the colors of shadow areas, midtones, and highlights by using a slider along the curves of the color wheels.

FIGURE 6.42
The Magic Bullet Looks Grad Exposure filter applied to the color-corrected shot with exposure drop-off applied from screen, graduated to the left end of the dashed line hovering near the middle of the screen.
(Still from NAU Marketing video, Chef and Melissa *by Jay Butler, Kurt Lancaster, and Jenna Lyter.)*

FIGURE 6.43
The Magic Bullet Looks Swing-Tilt effect applied to the shot (before color correction). Notice the foreground blur along the edge of the counter with the copper pots and pans, while the subject's face stays in focus. The horizontal solid line marks the depth of field, whereas the dashed vertical indicates the center point and angle of the tilt shift.
(Still from NAU Marketing video, Chef and Melissa *by Jay Butler, Kurt Lancaster, and Jenna Lyter.)*

correction tool, adjust the settings of the f-stop along a graduated filter, and see what happens when you apply the Swing-Tilt (similar to the Tilt-Shift lens effect) to a shot in post.

In addition, Magic Bullet works well with doing color correction with neutral "flat" settings. The frame grabs in Figures 6.44 and 6.45 were shot with Technicolor CineStyle on a Canon 5D Mark II and corrected using Magic Bullet Looks.

FIGURE 6.44
Frame grab of a shot utilizing Technicolor's CineStyle picture style. Note the washed-out milky look; the colors do not pop, but when put into Magic Bullet Looks, the richness of the colors comes out (see Figure 6.45).

FIGURE 6.45
Applying Curves removes the milky washed out flat look, adjusting Color Ranges adds a bit of red, while the application of Exposure provides an extra stop of open exposure to compensate for over-compensated underexposure occurring from an ND fader filter. The image pops with color and contrast. Notice the details in the highlights and shadows.

Here's some final advice on color grading. No matter what effect you use—from applying a little bit of tone to shaping a complex graduated exposure—as you go through your scenes, shot by shot, be sure to remain consistent in matching shots in a sequence, as well as when making the transitions between sequences. You don't want images to stand out because you improperly graded a shot or failed to match it with the previous shot. You may want to save presets in Magic Bullet, such as "Scene 1," so you have the look down for that scene and then apply it to the other shots in that scene. If the tones need to change from shot to shot, be sure you color grade by matching the skin tones of your performers from shot to shot. If the facial tones don't match, then the audience will notice it. Save the profile and apply it to the other shots in the scene.

This chapter covered the basics of working with a postproduction workflow to decompress your DSLR footage into a form that can be easily edited, and with increased chrominance and luminance color space—it makes it better for color grading. The chapter showed the steps for converting these files with Squared 5's MPEG Streamclip, Cineform's NeoScene, and Apple's Final Cut Pro. In addition, it provided the steps to sync up externally recorded audio using DualEyes and the sync feature of Final Cut Pro. It then shifted into the process to convert the look of your project using Magic Bullet Looks—a powerful postproduction tool to finalize the look of your footage so you can fully apply the final touches in achieving a cinematic look.

CHAPTER 7
Telling Better Stories with Your DSLR

HOW TO CREATE INTERESTING CHARACTERS

The key to finding your story is determining what your main character wants and what he or she does to get it. In a wedding video, a bride and groom want to get married therefore all of your choices, from the look of the film to what shots you choose to shoot must revolve around this dramatic need.

Jamin Winans' great internet short *Uncle Jack* is one of the strongest short films shot on a DSLR—due to the fact that it tells a powerful story. Jack wants to escape his pursuers while at the same time he wants to keep his niece happy by telling her a fairytale.

In summary, *Uncle Jack* takes the fairytale motif and updates it into a contemporary setting in which a man is fleeing a crime scene chased by thugs who want him dead. An unconscious clown sits in the passenger seat of the car, while a giggling woman screams with glee in the back seat of the convertible. Bullets fly and Jack's cell phone rings. Without listening to who's on the other end, Jack assumes it's one of his cohorts, and he warns him that the plan has been compromised and to, "Get out of there." The film cuts to a young girl on her bed, who quizzically says, "Uncle Jack?" He tries to ditch her, but she insists that he tell her a story because her parents are fighting and he once told her that she could call him any time when that happens. Not wanting to break his word, he tells her a fairytale, using his present predicament as the metaphor for the story. By the end of the film, Uncle Jack and his buddy in the clown suit are cornered in a costume shop, and the niece realizes what's going on and tells her uncle what to do to beat the enemy. After their defeat, Uncle Jack's niece tells him to stop gambling.

The story works well because the main character isn't just a shady character trying to avoid a gambling debt; he's a shady character who loves his niece and doesn't want to disappoint her. Good stories evolve from avoiding the stereotype that tends to drive the profit-motivated bottom line. The famed cinematographer Haskell Wexler, ASC, puts it this way:

> For me, artistic goes beyond the visual image or photograph; it's the totality of the philosophy, the ideas, the personality and the soul of people. Too often, the search for what seems to be commercial—the

things that grab people's attention—opens the door for celebrating antipersonal behavior, celebrating warfare, celebrating ways which do not elevate and serve mankind.[1]

Uncle Jack could have devolved into blockbuster violence, but Winan's takes the story to a deeper level by making Jack a conflicted character who represents something more than a stereotype. Wexler's advice extends to documentaries and news: what kinds of stories are you going to tell? The answer stems from the roots of why human beings tell stories in the first place.

HOW TO TAP INTO MAINSTREAM AUDIENCE'S EMOTIONAL CORE

There are probably as many reasons to be entertained by a story as there are people. The films of George Lucas and Stephen Spielberg tend to resonate with a wide audience because these filmmakers understand how to shape the images and stories that carry emotional and intellectual meaning for the viewer. Storytellers with broad appeal seem to naturally craft compelling stories that meet the needs or demands of a wide audience.

When storytellers strive to create and capture images that are unique to their own personal perspective, when they're tapping into the subconscious intuition, they can inspire viewers and perhaps teach them something about how to live their lives more fully.

In *Uncle Jack*, Winans taps into larger themes and not only provides us with an entertaining but tragically flawed character, but also uses the niece as the impetus to help change this character into something better than he is. "I liked the idea that the niece was just someone listening to the fairy tale," Winans explains in an interview, "but by the end you realize she's truly part of it and ultimately the knower of all. She's part of his world initially, but by the end, he's part of her world."[2] Being conscious when such change of character occurs is essential when crafting compelling stories—it's the hinge where your directing and cinematography revolves, since when you know when a character changes, you can craft images that highlight that change.

Whether we want to write our own scripts or shoot another's script, we should choose projects that resonate in some way with our need to tell *this particular story*. The art of shooting it well—shaping the look and feel of it—will be more honest and clear when we do a project that means something to us. This doesn't mean that when you choose to shoot a wedding or a commercial, for example, every moment of the work is imbued with deep psychological meaning. But a job can be more than a job when we endow it with our passionate view of how we perceive the world. Do we linger on a glance from the bride in

---

[1]Fauer, J. (2008). *Cinematographer Style: The Complete Interview, Vol. 1*, (p.297). American Society of Cinematographers.

[2]All quotations by Winans in this chapter were conducted by the author in June 2010.

One of the reason's Vincent Laforet's *Reverie* is powerful isn't that it was shot on a Canon 5D Mark II. It's that he opened with that romantic kiss between a couple and the guy blows it—he tries to pursue his love but loses it. The story contains power. It resonates with a universal theme of lost love, and most of us have experienced that loss in our own way. And in the hands of a good director-cinematographer (the DSLR shooter), the story can be translated into powerful images that resonate with an audience.

a tight close-up when she looks at the groom because we see in this moment a universal moment of truth … and we weld this image to the cultural belief that love can last forever? Maybe.

For Winans, the premise for *Uncle Jack* told through a fairytale lens was about shaping a point of view: "I strongly believe the world we see is a choice of perspective. Some of us see the laws of physics and some of us see magic. The fairy tale theme in a modern context was just choosing to see the typical action (cars and guns) sequence as magical instead." The perspective was shaped by the dramatic need for Jack to tell a story to his niece—not only to keep his promise, but eventually this act provides him self-realization about his own foibles and need for humility and change.

Uncle Jack and his niece—their conflicting dramatic needs that coalesce around a mutual desire to help each other out—express the core of Winan's short. How the characters react to the situation they're in defines who these characters are, and by having Jack become this father figure to his niece in her time of need provides her an opportunity to help save his life over the phone. And the dramatic needs of the characters are what an audience identifies with.

The story sets the tone and becomes the soul of the shoot. The camera is secondary. Philip Bloom, at a DSLR Hdi RAWworks Masterclass held in Los Angeles on March 6, 2010, discussed that it didn't really matter what lenses or camera you use if the content is "engaging"; it's the story that matters.

> Always start with characters—from them stems the conflict, thus the drama, and the audience will more easily get caught up in the story.

Always start with characters—from them stems the conflict, thus the drama, and the audience will more easily get caught up in the story.

Documentary filmmakers Brent and Craig Renaud have made such films as *Warrior Champions*, *Little Rock Central High: 50 Years Later*, *Taking the Hill*, *Off to War*, and *Dope Sick Love*. When asked about shooting short doc projects for the *The New York Times* after the earthquake in Haiti, they discussed the importance of finding stories that others avoid:

> We love to tell stories that won't get told otherwise or at least not in the same way. In one story we produced for the *The New York Times* recently we focused on

the young Haitian American Navy Corpsmen aboard the *USNS Comfort* hospital ship who have been called upon to be translators for victims of the earthquake in Haiti. With no training at all, these young men and women stepped up and became a lifeline for vulnerable Haitian patients coming aboard the ship, a foreign country really, unfamiliar and scary. The Corpsmen comfort the patients and attend to their needs, letting them know that the United States is here to help. Sometimes they tell the patients that their legs will be amputated, or even that they will soon die. Through the experience of these translators the viewer is given a totally different and interesting look at this crisis. These Corpsmen are national heroes, and had we not profiled them, very few people would have known it. Showing things like this to the world is something that makes us proud. (Lancaster, 2010, *Documentary Tech*. <http://documentarytech .com/?p=3489>)

One of their major themes revolves around the underdog doing something that deepens the human experience. The Renaud brothers capture these moments in their projects because something within compels them to bring back stories that mean something. And at the heart of it is the story—not what camera they shoot on; not the technology—but what story they are going to tell and what characters would compellingly help convey that story.

In our long form documentary work everything is about character. We are more likely to start a project with a character we like rather than an issue or a story. The short form news stories that we produce for the *Times* are a little different, but not a lot. With these stories often we are starting from a larger concept, like the Drug War in Juarez, or the earthquake in Haiti, but whereas most news stories are dominated by a correspondent either on camera or in voice-over, we are still looking for characters to drive the story. We do use some voice-over in these news pieces because it helps focus and keep the stories short. However we use as little as possible. We believe the look on a child's face, or a gesture from a politician, uncommented on can sometimes speak worlds more than an all knowing voice-over. (Lancaster 2010, *Documentary Tech*. <http:// documentarytech.com/?p=3489>)

The character is key because around that person is a dramatic need that tends to be universal by which the audience can identify and become engaged with the content—and they will more quickly fall in love with your images!

WHERE DO GOOD IDEAS COME FROM?

I tell my writing and production students that there is only one of them in the universe, and their job is to discover their unique voice and share that with others. Good stories come from storytellers who are honest with themselves and tell a story that's unique to their voice and passions. If you are going to shoot a scene in which a couple kiss, then you had better film it in such a way that comes from how you see the world—whether that's drawn from a fantasy dream vision, a nightmare, or from real life. In either case, it's rooted in how you feel and see the world. That's essentially what good filmmakers do and

FIGURE 7.1
The clever and powerful story of *Uncle Jack* revolves around fairytale themes in a few short minutes.
In this shot, a Pentax K-7 DSLR is taped to the steering wheel with a wide angle lens to shoot everyone
in the car. The car is set in a studio against a greenscreen. <Video at: http://vimeo.com/9578519>
(© 2010 Jamin Winans. Used with permission.)

helps guide them in shaping images that haven't been seen before. We haven't
seen shots quite like those in Laforet's *Reverie*. Although we've seen plenty of
chase scenes in film, we haven't quite seen the one Winans gives us in *Uncle
Jack* (see Figure 7.1). These scenes stem from the vision of how
these filmmakers perceive the world. It's their unique
voices that help provide power to those images.
Then their choice of cameras and how they shape
the look and feel of their scenes are coming
from the right place—the story.

> It's their unique
> voices that help provide
> power to those images. Then
> their choice of cameras and how
> they shape the look and feel of their
> scenes are coming from the right
> place—the story.

However, if the shots are too unique—not tapping into the dramatic action of a character
with wants and needs—you may end up putting together a pretty film, but you may lose your
audience. Without a solid story, you won't likely
capture a large audience.

In a personal example, when I directed a short written by a former
student of mine—*The Kitchen*, set in a 1950s farmhouse—the stifling heat of
August would bring in evening thundershowers. In probably every movie I've
seen, the sound of thunder always occurs simultaneously with the flash of
lightning. But that's not how I observed the world growing up during summer thunderstorms in Maine. There might be distant flashes of "heat" lightning with no thunder, and as it got closer, the lightning flash would always
occur first, until it was right overhead. After seeing a flash, we would count the

silence until the thunder to determine the approximate distance of the storm (five seconds would be about a mile). So when I crafted the sound design for this short around my experiences as a child in Maine, there would be flashes followed by moments of silence, the moments shortening as the storm intensified—and I paralleled this with the increasing emotional tensions of the film.

Winan's *Uncle Jack* "started with the idea of a character forced to stay on his phone through ridiculous circumstances and yet try to make it seem like everything was fine," the writer-director explains. "From there I asked the question, 'Who's the last person he should want to be on the phone with?' I liked the contrast of a clearly shady guy talking very genuinely and sweetly to a little kid. That quickly led to him translating his current situation into a bedtime story."

Developing Story Ideas by Michael Rabiger (Focal Press, 2006) is an essential read if you really want to tap into your original voice for finding and analyzing stories; it's useful for writers and nonwriters. In it, he presents dozens of writing exercises that will help you discover a unique voice in telling stories. "Discovering the source of your stories," he writes, "those you are best qualified to tell, means looking for causes and effects in your own life and grasping the nature of what you feel most deeply. … it regularly produces insights that make people more accessible and interesting—both the real people around you and the fictional ones you nurture into existence". The book includes exercises on discovering your voice and influences in life, conducting dramatic analysis, and assessing the feasibility and quality of stories. It also includes a series of writing projects covering tales from your childhood and family stories, retelling a myth in a modern-day setting, telling a story based on dream images, adapting a short story, adapting a news story and a documentary topic, writing a 30-minute fiction piece, and writing a feature film.

Having taught beginning scriptwriting for seven years, I determined the number of good scripts in my class hovered around 20–25 percent. After my students began using Rabiger's book, I saw the number of good scripts increase to 75–80 percent. The exercises work, so, as a professional educator, I wholeheartedly recommend the book.

Essentially, Rabiger guides you through a series of short writing exercises that tap into the your memories—whether it's a childhood memory, a story told in the family (such as about the time when my crazy uncle…). He has you write in the present tense in outline script treatment form. In addition, he provides tools on how to analyze a script for its story structure, as well as how to assess a story for its strengths and weaknesses.

I end this section with a couple of writing exercises that should help you find your voice and begin writing stories (or choosing stories that resonate with you). The first is drawn from Rabiger's *Developing Story Ideas*, and the second presents a way that I developed to write dialog. I include examples to help jump-start the exercises.

Exercise

Discovering Stories You Should Tell and Finding Story Ideas

Modified from Rabiger's *Developing Story Ideas* (Focal Press, 2006: 25–26).[3]

"Survey of Yourself and Your Authorial Goals"

1. Describe the "marks left on you by one or two really formative experiences"—ones that were life-changing or forced you to appreciate life in a different way. It can be happy and/or sad experiences—but it should be something that moved you to experience deep emotions. Keep these notes private. They do not need to be shared.

2. "Develop two or three *themes* connected with the marks that this main character carries. *Examples:* isolation; betrayal; the high cost of pretense."

3. "Think of three or four *types of characters toward whom you feel particular empathy*."

4. "Develop four *provisional story topics*. Make all four exploit a single theme from your answer to #1," and make each topic contain a main character, explore concerns you care about, and be as different from each other as possible.

5. If you want to work on a fiction piece, write a short three- to five-paragraph story in the present tense and showing only what an audience can see and hear (you can't see thoughts, so keep the story within the main character's point of view and what the audience can see on the imaginary movie screen of your mind). Craft the story around one of these story topics. Be sure to give your main character an agenda: she has a need, desire, or want that she must attempt to fulfill. Make her do it and put an obstacle or two in her way.

Example from one of my former students:

1. Psychological marks (private notes, not published).
2. Develop two or three themes
   a. Shame
   b. Self-destruction
   c. Misdirected anger
3. Three or four types of characters:
   a. Professional career people who obtained "everything" on their own and subsequently destroyed it all on their own.
   b. Someone who lost his/her identity due to self-indulgence (Gollum/ Sméagol from *Lord of the Rings*).
   c. Children who are emotionally abandoned and therefore never feel validated in their own emotions.
4. Four provisional story topics based on the theme of self-destruction:
   a. A motivated career woman who is secretly plagued by self-loathing and doubt but strives to be recognized and respected.

---

[3]This exercise was published in *Developing Story Ideas, Second Edition,* by Michal Rabiger, Chapter 3, "Artistic Identity," Copyright © 2006 Elsevier, Inc. Printed with permission.

  b. A daughter pretending that she's successful, happy & healthy in order to protect her mother from the truth about her addiction to drugs.

  c. A young thrill-seeker who hangs out with the Moab crowd to ride off cliffs with his bicycle and participates in various daredevil stunts—who is beginning to realize that he really doesn't care if he gets hurt or even dies.

  d. An animal rights activist & stray/abused animal rescuer who ends up getting overwhelmed and is finally arrested for animal abuse & neglect.

From this, we can see how this student evolved this theme into this story outline.

Scene 1: A 9-year-old girl named Millie wakes up and pads into the tiny kitchen of a dilapidated, wooden shack, clutching a ragged teddy bear. It is 1927 in rural Oklahoma. Millie sees her mother in the kitchen, staring wildly at the dirty pots and pans strewn all over the sink and table. Millie asks her mother what is wrong. Her mother tells her that ghosts came in during the night and messed up the pots and pans after she'd cleaned them, making breakfast for themselves and leaving before anyone in the house woke up. Millie tries to reason with her mother, but her mother emphatically tells her that she heard the ghosts clanking the pans and making a [ruckus] all night long. Millie presses the teddy bear close to her chest with both arms, turns around and goes back to her room.

Scene 2: Millie comes home from school during a cold winter day and sees that her little 4-year-old brother, Jake, is curled up in the corner, writhing in pain. She runs into the kitchen to tell her mother that something is wrong with Jake. Her mother continues to hum to herself and plod around the kitchen, making some kind of imaginary dinner for imaginary guests. Millie tugs on her mother's skirt, insisting that she come now and look at Jake. Millie's mother shoos her away and tells her it's not polite to interrupt adults when they're having a conversation—even though Millie's mother is the only adult at home right now. Millie runs back into the living room to check on Jake. He is pale and holding his belly. He emits a loud moan and her mother's voice can be heard from the kitchen, telling the children to pipe down and be quiet. Millie runs back into the kitchen once more, begging her mother to please come look at Jake, telling her that he's really, really sick. Her mother stares out the window while she holds an imaginary bowl of imaginary food in one arm and stirs with an imaginary spoon in the opposite hand. Millie runs back into the living room and props open the front door. She clumsily gathers Jake up in her tiny arms. He is almost as big as she is, so she has to pull him up several different ways before she finally gets a good hold of the boy. Millie carefully steps out of the house and down the rickety wooden steps, and sets off across the fields.

Scene 3: Millie toddles across the field with her brother in her arms. She knows the general direction of town and heads for it. She continues walking with Jake, having to set him down every now and then to catch her breath, then gather him up again to keep walking. The hospital is miles away. Millie carries Jake this way all by herself for the entire journey.

Scene 4: Millie finally arrives at the hospital. Nurses notice her as she stumbles up the walkway, exhausted. The nurses run out to grab Jake and help her up. They ask her what is wrong, and she can barely breathe, much less talk. One of the nurses, after one look at Jake, picks the boy up and hurries into the building. Millie is helped inside by the nurses and given a drink of water. Millie sits on the cold, hard wooden bench and waits, her water cup emptied, her dress and face filthy with dirt and dead weeds from the fields she had to cross. She lies down and curls up on the bench.

Scene 5: Millie wakes up. A doctor is touching her shoulder, trying to ask her questions about where her parents are and how she got there. Millie rubs her eyes and gazes up at the doctor, asking for Jake. The doctor informs her that Jake had a serious case of appendicitis, and that if she had not taken him to the hospital when she had, his appendix would have burst and he very likely would have died. The doctor tells Millie that Jake must spend some time in the hospital bed and that she should go home. Millie obediently walks out of the hospital and heads across the miles of fields that lead to home.

We can see the development of an original voice in this story, one that comes from this student's unique perspective on life. We can also see the development of the three act structure—the emotional arc mapping the change in character: the setup (the daughter notices that there is something wrong with her mother), complications (the daughter tries to get her mother to help the sick brother), climax/crisis (she takes her brother by herself to the hospital), and resolution (the brother survives).

Exercise

Writing Good Dialog

Give two characters conflicting agendas and place them into a scene that occurs in one location in one moment of time. As they speak, do *not* allow either of them to reveal their agenda through dialog—until the end of the scene (if at all), unless you want your story to sound like a soap opera! This will heighten the subtext—the underlying emotions and motivations of the characters—and will usually lead to good dialog. If you reveal the agenda too soon, the energy will likely dissipate quickly.

Example of dialog with hidden agendas by Margo McClellen:

```
Daytime, outside a posh restaurant on Sunset
Boulevard. PAULY is standing in front of
the doorway and lights a cigarette. He dons
a tacky blue jumpsuit and gold jewelry. A
strange looking man, an ALIEN, wearing a
tailored suit that could be Armani (if it
weren't for the fish-scale-like print) stoi-
cally walks up to Pauly.
```

> ALIEN
> Good afternoon. Please take me to
> your--

> PAULY
> Hey, is that a vintage Jag?

> ALIEN
> ... good afternoon. I would like for
> you to--

> PAULY
> Hey man, what kind of mileage you
> get in that baby?

> ALIEN
> Mile--

> PAULY
> Yeah I bet she guzzles, eh? But
> who gives a crap, right? That car
> is HOT.

> ALIEN
> Good ... afternoon ... I would like--

> PAULY
> You don't speak English too good,
> do ya?

Pauly glances up and down the street.

> PAULY
> Hey, my girlfriend's comin' out in
> a sec. She's gotta SEE this thing!
>   (toward restaurant entrance)
> Hey, SHEILA! Get yer ass out here,
> RIGHT NOW...you gotta SEE this!
>   (to ALIEN)
> Hey uh, do you have the time?

                    ALIEN
        Time? I--

                    PAULY
        HEEEY SHEEEILA!!!

SHEILA sprints out of the restaurant, glanc-
ing over her shoulder. She notices Alien and
smiles sweetly, then looks at Pauly urgently.

                    PAULY
        Here, baby, c'mon—you gotta SEE

        this CAR!

Pauly grabs her arm and starts to pull her
toward Alien's "car".

                    PAULY
              (walking around the car)
        Check this OUT, man!

              (to ALIEN)
        Hey, you wouldn't mind if we took

        it for a little spin would

        you? I'll give you FIVE HUNDRED

        BUCKS right now if you just let me

        take it around the block. All you

        gotta do is just WAIT HERE 'til we

        get back ...

                    ALIEN
        Wait ... here? You must take me to

        your--

                    PAULY
        Yeah yeah yeah I'll take you

        wherever you wanna go, foreign

        boy. After we get back.

He and Sheila exchange a knowing glance as
they get into the "car." The vehicle begins

to sputter, then starts violently flashing
bright yellow and orange.

> PAULY
> (from inside the car)

WHAT the--

The "car" winks out of existence. Alien just
stands there, staring at the empty parking
space.

> ALIEN
> Well ... crap.

We can clearly see the two different agendas: The alien wants directions to the
"leader," while Pauly wants to "borrow" the alien's ride and impress his girlfriend.
Although it's clear what both characters want, by having Pauly be the lead—taking
charge, *doing* what he wants, he is able to overcome the obstacle of the alien character. The alien, on the other hand, is clear on what it wants, but its agenda is so at
odds with Pauly's that it never gets a chance—which adds to the comedic flavor of the
scene. Good dialog is driven by hidden agendas.

Example of dialog with hidden agenda by Ed Crosby.

Will and Joe, two high school students, hang
out in the back of their school. They're
smoking cigarettes. Jennifer skips up to
them.

> JEN
> Hey Will.

> WILL
> 'Sup.

> Joe
> Hey Jen.

Jen doesn't take her eyes off Will.

> JEN
> Oh hey ... umm Will, how are you?

> WILL
> Fine.

> JEN
> Oh cool.

                    JOE
What's goin on with you, Jen?

                    JEN
Nothin much.

                    WILL
Man, I can't wait to get my leather
jacket.

                    JEN
Oh yeah that's a beautiful jacket. It's
gonna look really good on you.

                    WILL
Yeah, I know, I've been saving for
like a month but it's gonna be worth
it. Man I'm going to look so cool.

                    JEN
Yeah.

                    Joe
Hey Jen did you get that note I left
in your locker?

                    JEN
Huh? Uhh no ... I don't know.

                    JOE
Yeah well basically I'm going to
The Rat this weekend to see The
Unseen so I can pick you up a
t-shirt or a pin or whatever 'cause
I remember you said how you liked
them when we were talking about
bands at the pep rally.

                    JEN
What? Oh yeah that would be cool.

                    WILL
That punk rock shit, fuckin sucks.
They can't even play. Sounds like
shit.

                    JOE
It's not about musicianship, Will,
It's about raw aggression.

                    WILL
Yeah cause that's what gets girls
in the mood, "raw aggression."

                    JEN
Ummm, I kind of like it.

                    WILL
Whatever.

                    JOE
Yeah so if you want a t-shirt
They're only like 5 bucks but I can
totally spot you the cash. You can
pay me after or maybe you could buy
me a beer sometime.

                    JEN
Hmmm hmmm. Hey Will, uhhhh ...
Can you give me a ride?

                    WILL
You wanna ride in The Machine?

                    JEN
Yeah, I love The Machine.

                    WILL
Sure, babe. What you gonna do
for me?

                    JEN
Heh heh.

Jen looks at Joe who is looking at the
ground.

                    WILL
          God I love that car. It's like an

          extension of my personality. It's

          like you can look at my car and go,

          "Yeah, that guy is pretty cool."

                    JEN
               (turned off)
          Uhhh yeah.

                    JOE
          That's how I feel about my 10

          speed. One look at that thing

          and the ladies go wild.

Jen laughs.

                    WILL
          What, are you serious? No chick is

          into a guy who rides a bike.

                    JEN
          Yeah, I mean how old are you?

                    JOE
          16.

                    JEN
          And you ride a bike?

                    JOE
          Yeah, that's right I ride a bike!

                    JEN
          Okay, Jesus!

They all stand around shifting uncomfort-
ably. The schoolbell rings.

                    WILL
          Well, schools out. Gimme another

smoke, Joe. Come on, The Machine
awaits.

                    JOE
          (Looking at the ground)
I'm gonna walk.

                    WILL
What dude, you live like four miles
from here.

                    JOE
Yeah I know.

                    WILL
You're going to walk four miles in
those ratty tennis shoes. They're
going to fall off by the time you
get home.

                    JOE
I don't care.

                    WILL
Okay, come on, Jen.

                    JEN
Hey, you know, I just remembered
I have detention today.

                    WILL
Okay.

                    JEN
Okay see you guys later.

Jen runs off without looking at either of
them.

                    WILL
She is so weird. Alright, man, have
a good walk.

                    JOE
Thanks.

Will walks off. Joe, suddenly hauls off and kicks a garbage can, then he just stands there. He turns to walk away.

                    JEN
     Joe!

                    JOE
     Jen?

Jen walks out from behind the school.

                    JOE
     Will left already.

                    JEN
     Oh.

She looks around and fidgets.

                    JOE
     What happened to detention?

                    JEN
     Uhhh... cancelled ... yeah they

     cancelled it.

They both stand there looking uncomfortable.

                    JOE
     Well I was gonna go ...

                    JEN
     YES!

                    JOE
     Yes?

                    JEN
     I mean what were you going to say?

                    JOE
     I was gonna go home and listen to
     records.

                    JEN
     Oh that sounds cool.

                    JOE
     I mean you could come too if you

     wanted.

                    JEN

```
            Uhhh sure.

They walk off together smiling.
```

The subtext is clear, and we never have to worry about feeling as though the author is spoon-feeding how we should feel about the characters or let them tell us what their agendas are. Rather, the writer lets the emotional dynamics of the characters take over as they try not to say what's exactly on their minds, and we're led into a story that is entertaining because it forces the audience to guess what's going on, and this guessing is what keeps them interested.

STORY STRUCTURE

After you have a sense of character down and what the story may be about—and have a sense of how to write decent dialog—you need to think about story structure. This story structure is mainly shaped, or caused, by the main character, whether the character is initiating the action or reacting to it. In *Uncle Jack*, Jack wants to flee his pursuers, while trying to keep his niece happy over the phone. The structure of the story comes out of his need to escape while simultaneously using the changing scenes of his escapade to embellish the fairytale he's telling his niece.

Every action has a reaction. What occurs in one scene *causes* what will follow. A character does this by performing actions. He engages in actions because he wants something. Uncle Jack's niece wants him to tell her a story so she doesn't have to think about her parents' fighting. Uncle Jack reacts to this by telling her a story, while he simultaneously wants to escape his attackers. Neither character is static. For one thing, if a character is static, then there's nothing to propel the story forward; there is no dramatic need for an audience to gain emotional attachment and they'll look for other stories that hook them. And second, these actions, the dramatic needs of the characters, must be arranged in a such a way as to build emotions in the characters and, by extension, the audience.

Dramatic need drives the plot—the arrangement of actions. A bride wanting to get married would be the dramatic need in a wedding video, for example. So, when we're the DSLR shooters, what actions do we need to capture that reveal this dramatic need? In fiction, the dramatic needs of the character start with the writer but continue through production and into the postproduction phase of editing. But the principle applies to nonwriters, as well. The filmmaker, whether shooting a documentary on the fly or setting up a commercial, rock video, or wedding shoot, must understand the dramatic needs of the characters and subjects to be able to deliver useful shots for the editor (even if the filmmaker is the editor!); these shots need to move the story forward.

Typical story structures follow this pattern: hook, introduction or setup of the dramatic need of the character (some may refer to this as the *exposition*, the minimal necessary information needed by an audience to get the story), conflict or complications to the dramatic need that rises to a climax, and finally a resolution (the dramatic need is resolved).

A hook is an incident that grabs the audience's attention right away. We're given some kind of background or context or introduction to the character or situation. There's some obstacle the character must overcome to get what she wants; this conflict builds to a crisis point or climax where the character either gets what she wants or doesn't. Finally, the resolution reveals what the character learned from her experience.

This should not be a formulaic process, but rather one that's organic, rising out of the character's needs and wants as expressed by the writer (or filmmaker analyzing the story structure of whatever piece she's planning to shoot). The emotional changes a character goes through pivot around the setup, complications, and climax. These emotional changes in character (the character arc) typically revolve around three acts.

- Act 1 presents the setup, the introduction of the characters, their background, and setting. It may introduce the conflict—the central need or want of the character coming into conflict with something, someone, or even herself.
- Act 2 presents a turn of events for the central character in her quest to get what she wants; obstacles or complications get in her way, eventually escalating to Act 3.
- Act 3 comes at the apex of the story, the climatic point representing the strongest emotional moment for the character where she must face the final confrontation, the final crisis (the wedding vows and kiss at the wedding). She either gets what she wants or she doesn't, thus resolving the story.

In the Alien-Pauly story described in the dialog writing exercise, we can even see the emotional arc of the characters in a mini three-act structure; indeed, individual scenes will contain elements of the three-act structure (but usually not the resolution because the story continues into another scene):

- Setup of Act 1: The alien wants directions, while Pauly checks out the Alien's ride, thinking that it's a souped-up car.
- Act 2: This act adds the complication of Pauly deciding not to just look at the "car," but to call his girlfriend out and take the car for a spin, perhaps even to steal it—rising to the climax/crisis in the next act.
- Act 3: Pauly takes the "car," leaving the Alien standing on the sidewalk as the resolution.

In *Uncle Jack*, the emotional arc of the characters look like this:

- Setup of Act 1: Uncle Jack tries to escape thugs shooting at him. His niece calls him. He tries to get rid of her, but can't, taking us to…
- Act 2: This act adds the complication of Uncle Jack trying to tell a fairytale to his niece while he flees the car, enters a train, saves his buddy clown from falling from a building, and heads down a tunnel.

- Act 3: And they hide in a costume shop, where they are cornered by two gunman, while the niece explains to Uncle Jack how to escape the situation, thus resolving the story.

Why is this important for us as DSLR shooters? As the person responsible for setting the look of the shots and capturing them on camera, you, as the director (whether shooting it yourself or working with a cinematographer), must understand the story and know what images go where so the editor has everything needed to deliver a strong story. Gordon Willis, ASC, describes how the cinematographer "is responsible for the image. He is responsible for putting that magic up on the wall. He's the visual psychiatrist, moving the audience from here to there"[4]

If the cinematographer doesn't understand the story—the underlying dramatic needs of the character expressed over time—then how will she know what to shoot and how to shoot? This is rooted in the story. When a clearly written script maps the change of a character as he attempts to get what he wants (or even just a brief outline of the emotional change of the bride and groom in a wedding video), then it's much easier to revolve the story around a central character trying to get what he wants. If the story is vague, with a weak central character, the story doesn't move forward and the cinematography doesn't have a basis on which to shoot. Plus, you end up with random shots that might look pretty but don't move a story forward, moment by moment, shot by shot, and will likely bore an audience.

Get a script, write a script, adapt a story, or analyze and structure a rock video or wedding shoot around a story. If you can't think of a story, then modernize a fairytale and shoot it with friends. What would a short film look like if you rewrite and set the "Little Red Riding Hood" folktale in New York City or Los Angeles or a small town in middle America? Tell a story with your images.

Winans, the writer and director of the Internet short *Uncle Jack* (as well as the writer-director of 2009's fantastic independent film, *Ink*) believes that "story is everything" when it comes to narrative filmmaking. As a beginning filmmaker, he used to gravitate toward "cool shots, cool editing" without thinking too much about the story. "But after enough miserably failed films with really cool shots," Winans explains, "it became apparent that if I didn't have the script, and more specifically the story, then I was sunk no matter what I did with the camera." So as he honed his filmmaking skills, he focused on the story: "As the years have gone by, my focus has been less and less on the technical process and more and more about the script." He faced a hard lesson and realized that "filmmaking is way too difficult, expensive, and time consuming to waste on a bad script," he adds.

---

[4]Fauer, J. (2008). *Cinematographer Style: The Complete Interviews, Vol. 1,* (p.315). American Society of Cinematographers.

Until you're telling a story, you're not doing cinema but simply playing around with a camera.

Let's look at an example to see how this structure can be seen in Vincent Laforet's Internet hit *Reverie* (see <http://vimeo.com/7151244>), shot on a Canon 5D Mark II. This short piece (97 seconds, excluding credits), tells the simple story of a man forgetting to meet a girl at a specific place. He wakes up and realizes he's late, then flies out the door, grabs flowers, and races his way to her location in his car, but misses her. Finally, the search escalates as he rides a helicopter in order to find her, but he fails. The movie ends as it began, a man sleeping on a couch dreaming about a girl. He wakes up and rushes out to try and meet her in time, but his love is gone—or perhaps it was just a dream.

Let's map Laforet's short as a mini three-act piece on the graph, as shown in Figure 7.2.

Act 1: Hook, setup of dramatic need: The man wants the woman. We see a man and woman kissing. Man on sofa, sleeping, as TV flickers light onto him. He gets flashes of images of a woman dressed in red, waiting for him. The conflict is set up: he should be there, but he fell asleep watching TV.

Act 2: Rising action, further complications to his dramatic need. Man washes his face, rushes up stairs, grabs flowers, and races through the city, looking around as he drives. The woman stands and waits. There is a series of shots of the man driving, overcoming further obstacles; he's using the GPS—perhaps he's lost. He arrives, whipping off his sunglasses, but she's not there.

Act 3: Climax/crisis/final confrontation and resolution. The girl's gone. The man's arrived too late, and the flowers drop out of his hand. He sweats bullets. He drives around the city, looking for her. The sequence

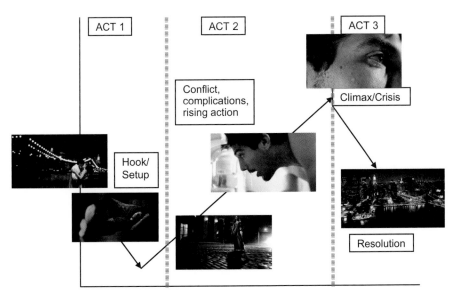

FIGURE 7.2
The three-act structure of Vincent Laforet's *Reverie.*

ends with a climatic shot of him in a helicopter as he continues to look for her. Panoramic shots of the city. The story is resolved as he realizes he's not going to find her. The short ends with him on his couch, waking up and rushing out the door—presumably the beginning of the film, or perhaps he's just dreaming about the encounter and failure to meet the girl. In either case, the story is resolved. He doesn't get the girl.

STORYTELLING SHOOTING EXERCISE

By Dave Anselmi

A good way to practice scriptwriting and see how what you write gets translated on film is to take a small scene from one of your favorite films and re-create it, shot by shot. Shoot a scene from one of your favorite films (make sure it's a good film that you can actually shoot—an action film with a lot of special effects may be too hard, but a good scene of drama can do the trick). By repeating the scene, by re-creating it shot-by-shot, you'll get a good sense of how good storytelling works on film. With this knowledge, you'll start to understand how to write better scripts.

Once the story is in place, a script written, then the cinematographer—in consultation with the director—determines the look and feel of the film, before shooting begins. In smaller projects, you may be the cinematographer and the director. In either case, the story should be your guide in determining how the film should look—whether you're shooting people to provide a snapshot of a city, wedding, commercial, music video, short, documentary, video journalism, or feature.

PART 2
Master DSLR Shooters at Work: Case Studies

This next part of the book examines seven strong story projects created by those with a flare for experimentation, a desire to push the capabilities of their DSLRs. Hundreds of others could have been chosen for the book, but these are the projects and people that fascinated me and represented some of the best cinematic documentary and short fiction projects in the DSLR world from an international perspective. Each chapter in this part explores a different aspect of filmmaking to reveal the capabilities of the cameras. It examines the approaches filmmakers took in attaining a cinematic look utilizing a variety of techniques[1]—from taking advantage of locations to engaging documentary cinema techniques to working with the blocking of actors.

In Chapter 8, Brazilian director Bernardo Uzeda, along with cinematographer Guga Millet and producer Isadora Sachett, envisioned a film look in their short *Casulo* that earned them a Brazilian Society of Cinematographers award. Their look relied on a strong primary color palette, the use of visual texture, and a postproduction process that not only included serious amounts of color grading, but also involved removing video noise from each shot. The process resulted in images of such pristine richness that one would be hard pressed

---

[1] I'm using film "look" in the titles to stay consistent with the book title—which is a useful marketing tool—but, of course, there is a difference, and a film look is not just one formula and refers to a variety of cinematic elements.

to say it wasn't shot on film—and, indeed, it was transferred to 35 mm film to screen at film festivals in Brazil (some viewers thought it was shot on 65mm!).

In Chapter 9, photojournalist Rii Schroer found the 5D Mark II a welcome fit to her intimate photography style, which includes building a rapport with her subjects, resulting in her characters shining through with not only cinematic flare, but with personalities that shimmer with depth. Furthermore, Schroer practiced a documentary style in her work that forthrightly challenges the need to engage in a TV news style, a style that looks and feels like video, rather than cinema. Schroer is a journalist who listens to her subjects, gives them a voice with respect, and at the same time weaves a story with strong images. Rather than let images simply illustrate a narration—as we typically find in TV news—Schroer practices visual journalism to be able to tell the story visually and cinematically.

Chapter 10 explores Philip Bloom's *A Day at the Races*. Bloom is a self-made guru of DSLR cinema and has become one of the strongest promoters of the HDSLR movement. In this short, he practiced his technique with a modified Canon 7D fitted out with high-end Cooke cinema lenses. He not only engaged his trademark style by covering his subjects with close-ups of faces, providing textural detail in the film, but captured the atmosphere of a horse stable and racetrack by doing so. His unique style stands out and he represents one of the most prolific powerful DSLR shooters working today.

In Chapter 11, Jeremy Ian Thomas, a colorist by day at Hdi RAWworks, and a director by night, put together the otherworldly feeling of *The Chrysalis*—taking advantage of California's Death Valley to evoke a purgatory for a young man who walks in between the liminal space of life and death. Thomas's wizardly skills in Apple's Color allows him to eke out a cinematic style from flat and superflat settings of Canon's 5D Mark II and 7D. In this project, he engaged the Cine Marvel picture style and integrated those images with CGI special effects.

In Chapter 12, Shane Hurlbut, ASC, teamed up with writer-director Po Chan to present probably the most engaging cinematic and heart-breaking short fiction shot on a Canon 5D Mark II to date with *The Last 3 Minutes*. It's certainly one of the most ambitious short DSLR films made—utilizing 18 different locations as we see an older man's life flash before his eyes (and all shot in five days). The impeccable detail in setting up each shot, getting the light perfect, choosing the proper lenses, and working with actors to shape the performance just so helped achieved a compelling cinematic look desired by so many aspiring filmmakers shooting digitally.

Ch. 13 explores how Kurt Lancaster and his students shaped a cinematic experience through a sound design in the Timpanogos Cave National Monument. They put into practice Walter Murch's idea of using metaphoric sound in cinema.

In Ch. 14, student Danger Charles created puppets and a miniature set in visualizing an Argentinian author's short story about how flies perceive heaven and hell. It's a great example of how script, mise-en-scene, and the cinematic elements of large sensor video helps shapes another world.

Note: All quotations of filmmakers in this section of the book are from interviews with the author, unless otherwise noted.

CHAPTER 8

Crafting the Film Look with Postproduction

161

Casulo (2009), directed by Bernardo Uzeda, Brazil, 17 min.

FIGURE 8.1
Still from Bernardo
Uzeda's *Casulo*
*(©2009. Used with
permission.)*

Technical data: Shot on a Canon 5D Mark II with Sigma 24–70 mm f/2.8 lens. Audio recorded with a Sennheiser MKH-416 microphone on an M-Audio Microtrack 2 digital audio recorder. Files converted to MPEG. Postproduction software: Final Cut Pro, Twister plug-in in After Effects (for 24P pulldown), Color Finesse 2.0 and the Tiffen DFX 2.0 filters, graduated NDs, vignettes, selective saturation, and so forth. Neat Video plug-in for noise reduction (Pro version). Images cropped and conformed to 1.85 aspect ratio for 35 mm film transfer, providing a 1920 × 1037 resolution, direct-to-positive or direct-to-print transfer at Technicolor USA using Cinevator (manufactured by a company from Norway called Cinevation).

Out of all the shorts shot on a HDSLR that I've seen online, *Casulo* is one of the strongest examples of video expressing the film look. Indeed, in 2010,

The trailer to
Casulo is located
at <http://vimeo.
com/13751287>.

the film earned the top cinematography award from the Brazilian equivalent of the American Society of Cinematographers: Associação Brasileira de Cinematografia. *Casulo*, reverberating with surreal echoes of David Lynch, tells the story about the complexities of obsession and death as a daughter spies on her mother who becomes obsessed by a male neighbor and a girl he is with. Although the narrative involves intricate levels of visual information and very little dialog, what stands out in the film is how the director and cinematographer captured those images and put them through a heavy postproduction process to shape a strong cinematic quality to the work (which was transferred to 35 mm film). The film was written and directed by Bernardo Uzeda, with cinematography by Guga Millet, and produced by Isadora Sachett. The project was shot on a Canon 5D Mark II in April 2009.

STORY IDEA

Uzeda's background is in film music and sound design, and at one point he made a documentary for film school. The doc earned several awards, which helped him raise money and gain the "confidence," he explains, to put together his first fiction. I thought of something that could be impressive visually and that could be done without a big budget or a big crew."[1]

Uzeda and producer Isadora Sachett shared a "certain distaste for the current types of features and shorts that were being made" in Brazil, he says. These stories not only shared similar journalistic style and themes, but also the "aesthetics, especially social/raw images" and most of which relied on dialog. Uzeda, a fan of visual cinema—in contrast to the dialog-heavy films produced in Brazil—wrote a murder obsession story with very little dialog. "Surrealistic images," Uzeda says, would drive the story, suspending it from realism. However, he admits that the film "can be confusing in a first viewing, but I like to think of it more as a dreamlike experience (this kind of experimentation is part of the fun when you are financing the whole project with your money)," he adds.

So he wrote his screenplay to shoot on a tight budget: "small crew, accessible locations, few actors, and so forth. Eighty percent of the film was shot in the facilities of my building (apartments, garage, swimming pool, emergency stairs, rooftops, balconies). So we only had to scout and pay for a couple of extra locations (which made principal photography considerably faster and cheaper)," Uzeda explains.

However, before he wrote the script, Uzeda looked at a variety of locations where he lived—ones that expressed "potential value for creating the atmosphere that I wanted. A recurring element in the shooting script is the POV shot," Uzeda says. "It was very important for the story to let the characters see and feel the atmosphere around them, and sometimes, they observe the other

---

[1]All quotations in this chapter are from interviews conducted by the author.

without being observed (something that was only possible after heavy location scouting, searching for places and corners that allowed this type of blocking effect)" (see Figures 8.2 and 8.3).

FIGURE 8.2
Still from *Casulo*, revealing how the production team utilized existing locations to help tell the story: a character peeks out a window, as she spies on a neighbor.
(Still from Casulo *©2009. Used with permission.)*

FIGURE 8.3
Looking unobserved conveys one of the principal themes of *Casulo*, which Uzeda sets up in this shot of a woman looking through a neighbor's window from her own apartment.
(Still from Casulo *©2009. Used with permission.)*

SHOOTING WITH TEXTURE AND COLOR

Because Uzeda focused on a story that would be told with images, he wanted to make sure the "details of its environments, [especially] the textures and the colors, was a key factor," he explains. His influences were photographers Sally Mann and Gregory Crewdson. "Both of them use extremely high resolution and contrast large format cameras," he notes. He also explains how his DP, Guga Millet, is "highly fond of John Alton, Conrad Hall, and Greg Tolland."

Money came from his own personal funds, as well as from producer Isadora Sachett. She also brought in DP Guga Millet and a number of other volunteer crew members. They "agreed to work for free just because they saw some potential in the project," Uzeda adds.

However, it wasn't a fast route to get the film made. They spent a year in pre-production and story development, which kept changing with a shrinking budget. But when they started shooting, their work was completed in five days. Postproduction took four months.

They were planning to shoot on Panasonic's HVX200, the tapeless P2 camera, jury-rigged with a 35 mm lens adapter. Guga Millet, the DP, owns the camera, so they could have used it free—a welcome hurdle to overcome with a low budget. But Millet told Uzeda that there was a better camera out there—the Canon 5D Mark II—that could shoot in 1080P and had the ability to change lenses, in addition to attaining "better definition, contrast, and color response in general," Uzeda continues, due to its full-frame sensor. Uzeda quickly got excited about the possibility. However, just as fast, he got "highly suspicious" when Millet said that it was a stills camera with a "film mode." Uzeda wondered if "this type of equipment could be up to the task of shooting the film which I had in mind." Neither of them had ever used such a camera, and there wasn't one to be found in Rio De Janeiro at the time.

Millet flew to Sao Paulo to check one out at a "photography tech-fair," Uzeda confers. "He then sent me some .mov files straight from the camera, and I was immediately impressed. That sharpness and depth of focus [were] exactly what I wanted for this project. We had to spend a large part of the budget buying accessories for the camera, but it was definitely worth it," Uzeda says. "The portability of the camera itself and especially the larger sensor made possible for us to save significant money in lighting gear and [and allowed us to get] other accessories like waterproof cases."

Once they had the evolving budget nailed down, the script finalized, and a camera chosen, they moved on to casting the actors. For Uzeda, "the most important factor [was] their faces," he says. "They had to portray immediate expressiveness without saying too much or even moving too much. They had to say a lot with only their eyes and subtle body language. I think the shot of the actor on the Laundromat room, with his lost gaze, is really representative of what the film is about" (see Figure 8.4).

FIGURE 8.4
The lost gaze of actor Charles Fricks in *Casulo*. The emotion expressed in this shot, says director Uzeda, represents what the film is about. Note the shallow depth of field in the shot and how the color grading allows the character to pop out on-screen. Also note that the character has a warm look to him, but the background remains cool, providing the sense of contrast and depth.
(Still from Casulo © 2009. Used with permission.)

Another image Uzeda had for the script was a red-head girl, who would be easily "differentiated from the others ([especially] on distant shots), not to mention the interesting underwater effect of her red hair on the shot when she dies in the pool," Uzeda notes. "I wanted the audience to be confused for a moment, as if her hair were blood floating on the surface, but in fact, it is just the red color of the hair with a strong backlight" (see Figures 8.5 and 8.6).

FIGURE 8.5
Actress Thaís Inácio becomes the red-headed girl that director Uzeda wanted in order to have her stand out in images.
(Still from Casulo © 2009. Used with permission.)

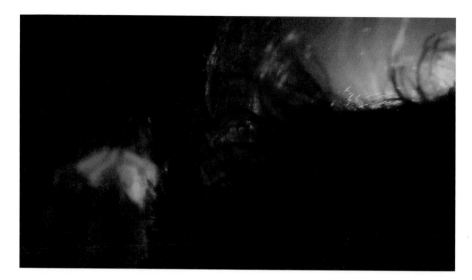

FIGURE 8.6
The red hair of Thaís
Inácio spills over into
a pool of water, backlit
so as to look like
blood—even if only
for a moment.
(Still from Casulo ©2009.
Used with permission.)

PRODUCTION NOTES

The production process went smoothly due to a tightly planned shooting script. Uzeda says he "spent months timing the movie inside my head with a chronometer. There was no time or budget for errors, so 80% of all the decisions were made during the elaboration of the shooting-script" in order to allow principal photography to "run smoothly and fast." But he allowed "room for new ideas and spontaneity on the set," he explains. "Guga usually came up with incredible shots and setups that I couldn't visualize until 10 minutes before rolling the camera. I spent one year talking to him about references from other movies, still photographers, painters, so our minds were pretty much on sync regarding the framing of the shots, blocking, and use of lights. There was little to no rehearsal with the actors (with the exception of the dialog between the mother and daughter, since it involved the performance of a child)."

Guga would typically begin his day talking to the assistant director to determine the order of the setups for the day's shoot, creating a map "of the locations and sets," Uzeda says, "marking where the camera would be and this helped me, Guga, and the art director to preview the setups and think some time ahead."

Because of the 5D Mark II's potential shallow depth of field, Uzeda used a focus puller. "Focus is a serious thing and it is not fixable in post," Uzeda warns. "Keep in mind that monitoring your video with a DSLR (at least in my experience with Canon) is not an easy thing. We tried using a Marshall monitor, but it didn't respond well to the real resolution of the camera (since we only had the option of using the RCA connector).[2] So, that left them with the small display

---

[2]The Canon 5D Mark II has an HDMI out for high-definition playback, but mysteriously only outputs in standard definition in live mode when shooting. The 7D does not have this problem.

of the camera itself to pull the very subtle focus of an image intended to be projected into the big silver screen—this is not an easy thing to do."

Another challenge was the limited first firmware build for the 5D Mark II. They were stuck with 30P and an automatic ISO (they shot before the firmware release that fixed this problem). "I was very afraid of losing the film look due to the frame rate," Uzeda says, "but I noticed that the progressive factor was much more important than the fps [frames per second] factor to attaining the feel I wanted for this project. In fact, I didn't care so much about emulating 35 mm film, but I also didn't want the 'video feel' due to small color/image resolution, interlaced frames, and so forth."

LIGHTING THE SCENES

The crew also spent a lot of time getting the lighting right—one of the key aspects of getting a cinematic look. "Sometimes the lighting setups took hours," Uzeda remembers, "due to our small crew and ambitiousness with the visual aspects of the film. So Guga usually made one basic light scheme that could serve all the camera setups (this took some time), but after that we only needed minimal adjustments from one setup to another."

FIGURE 8.7
Cinematographer Guga Millet sculpted light and shadow to provide us with this moody scene. He used the blue lamp, screen right, as a practical in lighting the girl's face. The arrow left points to the bounced light of a practical 3.2 K (tungsten color temperature) lamp on the floor pointed at the wall. Notice that a bit of this floor light hits the edge of the girl's shoulder and hair. This backlight separates her from the background, providing a sense of depth in the shot. The second arrow points to a blue lava lamp that reflects onto her face, shoulders, and wall. This is a soft key light. Images from the film were inspired by photographer Gregory Crewdson.
(Still from Casulo *©2009. Used with permission.)*

Part of the lighting design revolved around using practical lights. "Even though most of the film displays stylized and unnatural colors and lights," Uzeda says, "the shots ranged from working with very simple practical lighting, like the blue lamp as a fill light for the girl's face (see Figure 8.7), to completely artificial and extreme setups, like the last underwater night-shot; there we used a strong photoflood outside the water, to create the rays of light through the hair of the dead girl inside the swimming pool" (see Figure 8.6).

As Uzedo notes, he wasn't trying to emulate 35 mm film. Indeed, there is no formula for creating the film look. Different directors and cinematographers express different visions of how to set up an outdoor day or night shot, for example, based on the mood they're trying to set for the story. Following are a few case study lighting setups showing how director Uzeda and cinematographer Millet crafted a cinematic look during the production of *Casulo* with the Canon 5D Mark II.

ATTAINING THE FILM LOOK INDOORS—NIGHT

We can see how cinematographer Guga Millet sculpted light and shadow to provide us with the moody scene in Figure 8.7. Figure 8.8 shows the lighting setup.

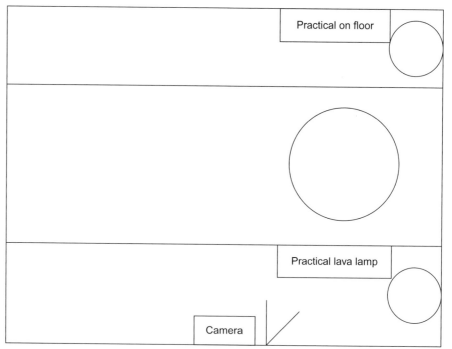

FIGURE 8.8
Floor plan of lighting setup for Figure 8.7.

Light and Shadow

DP Guga Millet describes how the director envisioned the shot in Figure 8.7: "The blue face shot was something that Bernardo wanted from the beginning. We did lots of tests with this blue lava lamp. I wish it was a little stronger though (although we fixed that in post), but we can really see that the light source is really that lamp." Millet explains how he lit the scene "like I was working with ISO 320 film with shutter at 1/60. The idea was to use only that lamp to light the actress. I also placed a 3.2°K in the background in order to create a backlight." He felt that blue light "would be too much and the lamp didn't have power enough to enhance her face. But I think it didn't work exactly the way I intended. The light was too low on the ground, and we couldn't raise it."

Exposure and ISO Setting

ISO 320, f/2.8, shutter 1/60.

"Actually," Millet explains, "I could not change ISO or shutter settings. The camera was in auto ISO mode in those days [when shooting in live mode]. I only had control over the f-stops"—because of the Sigma lens with a manual f-stop ring on it. They shot in April 2009 before the Canon 5D Mark II firmware that allowed manual control of aperture and ISO. The frame rate was stuck at 30 fps. According to Philip Bloom, the Canon 5D Mark II's sweet spot is at ISO 320, so they hit the best ISO setting for the camera.

Lens

Sigma 24–70 mm, f/2.8

Guga explains the lens choice: "When we shot the film, the camera was still in its first firmware, fully automatic 30 fps. So I used lenses for Nikon mount," allowing for manual control of the aperture on the lens.

Filters

No filters were used in the shot.

Camera Stabilization

The film was shot "on a kind of cinesaddle (which I like to call cinepillow). The camera sits on the bag and shapes itself around the camera through high-tech foam. It helps stabilizes the camera," Millet says.

ATTAINING THE FILM LOOK OUTDOORS—DAY

Uzeda notes how the scene in Figure 8.9 "was done completely at natural daylight (around midday or 1 p.m.)."

FIGURE 8.9
The arrow represents the direction of the sun.
(Still from Casulo ©2009. Used with permission.)

ATTAINING THE FILM LOOK OUTDOORS—DUSK

The silhouette in Figure 8.10 highlights the character's loneliness and isolation.

FIGURE 8.10
The silhouette highlights the character's loneliness and isolation. The setting sun is used as backlighting.
(Still from Casulo ©2009. Used with permission.)

Story Intention

The DP, Guga Millet, says how they "wanted to place her character in a world of her own. I think we achieved that with her silhouette against the blurred city." The time of day enhances her loneliness; the image would say something much different if it had been shot in the afternoon."

Light and Shadow

Guga explains the setup: "The woman silhouette shot was done only with natural light something like 10 minutes after sunset, at the magic hour. We raised the contrast in post to enhance the silhouette idea (in the flat image we could see more of the actress's face)." The silhouette also helps set the character apart and heightens her loneliness.

Exposure and ISO Setting

ISO 320, f/2.8, shutter 1/60.

Lens

Sigma 24–70 mm, f/2.8.

"The idea was to defocus the background as usual," Guga says, "with the intent of having a more dreamlike quality to the scenes."

Filters

No filters were used.

Camera Stabilization

Tripod.

AUDIO

Another aspect of production was how Uzeda didn't use location sound recording. "We shot the entire film without a sound recordist or location sound (with the exceptions of two small dialog scenes that were recorded on the set)," Uzeda explains. "This was another factor that helped to speed up the whole shooting process and keep us inside of the budget. Nevertheless, the postproduction months were loaded with intense work, but since this is something that is extremely cheaper than feeding and transporting 20 people with camera equipment from one place to another, I thought it was worth the time."

They used a Sennheiser MKH-416 hyper-cardioid microphone with M-Audio Microtrack 2 digital audio recorder, for the two dialog scenes.

GETTING THE LOOK IN POSTPRODUCTION

After completing principal photography, Uzeda moved into postproduction—where his specialty lies. "The 5D Mark II is also very sensitive to the color red; I saw myself removing red from almost 100% of the shots." The examples shown in Figures 8.11 through 8.13 reveal the redness in the originating shot.

Watch Out for Red

Shane Hurlbut, ASC, who shot a Navy SEALS movie, *Act of Valor*, on 15 different Canon 5D Mark II's, noticed different color balance settings in several cameras. Guga Millet shot *Casulo* on a 5D Mark II that ran red. Uzeda admits that although *Casulo* was "a great achievement in cinematography, I can't deny that 100% of the film was extremely color-graded in post, and we also did some RGB noise reduction, which saved some otherwise unusable shots." For color grading, he utilized Color Finesse 2.0 and the Tiffen DFX 2.0 filters. Noise reduction was accomplished by using "the incredibly cheap and effective NeatVideo plug-in by ABSoft."

FIGURE 8.11.
Thaís Inácio before and after color grading in postproduction. Uzeda says that this shot represents an "example of the Canon overcapture of red and magenta. The challenge here was to remove the exceeding red captured by the sensor, without ruining elements like the (intentionally red) hair of the actress and also returning her costume color to its original/intended tonality (blue)." *(Still from* Casulo *©2009. Used with permission.)*

Noise reduction software can be found at http://www.neatvideo .com/. The plug-in is available for After Effects, Premiere, Final Cut, VirtualDub, Sony Vegas, and Pinnacle Studio. A limited functionality demo is available free. The Pro version—which allows for HD 1920 × 1080 resolution—costs just under $100.

Because Uzeda wanted to transfer the digital film to a 35 mm film print, he had no option but to conform the 30P to 24P. "The pulldown process was done using two different methods," he notes, "which depended on the nature of the shot. Sometimes I conformed from 30P to 24P, which doesn't involve any sort of pulldown. Each frame is maintained. Only the speed is altered (20% slower), so we are actually reading 30 frames 24 times per second, which yielded a great effect in some shots (a smooth and dreamlike feeling), but this method is unusable for dialog scenes where the

FIGURE 8.12
Another example of how color grading in post helped achieve the film look in Uzeda's *Casulo*. *(Still from* Casulo *©2009. Used with permission.)*

speed of the movements of the actors could be distorted. The other method used a plug-in called Twixtor in After Effects."

POSTPRODUCTION WORKFLOW

After he transferred the files to the computer, Uzeda took the native H.264 .mov files from the 5D Mark II and decompressed them into MPEG files for editing purposes (although Apple Pro Res will work, as well). When he completed the final cut, he says he "reconformed the whole project to the original H.264 .movs from the camera and then went to After Effects. There, I processed the shots with (in this order): pulldown from 30→23.976 fps; digital noise reduction with NeatVideo; general color grading; miscellaneous filters (usually graduated NDs, vignettes, selective saturation, and so forth)."

FIGURE 8.13
In this scene set in the kitchen, director Uzeda explains how the DP "placed a cold light with a CTO (orange) gel, the resulting video in the camera (along with some color balance imprecisions on the 5D Mark II settings), was a *completely green* kitchen, so we had to fix that in post (note that the white/beige wall on the background turned purple because of this subtraction of green, which by the way, I think looks interesting)," Uzeda says.
(Still from Casulo *© 2009. Used with permission.)*

As noted before, Uzeda wanted to project on a 35 mm film print to attain the best possible viewing experience for an audience. "There's still no widely available digital projection that can match the color and pixel resolution of film," Uzeda argues. He also wanted to do a Dolby Digital 5.1 surround sound mix. "*Casulo* is a very sensorial and visual film," Uzeda exclaims. "Its sounds and images are everything in the experience. I could not afford making a digital exhibition copy and let the film end up screening in some festivals that only [have] two options: 35 mm or 'DV family tapes.'"

COLOR GRADING

When color grading and noise reduction was completed, Uzeda exported the final output to uncompressed .mov files at 1920 × 1080p/23.976 fps. But because the 16 × 9 widescreen format is at a 1.78 aspect ratio, he cropped his images slightly to be able to conform to an aspect ratio of 1.85 for 35 mm film transfer, providing a 1920 × 1037 resolution. He transferred the film at Technicolor USA "through a new technology called DTP (direct-to-positive or direct-to-print) using a machine called Cinevator (manufactured by a company from Norway called Cinevation)." Uzeda adds, "Through this method, there are no negatives involved. The digital files and your 5.1 mix in your MO-Disk are transferred directly to your final positive. You have less control since there is no color adjusting using the inter-negatives; nonetheless, it is a more affordable process for lower-budget productions, and I was very impressed and satisfied with the results."

SCREENING

The film was screened in fall 2009 at the Rio de Janeiro International Short Film Festival, in what Uzeda calls "a really nice theater, and that was the first time I could feel the power of the movie in a really large screen with a crowded audience which was very receptive to the experience. I hope to screen the film in other international festivals, of course, but nowadays with the overdose of short-films submissions, it's getting harder and harder to find a proper space for a 17-minute silent short thriller. My goal in creating the film was to have a first experience directing actors and working with a good DP, and it sure was unforgettable."

Uzeda plans to shoot his next project on a DSLR, again. "Things are getting better and cheaper. I think the cost-benefit result is amazing for lower-budget projects (although each day, more and more medium-/high-budget projects have DSLR cameras readily available for some miscellaneous shots)," Uzeda says. But Uzeda explains that a camera doesn't make a film. "The main thing will always be: it is not the camera that makes a good film, and not even great cinematography. We've all seen films shot with very little money and gear that impressed us, whereas every week there are lousy multimillion dollar features made with the best gear (and the best DPs) that are completely forgettable. Nonetheless, I suggest getting a very open-minded and experienced DP for shooting with a stills camera. Make tests and experiment in the locations where principal photography will occur if possible. Never think you are saving money having friends or nonexperienced people to handle important set functions like a director's assistant, gaffers, set production crew, and so forth."

"We've all seen films shot with very little money and gear that impressed us, whereas every week there are lousy multimillion dollar features made with the best gear (and the best DPs) that are completely forgettable. Nonetheless, I suggest getting a very open-minded and experienced DP for shooting with a stills camera. Make tests and experiments in the locations where principal photography will occur if possible. Never think you are saving money having friends or nonexperienced people to handle important set functions like a director's assistant, gaffers, set production crew, and so forth."

Uzeda faced these big drawbacks when using the Canon 5D Mark II before the firmware update:

- Problems occur with HD video monitoring, and no matte or reticules are available for monitoring on different aspect ratios or any kind of more-advanced image monitoring.
- Some strange artifacts can appear on fast-moving subjects, such as subtle ghosty motion blurs and things that you wouldn't see in the same image if shot on 35 mm.
- Subtle use of focus is very hard to do and demands an experienced and patient focus puller; otherwise, you can end up with a completely ruined film.
- Color sensibility of the sensor is still not uniform. Moiré-patterns show up.
- No matter how beautiful the image is, it is still being digitally compressed frame by frame.
- DSLRs generate more noise than most people think.
- Slow-motion implementation is poor or nonexistent.
- Audio implementation (at that time) is poor.

In any case, Uzeda feels that the "main [benefit] of shooting with a DSLR is, of course, the price vs. quality of image (full HD resolution, big sensor, possibility of changing lens, rich color, and contrast)." And if it's transferred to a 35 mm film properly, "you can get more than impressive results on the big silver screen."

After seeing Uzeda's film on 35 mm, some experienced postproduction people told him that they felt it contained "such sharpness and rich colors that it looked as if it was shot in 65 mm. I think this kind of a result for a camera that costs even less than the lenses and accessories we were using is quite a revolution," Uzeda says.

CHAPTER 9

Crafting the Film Look by Building a Rapport with Characters

16 Teeth: Cumbria's Last Traditional Rakemakers (2009), directed by Rii Schroer, England, 2:29 min.

FIGURE 9.1
John Rudd, one of Cumbria's last traditional rakemakers. Rii Schroer profiles John and his son, Graeme, in a short-shot doc on a Canon 5D Mark II.
(© 2009 Rii Schroer. Used with permission.)

Technical data: Shot on a Canon 5D Mark II (standard picture style) with Canon 24–70 mm/2.8, Canon 50 mm macro. Merlin Steadicam work with Nikon 28 mm and Canon adapter. Background audio recorded on the 5D Mark II, with additional audio recorded on a Marantz PMD660. The work was edited in Final Cut Pro with conversion to Apple Pro Res.

16 Teeth is located at http://vimeo.com/4231211.

FILMMAKER BACKGROUND

Born and raised in Germany, Rii Schroer followed the more practical route at university: economics and business administration. After getting her degree, she got a business job in Hamburg and moved there. As she worked for about six months, she became drawn to Hamburg's "vibrant photographic scene," where there were "lots of lectures and exhibitions," she says in an interview. She saw a presentation by Kent Kobersteen when he was the picture editor at *National Geographic*, and it changed her life. The lecture included a discussion about how the magazine's photographers work on stories. "It somehow clicked," Schroer remembers distinctly. "I decided that evening to become a photographer and went to a secondhand photographic fair a couple of days later to buy my first camera (a Nikon F90x)."

Schroer spent a year studying photojournalism and then moved to London "to work over the summer holidays." She says, "[I] was drawn into the amazing photo scene there, and started contacting the local papers to get some work experience and earn my first, although very moderate, money with photography." Schroer enjoys the "fast pace of news reporting, but also the technical aspects of photography. To work for the national papers doing news, but also work on feature stories, seemed to be a logical next step at that time."

Although she studied photography and found her passion there, Schroer said she was "interested in film from an early age, again being exposed to a brilliant cinema in my hometown, which showed all the classics and interesting European and Overseas releases." She played around with "little camcorders," but photography and cinematography didn't converge—as with many of the filmmakers in this book—until the release of the Canon 5D Mark II. "I often thought some stories I photographed for the papers would be better told with video or as multimedia pieces, so the new technical developments came as a blessing" and provided an "interesting way to tell stories," she explains.

At that point, "I took filmmaking seriously," Schroer says. Although she admits that there are "different thought processes and skills needed in doing photography or video," she finds that "there are more similarities than differences. At the end of the day, you are trying to tell a story, work with visuals, and have the joy of engaging with people from all walks of life, no matter the medium." So whether she shoots video or photography, the story (and outlet for it) will determine the best way to do it, whether shooting photo, video, or both in combination.

MAKING THE PHONE CALL

Schroer first saw the story about the rakemakers, John and Graeme, in a local newspaper. She called them to see what they were like and talked "about their work and lives in the remote village of Dufton in Cumbria, England." She discovered that "they were great, down-to-earth characters and the old, dark workshop and working practices he described sounded perfect for shooting this piece with a DSLR camera to make use of its low-light capabilities."

Once she had the feeling for her characters, Schroer decided that the "initial idea was to get a fresh take on an old tradition and to find those little quirky moments that put a smile on your face." With that, she had the beginnings of a story concept. Rather than writing a script, she and her assistant "formulated our interview questions." After speaking to John on the phone, she was almost ready to shoot.

ON LOCATION

Before pulling out her camera, Schroer remembered the first lesson in photo-journalism: "It is often crucial to be able to build a rapport with the people you meet in a very short amount of time," she says. This rapport comes easily for Schroer. It's in her nature. "I love to be with people from all walks of life and enjoy having the opportunity to peek into other people's lives. Wherever you are, a smile can open lots of doors," she adds.

And sometimes it does come easy. "John and Graeme gave us a great welcome and made it easy for us," Schroer explains. "I guess it was a nice change for them, to have us around for a day. And yes, we took our time in the beginning, had some tea and laughter before pulling out the camera. Our preparation was simple. Kind of a 'shut up and shoot' approach."

Schroer worked with Tansy Sibley, her assistant, who wrote an untitled article that would accompany the video on vimeo.com (see http://vimeo .com/4231211). They defined the questions for the interview. They also made sure the "equipment was in full working order, batteries charged, and so forth," which gave them the freedom to then "go with the flow."

THE DIFFERENCE BETWEEN TV NEWS AND DOCUMENTARY JOURNALISM

After getting to know their subjects and getting them relaxed for filming, "We decided that we should start with the sit-down interview first," Schroer says, "as it gave us a framework for the story and a guide to focus on certain visuals over the day" (see Figure 9.2). As they talked during the interview, Schroer says she "made mental notes of things that I found interesting for close-up shots, although a lot of them did not make it into the final edit, due to the time-constraints of the piece." After the interview, she took a series of stills, portrait pictures. Then they just "let them go on with their jobs, following them around. The 5D Mark II allowed us to keep it small and intimate during the shoot."

Schroer shaped part of her cinematic style by avoiding a TV/video news style and instead utilizing documentary film techniques. Video news often

- Involves a reporter's presence with a dominating voice narration and/or standup performance in front of a camera.
- Uses static shots with some pans.
- Uses shots designed to illustrate the story instead of showing the story.
- Filters the presence of the subject through the reporter's voice.
- Lacks the voice of a strong central character, and story depth is often shallow.

FIGURE 9.2
After getting her subjects at ease, Schroer conducts an interview, providing her with stories and ideas from her subjects before she starts shooting action footage to visualize her piece.
(©2009 Rii Schroer. Used with permission.)

By taking the time to build a rapport with John and Graeme, Schroer engaged a more cinematic "look" by utilizing these documentary film techniques:

- Backing off and allowing the subject to use their own voices (the "shut up and shoot" approach). This instantly provides a documentary film feel to the project because it no longer feels like a TV news piece.
- Engaging camera movement through the Merlin Steadicam, along with locked-down shots. Cinema *moves*.
- Using shots to tell the story visually. Cinema is a visual medium, and the story should unfold visually, rather than being told primarily through narration.
- Allowing the subjects' presence, their look, their feeling, their characters to come through as the most important elements (not the journalist nor the journalist's words or narration). This approach usually works well if the filmmaker builds a rapport with their subject.
- Allowing the characters and their voices to tell their story. This way, the journalist is placed in the background, off-screen, which provides room for developing a story that's much deeper than most TV news stories.

By following John and Graeme around as they worked, Schroer got "a lot of material," she explains, but "it was pretty clear whilst shooting which bits had the potential to go into the tight, short edit—for example, John talking about his worn shoe (see Figure 9.3), atmospheric shots, such as the silhouette whilst John is working in front of the window (see Figure 9.4), and so forth." These visuals—which include a photographer–cinematographer's keen sense of how light and shadow can be used to visualize and shape the mood of a story—add to the cinematic feel of the piece and show us what the characters do and feel. Rather than having a reporter tell us what her characters think and feel, we see and hear them.

FIGURE 9.3
John Rudd points out his worn shoe in Rii Schroer's *16 Teeth*. A 28 mm lens was used for camera intimacy, Schroer says.
(©2009 Rii Schroer. Used with permission.)

FIGURE 9.4
John Rudd passes in front of a window in one of Rii Schroer's powerful images in *16 Teeth*. Her images, shaped with an awareness of lighting, are used to show us the story.
(©2009 Rii Schroer. Used with permission.)

A PHOTOGRAPHER TRANSITIONS TO HD VIDEO

Schroer notes how easy it was for her to adapt to the HDSLR world. "[When I am] working as a press photographer, the camera feels like second nature to me and I have a wide range of lenses available," she says. However, Schroer hadn't mastered all the intricacies of the camera until later, such as the picture style. "As this was one of the first video stories being shot on it," she notes, "I used a standard picture style. I now use a 'user defined' picture style (sharpness and contrast all the way down, and saturation down by two notches) and do grading in post production." She's learned to shoot it "flat" in order to allow more room when color grading in post.

> "The camera looked more like a stills camera than a video one," Schroer explains. With the camera being less intimidating, she was able to build the intimacy with her documentary subjects, helping to provide that cinematic feel—especially with the use of close-ups.

In addition, the small size of the camera worked to her advantage, as Schroer believes the "5D Mark II rather than a regular video camera was less intimidating for John and Graeme." She also feels that the shape and size of the camera helped, as well, in making her subjects comfortable. "The camera looked more like a stills camera than a video one," she explains. With the camera being less intimidating, she was able to build the intimacy with her documentary subjects, helping to provide that cinematic feel—especially with the use of close-ups.

However, the hardest part for Schroer was "the lack of decent focusing controls [which made] accurate focusing challenging at times." Audio was also an issue, so they "decided to record the audio separately on a Marantz PMD660, and synced it with the piece in postproduction." Most of the shots were locked down on a tripod, while moving hand-held shots were done with the Merlin Steadicam "to achieve a more vibrant, intimate feel," Schroer says.

They also decided not to bring any lights, using "available light only (in contrast to the still pictures taken of them, which were separately lit)," Schroer explains. This also allowed them to "easily go with the flow and also test the camera's low-light capabilities," she adds.

For Schroer, composition "happens intuitively and is certainly based on my experience as a stills photographer. I make sure to film a good variety of wide, medium and close-up shots, and decide on the spot which lenses to use, depending on what is happening. For example, the opening shot of the rake was filmed on the 50 mm macro lens to make use of the shallow depth of field possibilities (see Figure 9.5). John's shoe scene was filmed on a wide 28 mm lens, being close to him (see Figure 9.3). It was important to us to achieve intimate sequences of them, so the wide angle seemed to be a good choice." Thinking about which lens to use to best tell the story places Schroer into the cinematographer's frame of mind, as opposed to that of the videographer, who shoots mainly to illustrate a story instead of shooting to tell the story visually.

Schroer also had to face dark conditions with automatic exposure—meaning that "most of the shots were automatically shot on the widest open apertures. Now I mostly shoot around f/5.6. It seems to be a good setting for not being too shallow, especially when moving, but gives enough depth of field to not have it look like video. For that reason I used a Nikon 28 mm lens with Canon adapter for the steadicam work to be able to select aperture settings at around f/5.6 and to be able to move without losing focus," she says.[1] The Nikon—with

---

[1] For journalists, if you can shoot at f/5.6, you can use cheaper glass. The most expensive glasses are fast, but if you don't need to go down to f/1.4, for example, you can use less expensive lenses.

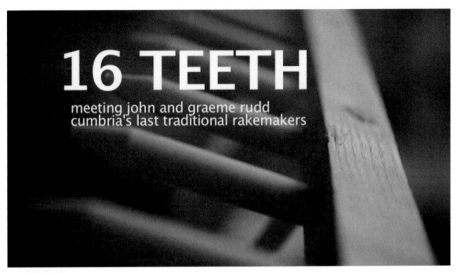

FIGURE 9.5
The opening title shot to *16 Teeth*. Schroer says she used the 50 mm macro lens to "make use of the shallow depth of field possibilities," a key function of cinematography. Take note of the narrow focal plane along the edge of the rake.
(©2009 Rii Schroer. Used with permission.)

its f-stop settings on the lens—was one of the options for which 5D Mark II owners had to adjust aperture manually before Canon's firmware update later in 2009.

Zoom lenses are an essential part of Schroer's toolkit, especially "if you don't want to carry too many lenses around and need to be rather flexible. I have found the Canon 24-70 mm a reliable workhorse for most situations, with the 50 mm macro lens for close-ups in the bag." But for her beauty shots, she likes to utilize primes: 24 mm f/1.4, 85 mm f/1.2, and a 100 mm macro. Using multiple lenses for a shoot also sets her into the film world and helps differentiate her work from typical video news pieces.

APPROACH TO EDITING

After getting her footage into the computer, Schroer transcoded them into Apple Pro Res. As she edits, Schroer looks "for those little moments I find surprising, fun, and visually entertaining. I have great respect for the craft of editing. As a one-man/woman operation though, you go with the flow and a lot of it comes down to intuition and recapturing the fresh thoughts you had" after you left the scene, she explains.

"What did you find surprising or did not know at all, what made you laugh? It is simple questions you try to answer and then put together, to make a piece that feels authentic to your experience," she notes about her process when editing.

> "… As a one-man/woman operation, you go with the flow and a lot of it comes down to intuition and recapturing the fresh thoughts you had" after you left the scene, she explains. "What did you find surprising or did not know at all, what made you laugh? It is simple questions you try to answer and then put together, to make a piece that feels authentic to your experience," she notes about her process when editing.

At first Schroer considered showing the story of rake making, but in the end focused on the characters. "We did film all the steps of how the rakes are made, but in terms of the story, we were more interested in showing Graeme and John's characters and their love of what they do, than, for example, creating an informational piece about a dying tradition."

In the end, the editing choices revolved around her goal "to capture the kudos of Graeme and John, their warm, down-to-earth characters, and their joy and pride in the work they do."

DSLR ADVANTAGES OUTWEIGH DISADVANTAGES

Rii Schroer loves the adventure and flexibility in shooting with a DSLR camera that can both shoot stills and high-quality video. "For my line of work," she explains, it "opens up amazing possibilities in offering full multimedia packages to clients, shooting stills and full-frame HD video with one device, achieving cinematic quality in a small or one-man/woman team. The system is very adjustable. It can be used small for a 'fly-on-the-wall approach' with not more than a tripod or small rig, or used more elaborately on rigs with focus pulling, glidetracks, jib-arms, whatever one can think of."

> "For my line of work," she explains, it "opens up amazing possibilities in offering full multimedia packages to clients, shooting stills and full-frame HD video with one device, achieving cinematic quality in a small or one-man/woman team. The system is very adjustable. It can be used small for a 'fly-on-the-wall approach' with not more than a tripod or small rig, or used more elaborately on rigs with focus pulling, glidetracks, jib-arms, whatever one can think of."

Like other 5D Mark II shooters, Schroer found getting accurate focus, "especially in low-light conditions challenging," as well as the audio issues. But because "there are ways of getting around these challenges to create the story you want to tell," Schroer feels the quality of the image outweighs the disadvantages.

By taking advantage of images—by telling the story through the lens of the DSLR camera rather than a reporter's voice, allowing her subjects to take center stage, and engaging a cinematographer's eye for lighting to help set the mood—Schroer provides a short digital film that's far more cinematic than reports found on TV news. And that's a goal more video journalists should try to attain in their work.

CHAPTER 10

Crafting the Film Look with Cinema Lenses

A Day at the Races (2010), directed by Philip Bloom, United States, 6:00min.

Technical data: Shot on a Canon 7D with PL Mount in a neutral picture style with Cooke S4 25mm and 100mm lenses and a Tokina 11–16mm lens. Audio was recorded on a Zoom H4n with a Rode shotgun mic on a boom. The 7D was also modified with a 6 × 6 Mattebox and 0.9, 0.6, and 0.2 ND filters. Edited with Final Cut Pro. Color grading with Apple Color.

A Day at the Races is located at http://vimeo.com/9978341.

MEETING PHILIP BLOOM

Bloom, hailing from England, arrives late at Venice Beach's famed Sidewalk Café, where you can find a Louis L'Amour hamburger on the menu, as well as homeless teens with their dogs intermingling with circus act characters roaming along the boardwalk. But he's always jolly and can win you over in moments with his charm.

FIGURE 10.1
Still from *A Day at the Races* directed by Philip Bloom, showing off his trademark close-up of people's faces.
(©2010 LumaForge, LLC. Used with permission.)

Bloom came out of the ranks of Sky Television in England. He begged to be a camera operator and actually found his break when a sound crewmember left. He filled the opening and Bloom says he "learned to shoot from some of the best cameramen I've ever worked with." He also learned to work efficiently and quickly by shooting news. "I would have to say that some of the greatest training for people to learn to shoot fast and shoot efficiently is to work news. Because you really have to get stuff done fast," he notes. "I will walk into a room and it is almost like a Terminator-style scan," he quips. "I'll look around the room and within about 30 seconds I will put any additional lighting where the subject is going to be and where the camera is going to be." He stayed with Sky Television for

> Some of the greatest training for people to learn to shoot fast and shoot efficiently is to work news.

FIGURE 10.2
Still featuring Ishan Tankha from a 90-second spot, "Voices of Change" directed by Lucy Campbell-Jackson and shot by Philip Bloom on a Canon 5D Mark II. Note Bloom's oblique composition capturing the depth in the shot. *(©2009 Greenpeace.)*

17 years, traveling the world producing documentaries for his last three years at Sky. "It was great fun," he smiles.

After leaving Sky, he went independent. And found DSLRs. But he first balked at their potential. He tossed the Canon 5D Mark II aside. After seeing some footage over the summer of 2009, he began to change his mind. "Initially I thought the weaknesses outweighed the strengths, but by progressively using them, and with new cameras coming out and more importantly with new firmware coming out, it feels like it is going the other way and the strengths are outweighing the weaknesses," Bloom explains.

Bloom shot some projects with it, including a commercial for Greenpeace (see "Greenpeace: Voices of Change" at http://vimeo.com/6695584; see Figure 10.2). He quickly became one of the foremost gurus of DSLR cinema, even hired by Lucasfilm to show the Lucas team the cinematic potential of the cameras and then later brought on the set of *Red Tails* (2012) to shoot some plates and pickup shots with Canon DSLRs (see Figure 10.3).

See the following:
Philip Bloom's Greenpeace commercial, "Voices of Change" directed by Lucy Campbell-Jackson: http://vimeo.com/6695584; Philip Bloom's timelapse video, "Lucasfilm's *Red Tails* on set Timelapse": http://vimeo .com/12148053; Philip Bloom behind the scenes of *Red Tails*, "Behind the Scenes on Lucasfilm's *Red Tails* with the Canon DSLRs": http://vimeo .com/11695817; Philip Bloom's video, "Skywalker Ranch": http://vimeo .com/8100091.

"When you see them on the big screen, you can understand why Lucasfilm is so amazed by these cameras," Bloom explains, "and the whole industry is so interested in buying them because filmmaking is an expensive business and a big part of that is cameras and big parts of that [are] the amount of crew that is needed."

Bloom admits he's not an expert in the design of Canon lenses or the technical aspects of how everything works inside the camera, but he does say, "I'm just very passionate about using them and I use them prolifically and that is why people come to me. They come to me because of my experience."

He's distinctly known for a style that captures intimate portraits of people's faces, a style that strikingly echoes with the composition of Bingham's *Mississippi Boatman* (see Figure 10.3). And for *A Day at the Races*, the Cooke lenses add compositional strength to Bloom's project.

FIGURE 10.3
George Caleb Bingham's
Mississippi Boatman
(1850).
Photo of painting by
Kurt Lancaster. National
Gallery.

But what is more interesting is how some of Philip Bloom's images from *A Day at the Races* (including many shots from his people series), captures a similar style and composition of Bingham (see Fig. 10.4).

FIGURE 10.4
Philip Bloom captures
emotion with a close-up
in *A Day at the Races*.
*(©2010 LumaForge, LLC.
Used with permission.)*

Although I don't believe Bloom has studied Bingham's art, many cinematographers do, and what Bloom instinctively conveys is a keen concept of composition that echoes what a master painter does with composition—all of which provides cinematic strength to his HD videos. Bloom's shots not only convey the compositional sensibilities of an artist (such as Bingham's work from 160 years earlier), but they also engage what good artists always do—capture the essence of humanity in moments of unvarnished truth, the rawness of the human condition filtered through the artist's eyes with aesthetic prowess.

SHOOTING WITH CINEMA LENSES

In early 2010, Neil Smith, founder of the digital post house Hdi RAWworks asked Philip Bloom to come to Los Angeles and shoot *A Day at the Races* as a proof-of-concept piece—that the Canon 7D can be utilized as a cinema camera by fitting it out with Cooke lenses (S4i; see Figure 10.5). These lenses are meant to be rented, unless you have an extra $20,000 lying around. "As a serious professional post house, the first time I came across HDSLR cameras I totally pooh poohed them," Smith laughs. "I thought we would never use them. They would never be used in" cinema projects.

Neil Smith hired Philip Bloom not only to shoot a short with a 7D fitted out with Cooke cinema lenses, but to present a master class workshop at The Lot in March 2010. It was a way to prove how these cameras can be utilized by a small crew and still attain a cinema look for film projects. It's a way of "making things simpler and more streamlined. And that's certainly [... what] these cameras are very good at doing," Bloom says.

Bloom explains how he initially conceived the story with Neil Smith. "He wanted the majesty of the horses through the morning mist running on the race track," Bloom remembers. But "the longest lens I got was 100 mm" and there was no mist. "Filming horse racing with one camera and the longest lens [at] 100 mm, you aren't going to get much," Bloom remarks. "I was expecting longer lenses, and I didn't get them, so as soon as I saw the lenses I had, I completely changed the plan. I said, OK, we are going to do the detail behind the racing. We are going to capture the life around the racing instead of the racing itself."

FIGURE 10.5
A Canon 7D fitted with a PL mount, sports a $20,000 Cooke lens. *(©2010 LumaForge, LLC. Used with permission.)*

This became the story—an immersion into the environment surrounding the horse races, such as the stables, rather than the race, itself.

RETROFITTING THE CANON 7D

Hot Rod Cameras (hotrodcameras.com; Illya Friedman, President) designed a PL mount for the 7D, allowing professional cinema makers to mount cinema-type lenses, such as the Cooke modeled in *A Day at the Races*. It's not cheap for low-budget DSLR shooters, but for $3,250, the company will take your 7D and modify it so that it can take the PL mount. For *Races*, Bloom utilized two Cooke S4 lenses, 25 mm and 100 mm, as well as a modified Tokina 11–16 mm. Bloom loved the way the images with the Cookes turned out. "What a gorgeous image these lenses give you," he explains on his blog. "Yes it was a lot more fiddly and time consuming using these lenses with a mattebox for NDs than my normal 'run and gun' setup but it was worth it. The images ... speak for themselves!"[1]

---

[1]http://philipbloom.co.uk/2010/03/04/shooting-7d-pl-with-cooke-lenses-for-saturdays-la-masterclass/, accessed 26.04.2010.

ON LOCATION

Bloom shot in and around horse stables at Hollywood Park for two and a half hours; then he and his team shot for a couple of hours at Santa Anita racetrack. It was a 5 a.m. shoot. Smith explains, Bloom "shot only in available light. He captured some beautiful images of the race horses being put through their morning training before sunrise and then in the afternoon at an actual race at the Santa Anita track."

The only shots where they used the mic were with the interviews and the man playing the trumpet. All the ambient noise was recorded in-camera, including the shoveling of the hay (see Figure 10.6). If the level is low enough, editor Jeremy Ian Thomas says, "it's good enough" to use in the project. However, if the levels are too high, "then you hear that kind of tin can feel," Thomas adds. (Which is why recording on a separate audio recorder is preferable.)

FIGURE 10.6
You can hear the scooping of the hay beneath the music track in *A Day at the Races*. The audio for this shot was recorded on-camera.
(©2010 LumaForge, LLC. Used with permission.)

Despite the fact they didn't get long lenses for the initial plan of shooting a race, Bloom felt it worked in his favor by covering the backdrop of the races so that they could focus on the people setting up the event, the ones working in the stables. "That is the kind of thing I do anyway," Bloom explains. "We had the horses in there as background and that worked so much better. I was really happier with it."

Jeremy Ian Thomas, the editor of the piece, was on location with Bloom, who explained to Thomas that the story "wasn't going to be about the majesty of the horses, but the life swirling around the horses, and that there's this whole other world" where "the horses are actually innocent bystanders in a much more human" story, Thomas says. "It's not really about the horses. They're beautiful and humble and quiet, but around them is a whole industry of gambling, and

Philip and I were very cognitive of that early on in the storytelling. He and I were looking at each other like, 'We need to stay here in the stables.'"

But Neil Smith originally "wanted to go shoot the horses running," Thomas explains, "but Philip said, 'Let's stay here' [in the stables] and I agreed with him. 'Let's stay here and let's capture the light here, and then we'll move on to the horses.'"

Thomas continues, "Anybody who [watches] it will see that the horses are quite out of focus in a lot of it (see Figure 10.7). They're behind the people, and it's more about the life around it, and I thought that was brilliant." Thomas pauses. "Horses are great and I think horses are amazing, but there's been a lot of movies and documentaries about horses, but there hasn't been any, that I've seen, about the life around the race horses. And I thought that was pretty cool."

FIGURE 10.7
A woman poses in front of a horse revealing the shallow depth of field in natural lighting of the Canon 7D in *A Day at the Races*.
(© 2010 LumaForge, LLC. Used with permission.)

Philip Bloom remembers arriving at "the ungodly hour of 4:30 a.m." They started with Mike Mitchell, a trainer at the Hollywood stables. Bloom remarks on his blog how he has a "family in the racing business in England, and the people working in the stables are *generally* young blonde students (huge sweeping generalizing there!)," but at the Hollywood stables, "they seemed to be Latin American guys with MASSIVE filmic moustaches. Much more fun for me to film, as people know I tend to film interesting looking people than the obvious pretty ones!"[2] And one of Bloom's trademark styles is to gravitate toward the close-ups of these faces (see Figure 10.1).

For most of his previous projects—and all of his personal ones—Bloom typically edits. But due to the time constraints on this project, he passed off the

[2]http://philipbloom.co.uk/2010/03/04/shooting-7d-pl-with-cooke-lenses-for-saturdays-la-masterclass/, accessed 26.04.2010.

task to Jeremy Ian Thomas of Hdi RAWworks. "It is so nice to see someone else take your work," Bloom says, "and Jeremy was so tuned in to what I wanted. It worked brilliantly."

After dumping the footage into the computer, Thomas crosses his fingers and says he "hopes this footage is good"—and he speaks from being one of the people on location that day. "I hope we didn't mess up," he laughs. He's seen Philip Bloom's work and knows what he's looking for. "I like Philip's editing style," Thomas says, "but it is different than mine, and I thought, 'Okay, I don't want to go too far left field and have to re-edit it because he doesn't like it.' So I kept in mind what Philip might want to see." But when it came to pacing the film, Thomas took "a lot of liberties."

Thomas did not want to mimic Bloom's work found in much of his personal short DSLR projects. "His stuff tends to be dissolves—long dissolves, beauty photography of trees and deserts and stuff, and I wanted this to feel more narrative—like it was building and building and building," Thomas remarks. "I wanted it to feel a little more hypnotic," while at the same time sticking "pretty close to what [Bloom] was used to seeing."

Bloom explains how he is drawn to "real people's stories. That's my favorite. I like real people, just telling about their life. Because everybody's got fascinating stories to tell." Although not in-depth character studies, the stories Bloom creates tend to revolve around people's faces and the environment they're in.

One of the images that stood out to Thomas included a shot "where you see something spinning, and you don't quite know what it is yet, and then the horse comes in frame. I knew that was going [to] be either the opening shot, or one of the opening shots, because I thought it was nice. I liked the abstract feel of that. And then the horse shows up and you go, Oh, okay, it's—and then we go wide, and you see the whole stable" (see Figures 10.8 to 10.10).

FIGURE 10.8
Jeremy Ian Thomas originally conceived this abstract object motion as the opening shot of the film. It appears about 30 seconds into *A Day at the Races.*
(©2010 LumaForge, LLC. Used with permission.)

FIGURE 10.9
As the shot proceeds, it goes a bit wide and we see a horse.
(Still from A Day at the Races. *©2010 LumaForge, LLC. Used with permission.)*

FIGURE 10.10
A full wide shot reveals the horse tied to an exercise carousel.
(Still from A Day at the Races. *©2010 LumaForge, LLC. Used with permission.)*

FIGURE 10.11
Philip Bloom eyes a shot in *A Day at the Races* on a Marshall monitor attached to the Canon 7D.
(©2010 LumaForge, LLC. Used with permission.)

Thomas explains how he edited in "my mind where I thought shots would go" as he "was watching that [scene] when [Bloom] shot it" (see Figure 10.11). Thomas says that's what he does when he directs a project. "I edit in my mind. When we shoot, I already am piecing it together."

Thomas feels that color grading is a process that should begin with the cinematographer. "If you're working with a good DP like Philip," he says, "you're lucky, because you're starting out with a really good color palette to begin with." Whether DPs realize it or not, Thomas believes they are "being drawn to the color of an image a lot of times, even more than a composition." In the case of *A Day at the Races*, what Bloom shot contained "heavy, heavy color tones already," Thomas observes. "Every image he grabbed had something in it already that I liked" as a colorist. "So I would either enhance what was already there, or I would dial it back if there was too much of it. Some of the stuff inside the stalls was too yellow, so I would have to dial the yellow back and bring some more earth tones beneath the yellow" (see Figure 10.12).

FIGURE 10.12
A shot from inside a stable, which for Jeremy Ian Thomas was too yellow, so he, as the colorist, "would have to dial the yellow back and bring some more earth tones beneath the yellow," he explains. *(Still from* A Day at the Races. ©*2010 LumaForge, LLC. Used with permission.)*

But this process isn't always easy, especially with some other DPs who are not looking at colors. "When you're not working with someone like Philip, and there's not a lot of color, you have to really make the DP look good, [as if] he saw that color already," Thomas explains. "But all I really did with *A Day at the Races* was keep the skin tones intact by doing a desaturation of the skin tones, and then I would saturate everything around the subject, because the colors were already so beautiful. There were these really nice greens, mid-level greens, and there were these really beautiful pink hues across the mid-tones at the stables. And there was a nice yellow, and some pink." When he saw a person in a shot, Thomas said he "would make sure their skin tones were right. But everything around them was popping, and colorful" (see Figure 10.13). Overall, he felt that it was "a really good grading experience."

In the end, Bloom was happy with the project. He gave some notes to Thomas after seeing the rough cut, and additional changes were made. Bloom wouldn't have chosen the particular piece of music for the piece and would have taken a different approach for the final edit, he explains, but he admits that "it's always great to see how someone else interprets your work."

Bloom also enjoyed using the Cooke lenses on the 7D, but at the same, "I honestly feel for the type of shooting that I do, like this piece, that using Canon or Zeiss lenses would have been just as great."

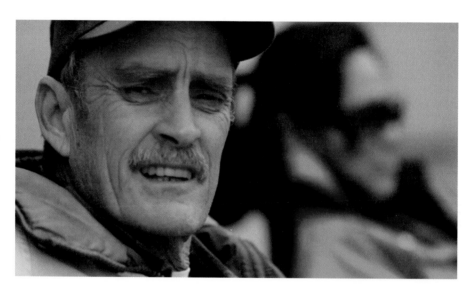

FIGURE 10.13
The colors would "pop," as Jeremy Ian Thomas explains in observing *A Day at the Races*. He would make sure the skin tones were correct and then bring out the colors by saturating them a bit.
(©2010 LumaForge, LLC. Used with permission.)

Neil Smith was pleased with the work that Bloom and Thomas did: "When we screen the movie in our theater," Smith boasts, "people are truly amazed at what Philip was able to capture with the low-light capability of the 7D and with a documentary style of shooting." In short, Smith explains, "the real purpose behind the film was to show how HDSLR cameras can be used to help creative filmmakers tell their stories, easily and cheaply without sacrificing production value."[3]

---

[3]Cheap in relationship to the cost of a cinema film camera, as well as film stock. The lenses, however, are not cheap, but this film shows that a modified Canon 7D can utilize a high-end lens package that can be rented without having to use a full-size cinema camera.

CHAPTER 11

Crafting the Film Look with Location and CGI Art

The Chrysalis (2010), directed by Jeremy Ian Thomas, United States, 6:54 min.

Jeremy Ian Thomas, a professional colorist at Hdi RAWworks, sits in a cramped space around the corner from the Douglas Fairbanks building in The Lot in Hollywood, a site that resonates with film history—Mary Pickford, Charlie Chaplin, D.W. Griffith, among other names—a site where black-and-white silent films expressed the cutting-edge 90 years ago. Thomas sits on a swivel chair in front of an L-shaped desk in the middle of the room as he conceives the cutting edge with DSLRs in 2010. Behind him are two couches.

The Chrysalis can be found at http://vimeo.com/11367602.

FIGURE 11.1
The color palette of *The Chrysalis* was browns, blues, and whites. Actor Mike Wade walks across salt flats in the midground of California's Death Valley.
(© 2010 Hdi RAWworks. Used with permission.)

Shelves are full of production knick-knacks. There's barely room to pull up a chair because one has to walk over gear bags and LitePanels in order to chill. On the wall hangs a 10-bit plasma screen, the output to a fully decked-out Mac Pro containing more filmic energy than Charlie Chaplin. Here, Thomas makes HDSLRs and other digital films look really good.

Philip Bloom calls Thomas a wizard at color grading—but he doesn't look like Gandalf. A tall, large man with boyish looks, Thomas expresses an infectious passion for filmmaking at all levels—from sound design, color grading, producing, and directing. Thomas attended the LA Film School and fell into color grading as a way to earn a living. But he loves getting a talented team together and putting projects together; he faces a team of people for a short he outlined with Robert Lehman, *The Chrysalis*, to be shot over the weekend in California's Death Valley.

The Chrysalis was conceived as a short fiction project to prove the cinematic capabilities of the Canon 7D. Neil Smith, the owner of Hdi RAWworks and the producer of this film (as well as producer on *A Day at the Races* profiled in Chapter 10), says that both projects "demonstrated that HDSLRs when combined with professional grade cinema lenses—from the high-end Cookes to the less-expensive Zeiss ZE primes—are capable of a wide range of visual storytelling." Smith calls the project a shooting exercise, to push the capabilities of the Canon 7D. "We sent the film-crew out into Death Valley with a single African American actor and a standard 7D fitted with Zeiss ZE primes," Smith says. "The crew filmed in the glaring sun of the desert for three days and then combined the footage with a very clever visual effect shot of a large spinning glass orb to produce an illusion of some magical transformation taking place out in the wilderness."

The project essentially would answer these two questions: Could the Canon 7D hold up to the contrast of desert daylight and can it deliver a scene with CGI art?

With the producer's go-ahead, they had to find a DP to shoot the project. Jeremy Ian Thomas met Dave Christenson when he came to Hdi RAWworks to talk to Neil Smith and Thomas about using the Canon 7D for a documentary he was shooting in Nepal. After Thomas saw Christenson's footage, he asked him to DP this super-low-budget weekend project. It would include special effects CGI created by Kris Cabrera. But the microbudget of $1,000 meant nobody got paid, so the love for cinema and the love for shooting with DSLRs drove the crew to jump on board the project. Thomas explains that "they are all getting paid in hugs and we've got fruit snacks," the crew around him laughs. I observe the preproduction meeting for the film.

Sponsors donated equipment, such as a Red Rock Micro shoulder mount, Lite Panels for lights (which they did not end up using), and Zeiss lenses (see Figure 11.2). Despite the sponsors, Thomas emphasizes that "it's more important for us to come back with a really great little short than for us to utilize all the gear that was given to us and come back with a [weak] short. Let's try to use everything we possibly can, but never ever let it hinder what we're doing."

FIGURE 11.2
DP Dave Christenson looks through a Zakuto viewfinder with a kitted-out Canon 7D. Director Jeremy Ian Thomas looks on (screen right). *(Photo by Hunter Kerhart. ©2010 Hdi RAWworks. Used with permission.)*

THE PREPRODUCTION VISION OF JEREMY IAN THOMAS

The Chrysalis tells the story of a man going through a "spiritual experience," Thomas explains to the actor and his crew. It's "going to feel like a survival flick for the first three minutes" or so. We'll see a "guy wearing Army" fatigues with a "backpack on and little camping stuff hanging off" (see Figure 11.3). He's "going to be eating out of a can of beans, very kind of Mad Maxist, wide desert survival feel."

Thomas turns in his swivel chair, his Mac behind him, and spreads his arms out as he shares his vision of the opening scene. "He's going to be sweating, he's going to be tired; he's in the desert and he's going to see this piggy bank sitting in the middle of the desert salt flats. He knows that's what he's been looking for, but he doesn't know why. So he runs up on the piggy bank and he looks at it and he obviously has an emotional connection to this specific piggy bank" (see Figure 11.4).

"He sits down Indian style and he empties his backpack and then there's a time piece, a camera, a stuffed animal (see Figure 11.5)," Thomas turns to the actor, Mike Wade, "and if you bring in any knick-knacks, it's going to be a bag of certain things, and he's going to set them up in a half circle." He has "an epiphany of what his life has been about. And then he realizes, there's something about the piggy bank that's not right, so he crashes the piggy bank on the salt flats and shatters it and inside is a note [see Figure 11.6]. He opens the note and it's a hand drawing, and it says 'Me and Daddy' and so it's from his son, and you'll hear some audio stuff that goes with that, maybe his son calling his name."

FIGURE 11.3
Equipment hangs off actor Mike Wade as he pauses on the salt flats in *The Chrysalis*. We'll see a "guy wearing Army" fatigues with a "backpack on and little camping stuff hanging off," director Jeremy Ian Thomas says in a preproduction meeting.
(©2010 Hdi RAWworks. Used with permission.)

FIGURE 11.4
Actor Mike Wade reaches out to a piggy bank in *The Chrysalis*. "He knows that's what he's been looking for, but he doesn't know why," director Thomas discusses to his crew and actor in a preproduction meeting. "So he runs up to the piggy bank and he looks at it and he obviously has an emotional connection to this specific piggy bank."
(©2010 Hdi RAWworks. Used with permission.)

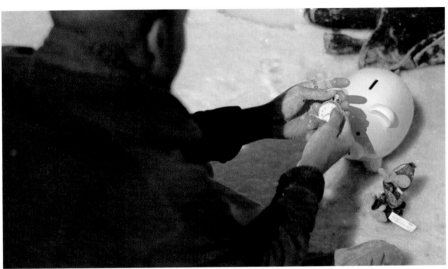

FIGURE 11.5
Actor Mike Wade empties out his backpack and holds an old timepiece in *The Chrysalis*. "So he sits down Indian style and he empties his backpack and then there's a time piece, a camera, a stuffed animal," Thomas explains in the preproduction meeting.
(©2010 Hdi RAWworks. Used with permission.)

FIGURE 11.6
Actor Mike Wade smashes the piggy bank and pulls out a glowing necklace. Originally, as discussed in the preproduction meeting, Wade was going to pull out a note, "a hand drawing, and it says 'Me and Daddy' and so it's from his son, and you'll hear some audio stuff that goes with that, maybe his son calling his name," Thomas says. But the change to the glowing butterfly necklace worked because it "represents the rebirth of this man growing from a moth to a butterfly," Thomas explains to me later. The glow was created using After Effects.
(©2010 Hdi RAWworks. Used with permission.)

FIGURE 11.7
Actor Mike Wade runs up to a spinning reflective sphere in *The Chrysalis*. The sphere was created using 3D Studio Max by Kris Cabrera.
(©2010 Hdi RAWworks. Used with permission.)

FIGURE 11.8
The raw footage of the scene, before color grading and CGI art. See Figure 11.7 to see the shot with the crystal and the blue added using Apple's Color. Thomas worked with Kris Cabrera, who crafted the reflective sphere. Normally, they would use a C-stand and stick a green tennis ball on it, but they didn't have a large enough crew to carry it, so they ended up using a tripod. "Because it was all white and it was so contrasty, we were able to just use the tripod out there. It was contrasty enough so that [Kris] was able to track off of that" in 3D Studio Max, Thomas explains.
(©2010 Hdi RAWworks. Used with permission.)

At this moment, Thomas continues, "off in the distance, you'll hear a bit of a pulse, a pulsing noise low end that catches his attention and he packs everything up and it's a crescendo. He's pushed and motivated to do these things, but doesn't know why. So he runs up on this sound, and that's where 3D guy comes in," he smiles at his CGI artist, Kris Cabrera. "There's going to be a reflective sphere that's floating above the salt flats that's spinning, and you'll be able to see a reflection of the desert and everything on it, and he's obviously going to have this moment with this sphere; he's going to walk up on it."

Thomas pauses. "We haven't quite decided what we're doing with the sphere, but he's going to touch it (see Figures 11.7 and 11.8), and it's either going to expand into smaller balls and fall to the ground or turn into sand and go up his arm. But then we're going to cut out of that immediately and—the ending is a bit up in the air—but he's either going to be on a street corner with blood coming out of his nose taking his last breath as the camera pulls up and his wife is going to be over him trying to revive him, or he's going to wake [up out of] a coma in a hospital bed and see his wife and child and realize that the greatest things in life aren't things at all."

The story takes place in "the space between life and death. And he's learning in this place … so the time piece represents time; the piggy bank represents money or belongings; the camera, memories; they all represent something," Thomas explains. The camera was dropped; instead, a stuffed animal provided by Wade was prominent in the scene.

Ultimately, Thomas and his crew "wanted to see what we could do in a big white space," he explains. "It is about the story, but it is more about the techniques to tell that story" that they're testing out in the hopes that they can do future projects together and get paid for it.

They continue to talk and ask questions in the preproduction meeting. Thomas listens and is open to ideas from his crew, but he's adamant about holding to

3D Visual Art with the Canon 7D

Kris Cabrera

For this shot (see Figure 11.9) I used 3DSMAX and Vray for rendering. For the salt I used a plug-in for 3DSMAX called Krakatoa, which pretty much renders as many particle points you want, and for compositing I used NUKE.

Workflow with the 7D was pretty straightforward. Since I have used footage from the 7D before, there weren't really any surprises. I knew as soon as I heard the 7D was being used I was thinking in my head, "All right, whatever is going to be done in CG, it has to be perfect," just because every little detail would show up. Making a sphere and having it fit into that space was a little tricky, just because it was a big sphere! For lighting I received about six 4k plates that I ended up stitching up in Photoshop and creating a reflection plate. There was really no light except for sunlight. So the hard work went into the compositing side.

FIGURE 11.9
Actor Mike Wade holds up the glowing necklace and touches the sphere. The glow and debris were created using After Effects.
Jeremy Ian Thomas explains how he originally conceived this shot in the preproduction meeting: "When he reaches his hand in, the
tips of his fingers are the focal point, and where he is reaching, that is the sphere and we hear a 'whoo whoo' sound, and where he is
touching the sphere, we'll have the sand be reflective little beads of sand trying to crawl up his body."
(©2010 Hdi RAWworks. Used with permission.)

an opening shot he wants: "All I absolutely have to happen for me—and I'm wide open to trying a whole bunch of other stuff—is that I want to be there an hour before the sun comes up. And I'm a little crazy, but I've started to sound design the opening shot without any pictures. I put some music and some wind chimes" together, he tells his crew.

In this moment, "I see him, a tight shot of him against that blue light that starts to happen before the sun comes up with that big open desert sky," Thomas continues. "I see him cracking a can of beans and start eating the beans with the sound behind it. We go wide, and I want it to be very abstract where you can't fully make it out who he is, where he is until the light starts to show itself. That I absolutely want." However, despite the fact that they did shoot the scene, they did not end up using it in the final cut. "We actually shot Mike eating the beans. It was an amazing shot and really worked, but within the context of the whole movie, we felt it wasn't needed. The movie is very ethereal and contemplative and the pace is very deliberate, so upon watching it again and again, [we decided] the beans scene was the only one we felt we could take out, and once we did, it just pushed the action along much quicker."

I met up with Thomas after the shoot. They got out in the desert at 4 a.m., and walked several miles to their location. It was freezing at 30° Fahrenheit, and when the sun came up, it reached 80°. Thomas says he "actually started to feel pretty dehydrated. I had to start really drinking water, and I couldn't keep the water down. I was throwing up the water, and I got really worried. It's four miles back to the car, and there is not even any solace from the weather back at the car. That's why on big shoots there are tents so people can cool off. We were eating crackers and drinking water; it reminded me of when I was in the military. I had to push through that emotionally."

In the end, Thomas felt it was a good experience for the story, and for the actor. "It was good for the actor because being out there, you start to think, 'Dude, what if I was actually lost out here and that was what the story was about.' It was an amazing experience. It was an eye opener in a lot of ways."

Working with the Actor

The realism helped because Thomas said they did not work off a script. He talked to the actor, Mike Wade, "about what needed to happen to move the story forward." About the facial expressions, that "was all him," Thomas explains. "I gave him the parameters and said, 'Action.' He's a really, really good actor." When Wade was walking through the salt flats, Thomas gave him this parameter: "Imagine just being stuck here, and that's all the water you have in the canteen. That was enough. That got him to the place that this is life or death, because that's what it is about." Thomas would talk to Wade if there was a beat in the performance that didn't feel right. "For the most part I let him interpret what we had talked about," Thomas says.

Most of the scenes they did in two takes. The last scene with the sphere took about 10 takes, Thomas explains. "It was hard, because it wasn't fear, so much," so he had to get Wade in the right frame of mind. Thomas pulled out C.S. Lewis from memory. "There's a book by C.S. Lewis called *The Problem of Pain*, and he talks about the idea of "fearing God." Thomas adds: "The word, *fear*, in the Hebrew is more like reverence, awe. And it's hard to explain something like that [to the actor]. So that took a little while to say, you're not afraid, you're in awe. So it was difficult to get to that emotion. But we eventually got there."

One of Thomas's favorite shots was the sunrise (see Figure 11.10). "Right as the sun started to come up across the mountains, it was this nice bluish-pink light and the actor had a garb on all the time, a head wrap, and he had it over his head like this, and he's standing waiting for direction because we are getting our next camera set up. So he's just standing there and the garb is flowing forward in the wind. He's just standing, pointing the way the wind is going and I'm like 'roll on that.'"

Postproduction on a 10-bit Plasma Screen

Thomas was pleased with the performance of the Canon 7D. "We couldn't have pushed it any more than we did—all white with a black actor. Between the sky

FIGURE 11.10
One of Jeremy Ian Thomas's favorite shots in *The Chrysalis* reveals actor Mike Wade standing silhouetted in front of a mountain sunrise. "Look at that," Thomas exclaims as he puts the image up on the 10-bit plasma screen. "Isn't that gorgeous? How do you see everything, that's not blown [out], there's detail there. Isn't that amazing? It is almost like he's contemplating whether he is going to traverse or not. That is one of those happy accidents as a filmmaker. I'm like, 'Wow' I wouldn't have set that shot up like that and it just happened," Thomas explains. The details are in the craggy ground and the folds of the head garb. *(©2010 Hdi RAWworks. Used with permission.)*

and the ice, it was probably a nine stop difference. So the fact that Dave got it all exposed is amazing. The stuff that we are going to end up using, barely anything is blown out," he says during the early phase of postproduction. "There is only one shot where the sky is blown out. We shot it in a neutral way so it is all milky, which I think works. I'm going to do some grading, and I'm going to play around with it, but there is not a ton of latitude" in that shot. The color palette was limited, Thomas explains. He points at the 10-bit plasma screen in his office as he punches buttons on his Mac. We see a shot of the desert. "This is literally white, blue, and brown, so you can't really push it real, real far, so I'm going to go drastic with the look and make it all blue," he explains.

Thomas is a wizard on the computer. He pulls up a daily, shot with a 100 mm Zeiss. "That's him walking towards the flats. The movie's going to open with the wind and music and stuff playing here. See how bad the wind was on the edges of the frame? So bad, you'll see it moving. For the first 20 seconds, it is just going to be this and you'll think, 'What is going on?' And then here he comes. It is pretty cool stuff."

The salt flats look like snow and ice. It "was almost like shooting a movie on a mirror," Thomas muses. "A lot of people will think that is ice, which is fine. See how the water was reflecting; we've got some of that." But no matter what people think it is, the scene, Thomas smiles, is "otherworldly, dude."

But as he gets into color grading, Thomas reveals that Marvels Film Production's cine-gamma curve picture style they used hindered his vision.[1] "Both my DP, Dave [Christenson], and I agree that we should have shot more neutral. We shot MarvelCine, which at the time seemed like it would be fine. But that's where some of that magenta's coming from, too." They didn't use SuperFlat—which Thomas typically favors with the Canon DSLRs—because "we were fighting off so much light [from the salt flats] that trying to add more light via the SuperFlat (which means we want to see further into the shadows) would have screwed up our gamma [curve]—which is our midtones. We would have had way too much milk in the midtones—too much dynamic range." He would have liked to have shot it straight neutral. "The MarvelCine adds a little bit of color, and now in retrospect it dictated where we went with the color. If it was [shot in] neutral, I could have gone further in a different direction, because it already had a red tone to it and trying to fight off red with blue [in color grading] always gives you magenta, so that's why it looks a little magenta," Thomas explains. For the sake of the story, he adds, there's really nothing wrong with that, but from the purity of the image, it doesn't work for him.

In addition, Thomas admits that they ran into some aliasing issues because of a lot of square-type images they were shooting, "but it wasn't enough that we couldn't tell our story," he says to an audience at a Hdi RAWworks screening on May 1, 2010.

"The first time we showed it, I don't think people knew how to respond to it. It was just dead quiet. One person clapped, and I was like, 'uh-oh.' In my mind, it was like, 'We're in trouble.' But by the third time we showed it, to the third set of people, it went really well. People come here [at Hdi RAWworks], because they want to see pristine imagery. What we made isn't—it's beautiful, but it's not *The Last 3 Minutes*. It's not supposed to be like that. It's supposed to be otherworldly and gritty in ways, which is our style. Overall, I'm happy. This is the first time when I made something that I'm okay if people don't like it, because [the project's] coming from an honest place. I know what the parameters are. I know what our limitations were. That's enough for me."

The reaction may be tied not to its gritty look, but to the fact that the film lacks a decisive ending—which was due to a budget shortfall. As is often the case in filmmaking, limited budgets can compromise artistic vision and hinder storytelling. The film, as originally conceived, was supposed to end with the character waking up on a street corner and dying with his wife over him as Thomas noted earlier during the preproduction meeting. "What we wanted to do was just unattainable," Thomas explains. "I would have liked to have ended it a [multitude] of ways," he says.

In the meantime, Thomas will tinker with the film to perfect the story he's trying to convey. "We're going to add some matte paintings. So a lot of those

---

[1]The Marvels Cine style can be found at http://marvelsfilm.wordpress.com/2009/10/19/canon-7d-picture-style-with-cine-gamma-s-curve-free-download/.

wides where he's walking and the sky's open—as if civilization's been depleted, there will be an old wind turbine back there," he gestures with his hands as if he sees the image already fixed on-screen. "Or there may be an old Ferris wheel with moss on it, like the end of the world already has happened. This will help people cue into the sci-fi feel of it early on, because I'm not sure—." Thomas collects his thoughts, thinking about his audience. "After seeing it today, we led [the audience] to believe that it's a survival movie at first. Once he crushes the piggy bank, it's a little bit too much for people, too quick. I think we have to cue them earlier that other things are going on." The matte painting will help foreshadow the surreal shift in the film.

In addition, Thomas would like to add an ending where the character "dies on a street corner after being shot, taking his last breath." At the time, the producer, Neil Smith, "felt it was too dark and suggested we shoot something sweeter and more of a Hollywood ending," Thomas admits. That's when they conceived "the idea [of] him being brought back to life in a hospital" with his wife leaning over him with the butterfly necklace we saw him find earlier in the broken piggy bank—but it ended up being too expensive to shoot.

Thomas would still like to go back and shoot his original ending. "I would like to do a jib shot from his eye up to reveal that there's this whole scene unfolding in an urban environment. So it starkly contrasts from this surreal otherworld we lived in for most of the movie, and he's coming to, taking in his last breath with his wife over him, and other people scurrying around."

Whether this ending gets made or not, what can't be denied is how the Canon 7D was able to cinematically deliver the evocation of an expansive emptiness with high contrast (an African American actor against white salt flats) and how it holds up with the insertion of high-quality CGI effects.

CHAPTER 12

Crafting the Film Look with Light, Composition, and Blocking

The Last 3 Minutes (2010), directed by Po Chan, director of photography Shane Hurlbut, ASC, United States, 5:18 min.

LENSES AND CAMERA SETTINGS

The Canon 5D Mark II was used on this shoot. The following Canon lenses were used in the making of *The Last 3 Minutes*:

- EF 24 mm f/1.4 L II USM
- EF 35 mm f/1.4 L USM
- EF 50 mm f/1.2 L USM
- EF 85 mm f/1.2 L II USM
- EF 100 mm f/2.8 L Macro IS USM

The Last 3 Minutes can be found at http://vimeo.com/10570139.

Picture Style

- Neutral, with −4 Contrast and −2 Saturation

FIGURE 12.1
Shane Hurlbut, ASC captures the beauty of Eli Jane in a sunset shot in *The Last 3 Minutes*. The sun provides rim lighting from a ¾ rear key position.
(©2010 Hurlbut Visuals. Used with permission.)

Shutter Speed

- 1/50th sec

ISO Settings

- Day exteriors: 160 (with Tiffen ND filters)
- Interiors: 320 and 640

Most of the shots were either handheld (free) or the camera was attached to a helmet, for first-person perspective.

SUSHI WITH SHANE HURLBUT, ASC

Shane Hurlbut, ASC, is a tour de force. We sit at a sushi bar in Malibu Beach as the darkening spring sky brings out twinkling stars. It's been a long week shooting a short fiction written and directed by collaborator Po Chan, with 15-hour shoots the norm, a demanding task for a low-budget film for Canon in a bid to show off the 5D Mark II's capability as a cinema camera. Exhaustion ebbs around Hurlbut's eyes, but his effulgent passion for cinematic storytelling, his jovial flare of expression, isn't tempered by fatigue. He insists that I try yellowtail touched by cilantro and fire sauce—which sums up his enthusiasm for life. "It's killer," he remarks with a laugh. He knows when to party and is quick to laugh on set but sometimes impatient with those not firing as fast as he is.

Shane's unfailing work ethic grows from being raised on a farm in upstate New York. "I was on the tractor at eight years old. I'd wake up in the morning around 5:00 a.m., and I'd get on the tractor. Then around 7:00 a.m., I would come in and grab some breakfast and head off to school. My day would not end there. I'd practice sports after school, and then it was time to get back on the tractor, where I'd work till 10 or 11 at night." When did he have time to complete his homework? "Well, my dad welded this bookstand [onto the tractor] so I could read while I was driving it." His mother was a sixth grade teacher, who became president of the teacher's union. "I grew up seeing my parents work very hard and have a passion for what they did."

His parents, with what "little they had," were willing to pay for college, Shane says. "I wanted to make sure I didn't spend their money foolishly, so I initially chose a junior college to make sure my career choice was something that I wanted to do with my life." The first year he studied radio. "I loved it." The second year "was TV and I loved that even more." In high school, his focus had been all about sports, and Hurlbut earned B grades. "College was different because I was passionate about what I was learning and graduated magna cum laude with a full scholarship to complete my studies."

But his motivation to earn better grades didn't just revolve around his work ethic. There was a girl, Lydia, whom he'd known since he was three. They started dating when Hurlbut was in tenth grade. She went to Simmons College in Boston, a move that was encouraged by her parents to separate them because this was the first serious guy she had ever dated. He says, "I remember walking in to the guidance counselor's office at Herkimer County Community College and [saying], 'Help me to find the best film school in Boston!'"

"I went chasing after the girl," he laughs. Hurlbut enrolled in Emerson College in Boston and studied mass communication, but switched to film after helping out a hometown friend from USC, Gabe Torres, who shot a project over a summer break in Aurora, New York, where they both had grown up.

"I worked on Gabe's project and fell in love with film. It was so different from TV, and I thought, 'My God, this is it.' So I went back that next semester, and I changed everything I had from TV and mass communication to film, and then I did a four-year film degree in one year."

After graduating from Emerson and getting engaged to Lydia, Shane thought that getting a job would be easy after college, since he had all of these contacts. That false sense of security quickly faded after every job opportunity was met with, "You need more experience." His parents knew what was best and insisted that he get any job just to get hands-on experience in the workforce. He swallowed his pride and worked at a film rental house in Boston, where he had formerly worked as an intern. "I started out packing trucks, and within six months I was running the whole lighting and grip department." But he realized that Los Angeles was the place to be for high-volume film production.

He convinced Lydia that they should leave both their families on the East Coast and move to California. She got a job at Children's Hospital, Los Angeles, when there was a nursing shortage and they helped pay for the move. "I got a job at Keylite, a rental house, and it worked really well because I worked my way up the ladder just like I did in Boston," Shane explains. "Three months later I started on the movie *Phantasm II* [1988]. It was an amazing experience because it changed the way I thought." At first, he didn't plan to be a DP. He wanted to be a storyteller, a director. Lighting wasn't his first priority. But it all changed in a flash of inspiration. Shane worked as a grip truck driver on the movie, and one day was racing a flag into the key grip when his friend Brian Coyne, best boy electric on the project, asked him if he would be scared when sitting in the theater with the lighting that was being done on the crematorium set. "Brian said, 'Look, there are no shadows. You can see every nook and cranny in this place. Where is the mystery? It's just not scary.' Snap! A light bulb went off in my head, and from that point on, everything I looked at was light. That was 1988." Shane fell in love with cinematography. By 1991, he shot his first music video. "Then I became a commercial cameraman in 1994 and then shot [my] first feature in 1998."

Hurlbut was offered *The Rat Pack* (1998) for HBO as his first feature. That break came when director Rob Cohen had seen a Donna Summer music video that Shane shot for Rob's film *Daylight*. He was thrilled with the visuals from that music video and decided to take a chance on Shane. Hurlbut went

Hurlbut's approach to cinematography is to observe what's around him. "I just looked at light wherever I went.... I think the best lighting comes from just observing. Then, when I am asked to bring a director's vision to life, I pull from a variety of personal experiences and incorporate those visual references in my head into my lighting."

on to receive a cinematography award nomination from the American Society of Cinematographers.

Hurlbut's approach to cinematography is to observe what's around him. "I just looked at light wherever I went.... I think the best lighting comes from just observing. Then, when I am asked to bring a director's vision to life, I pull from a variety of personal experiences and incorporate those visual references in my head into my lighting."

The Last 3 Minutes became a project where Hurlbut wanted to showcase the cinematic capabilities of the 5D Mark II. "I wanted to have the opportunity to show Canon what the Hurlbut Visuals Elite Team and I could do with the 5D in a short narrative piece.[1] Lydia negotiated the deal with two Canon departments: education and marketing. The behind-the-scenes segments were just as important to Canon as the footage itself." They worked out the timing, gave Hurlbut the 24P firmware update, and presented it at the National Association of Broadcasters in Las Vegas in April 2010.

PO CHAN'S STORY: FROM HONG KONG TO HOLLYWOOD

The story of *The Last 3 Minutes* revolves around a weary 68-year-old office janitor who dies from a heart attack. His life passes before his eyes, and he lives through memories, both regrets and celebrations, starting from when his wife left him and then going back in time to when he was born. Typically, when there's a story about someone's life flashing before his eyes, Hurlbut explains, "It's always the perfect light and it's always at sunset. And that's awesome, but we wanted to take this very mundane man" and show his "absolutely dead existence." But beneath this surface, there are "many layers behind his life, and those layers are extraordinary," revealing choices made, good and bad, that led to the present moment.

The inspiration for the story came from Po Chan, the writer and director of the film, reflecting her own philosophy about life. She explains, "I believe that life is like a *big circle*. We are all born *innocent*, and no matter how many right or wrong things we have done, how many wrong decisions we have made in life, at the last minute, right before death, we will again become innocent." She

---

[1]Elite Team members include professional filmmakers embracing DSLR technology who work for Hurlbut Visuals for specific projects: Chris Moseley, Derek Edwards, Tim Holterman, Rudy Harbon, Mike Svitak, Darin Necessary, Marc Margulies, Bodie Orman, Dave Knudsen, and John Guerra (see bios at http://www.hurlbutvisuals.com/team.php).

infused this theme into her film, a theme that she feels comes from being born and raised in Hong Kong. "I grew up in the Eastern culture, surrounded by Buddhism philosophy. We believe everything comes in full circle—what goes around comes around. It's like yin and yang, so to speak."

Besides the concept of the story, the second most important element in this film for Po is the music. She explains: "I think our memory is like the annual circles of a tree. The new memory will grow on top of the older one; as we grow older, our memory layers will grow thicker. I believe that the memory of music is in the core layer of our memory, especially the music that we heard when we were children. So the music in this film is the representation of the core memory of my main character." Po turned to a friend for bluegrass music suggestions "because my main character was born right after the Great Depression." After listening to over 1,000 tracks, one caught her ear, "Across the Wide Missouri," a traditional American folk song about a roving trader in love with the daughter of an Indian chief. Timothy Godwin, a talented musician and friend of the Hurlbuts, listened to the song for inspiration and then created the soundtrack for *The Last 3 Minutes*.

Po enjoys the shift from living and working in film in Hong Kong to the United States. "When I was growing up, I was taught to follow the rules, not the dream," she explains in her Cantonese accent. "When you finish school, you go find a stable job and make money. It never occurred to me to become a filmmaker, even though I always loved film. And I remember my very first film I saw in the theater when I was little; it was the *Close Encounters of the Third Kind* [1977]. I fell in love with that film; it blew my mind, and then I realized that it completely transformed my life in that two hours."

Like Hurlbut, Po had one of those Hollywood moments, where her experience with watching *Close Encounters* would come full circle years later. "I remember we did a job with Mr. Spielberg, and I was so shy, 'O My God, it is Mr. Spielberg, the director [of] *Close Encounters of the Third Kind*, right?' So I was hiding in a corner, and all of a sudden he walks up to me, and he asks me what I do … and I said 'Oh, I am a camera assistant for this job.'"

"And he said, 'What *do* you want to do?' That is what he asked me, and it came out of nowhere—Mr. Spielberg walked up to me and just asked me this question."

"And I said, 'I want to be a director, I want to be a filmmaker,' and he put his hand on my shoulder and said, 'Don't give up, girl.' I just stood there frozen, thinking God has sent him here to tell me that. And you know what? I will not give up."

As for the process in writing the story for *The Last 3 Minutes*, Po explains how her creative brain works. "Most people like to capture interesting things or ideas by writing them down. I don't. I purposely don't write them down. The reason is that I want it—whatever the entity is—put in my brain and this machine is going to mold it, change it into something else. Or combine it spontaneously with other random events I grabbed two days ago. It works better for me that way. Once I have the core concept, the rest of the detail will come to me naturally, because they are all in my brain, filtered, molded, and ready to go. The most important thing is I already have feelings for all of them because they have been living in me. We breathe, we eat, we live, and sure, we will die together."

Hurlbut has collaborated with Po Chan on about nine different movies, he says. He met her on the set of the HBO series *Deadwood*. Hurlbut was hired by HBO to shoot some promo pieces for the show. "And so Po was driving the producer from Beverley Hills out to the set," Shane remembers. "I saw her dropping the producer off and I wondered, 'Who is that?' I'm starting to line up a shot inside the set, and I remember her coming through the swinging doors, walking over while I was doing a shot and questioning why I chose a particular lens."

"I turn to the producer and said, 'Who is this person?'"

"'That's Po Chan.'"

"'What does she do?'"

"'Well, she's from Hong Kong; she loves film. She loves it, breathes it.'"

They hit it off—Shane respects fearless and direct people. He hired her as his assistant, and they became collaborators. In *The Last 3 Minutes*, a script that Po wrote in one day, he talks about how "she had incredible vision in the way she worked with actors and designed the shots. She was very thorough with story-boards and a treatment that was so detailed. It made my job very easy."

SHAPING A POINT OF VIEW PERSPECTIVE

So the story evolved into a script treatment that's bittersweet (see Appendix 5). Hurlbut emphasizes that we see William's life in three minutes: "the girl that got away, the best friend who dies, the celebration of different life events. We see the tender moments, the sad moments, but [the flashbacks] didn't have to be perfect, and the light didn't have to be perfect." For example, in the sunset scene, "it's much more from a sense of how he would see it from his memory." Visually, Hurlbut wanted to "capture the emotion of each character through William's eyes"—from his point of view with the use of the small format Canon 5D Mark II.

What amazes Hurlbut the most is how the small form factor of the camera allows him to get the kinds of shots he could never do with a 35 mm cinema camera. "Never before have we been able to cinematically do a helmet cam, do something that really puts the viewer in a first person perspective," Hurlbut emphasizes. "And that's what this camera really has enabled me to do. Tonight, we were on the beach (see Figure 12.2), and my camera assistant is wearing the helmet and he is able to look at her and caress her arms, and then she turns and runs into the ocean. We start on a close-up of water dripping

FIGURE 12.2
Shane Hurlbut looks through the Canon 5D (with a Z-Finder), the camera attached to a helmet worn by camera operator Bodie Orman, as they set up a shot on the beach with Eli Jane. Director Po Chan leans in screen right, with producer Greg Haggart observing in the background. An assistant uses water from a water bottle to moisten Eli's hair, for the close-up of water dripping off her hair.
(Photo by Kurt Lancaster).

FIGURE 12.3
First-person perspective from William's memories of stroking his girl's arm as water drips from her hair, from *The Last 3 Minutes*
(©2010 Hurlbut Visuals. Used with permission.)

off one strand of her hair into a wide shot of her running on the beach" (see Figures 12.3 to 12.5).

Hurlbut explains that for first-person perspective, the Canon 5D Mark II "is the device to do it. We used depth of field to make it filmic, and we took the audience on a life ride." Po Chan explains how, "I do not want the audience just watching the film. I want them to be able to feel the film. I want to enable the audience to feel what I feel. All the elements in this film, from the casting and

FIGURE 12.4
Actress Eli Jane looks into the camera to engage a first-person perspective of William looking back at his memories in *The Last 3 Minutes*.
(©2010 Hurlbut Visuals. Used with permission.)

FIGURE 12.5
Actress Eli Jane, who plays the love of William's life, coaxes him on by looking at the camera in a first-person perspective in *The Last 3 Minutes*.
(©2010 Hurlbut Visuals. Used with permission.)

the music to the wardrobe; from makeup (the choice of lipstick) to the hairstyles and hair colors; from the patterns and textures of the set dressing pieces to the looks of the crystal itself, are all carefully chosen so that they all work in harmony to tell the story."

LIGHTING THE BEDROOM SCENE

In one scene, after the main character's wife decides to leave him, she packs her bags and heads out the door. There is a dress lying on the floor. William goes over to pick it up, and time slips back into a memory of when, according to Chan's treatment, he sees from his point of view, "his wife wearing the

FIGURE 12.6
Actress Eli Jane presents
a seductive look to the
camera, starting "close,"
in Hurlbut's words, "on
the beautiful face" in *The
Last 3 Minutes.*
*(©2010 Hurlbut Visuals.
Used with permission.)*

same dress. She seductively takes off the dress and crawls under the sheet with William…" (see Appendix 5).

Hurlbut explains how he wanted to keep that scene "very intimate," but at the same time not make it look like a romantic "setup," such as turning "the lights all down, and make it candlelit with soft focus—edgy. Everything's dark, and now I'm going to take my clothes off. That is the exact opposite of what I wanted to convey here."

By avoiding the temptation to go for the moody "perfect light," Hurlbut crafted a scene where "the lights were on. It's nighttime and they just got back from an evening out, and she's still in her dress and he's reading a book. She's coming in, and starts to play with him. So the lights are up, he's reading, then all of a sudden we're in a strip tease scene. That's what I wanted to convey. Out of nowhere the guy is reading his book and all of a sudden looks up, and he's got a beautiful woman in front of him with the dress she just wore out to the movies and now she's taking it off."

To tell this story visually, Hurlbut explains, "You start close, start on that beautiful face. She walks away from the camera; she starts to perform a strip-tease act for her husband. You create that suspense where you think you're going see her but the sheet flies up into frame and blocks your view; then all of a sudden she slinks up under the sheets into a rocking close-up and tells William that she loves him" (see Figures 12.6 to 12.8).

Hurlbut feels that this is one of those scenes where it feels shorter than it really is. "No matter how much Po and I tried to cut that scene down to fit within her 8- to 10-second window," we couldn't do it, he says. "When I was watching

FIGURE 12.7
Hurlbut says, "She starts to perform a striptease act for her husband. You create that suspense where you think you're going see her strip, but the sheet flies up into frame and blocks your view"...
(Still from The Last 3 Minutes *©2010 Hurlbut Visuals. Used with permission.)*

FIGURE 12.8
Hurlbut continues, "Then all of a sudden she slinks up under the sheets into a rocking close-up and tells William that she loves him."
(Still from The Last 3 Minutes *©2010 Hurlbut Visuals. Used with permission.)*

it happen [during the shoot], I thought it was 8 seconds" long, but the actual take was 32 seconds. The final edit has it at 20 seconds. "That's when you know you have something great," Hurlbut smiles, "because when it feels shorter than it really is, you know you've struck a nerve."

FIGURE 12.9
Camera operator Bodie Orman gears up with the helmet cam. The 5D Mark II's LCD screen shows the scene about to be shot in *The Last 3 Minutes*.
(Photo by Kurt Lancaster.)

LIGHTING WITH SPECIAL EFFECTS AND BLOCKING NOTES TO AN ACTOR IN THE VIETNAM WAR SCENE

In the Vietnam War scene, William discovers his wounded buddy dying in the middle of explosions. Hurlbut did not want to mimic the style found in *The Thin Red Line* (1998), created by John Toll, ASC, nor did he want to reinvent what Bob Richardson, ASC, did in *Platoon* (1986). "These guys really knocked the genre out. What I wanted to convey was the sense of the audience being immersed in the action and using debris mortars to change and filter the sunlight (see Figures 12.10 and 12.11). We start with an explosion, and he goes down for cover. He gets up, realizes his friend's been hit, and he runs to him. We blow off this huge mortar explosion, because I wanted the world we've seen—this backlit sun dappled through the trees—to go completely overcast, forcing a mood change. So in an instant, you have a beautiful backlight, completely soft ambiance, and when the explosion goes off and he starts moving towards him, the sun is taken out. It goes dark. The tonal range changes, dropping four to five stops in the lighting. And the camera did so well digging into the shadow areas. And then the sun comes back out once the explosion subsides" (see Figures 12.12 and 12.13).

Hurlbut explains how he collaborated with the special effects team to light the scene. "We positioned spot fires to add color, we sent debris mortars into the

FIGURE 12.10

The special effects crew sets up the spot fires around actor Alex Weber, used to help light the scene in *The Last 3 Minutes*. Pyrotechnic gear and supplies in the foreground, with crew to the right.
(Photo by Kurt Lancaster.)

FIGURE 12.11

"We positioned spot fires to add color, we sent debris mortars into the air to diffuse the sun, and we used lawnmower smoke to cover up the brown tones in the scene that were not realistic to a Vietnam jungle," Hurlbut explains in this sequence from *The Last 3 Minutes*.
(©2010 Hurlbut Visuals. Used with permission.)

FIGURE 12.12
Actor Alex Weber raises his hand in the midst of explosions in *The Last 3 Minutes*.
(©2010 Hurlbut Visuals. Used with permission.)

air to diffuse the sun, and we used lawnmower smoke to cover up the brown tones in the scene that were not realistic to a Vietnam jungle." While working on *Terminator Salvation*, he learned about different mortar explosions, including trapezoids, flash pods, and a square pan. "You start to understand the terminology," Hurlbut says, "and then you use it to your advantage for lighting. I wanted to take the sun away. So with one explosion it went away. And then it comes back right as William's friend died. The timing was just perfect; it was like a sunray from heaven during the death sequence" (see Figure 12.13).

In the rehearsal for this scene, Po Chan explains the importance of a love letter to actor Alex Weber, who plays William's best friend in the Vietnam War (see Figure 12.14).

Po says to him, "Now you're trying to reach the letter. Which pocket will you go in and take it out? You look at it; then you're gone." That's the physical action she relays to the actor. She then layers this with an emotional note: "You're expressing the feeling of the last minute [of your life]. The blood is gone. No pain. Your soul is slowly running out of your body."

Po explains that the "the letter is the most important element in this scene. The scene that comes after this scene is the night before when he is writing a letter to his girlfriend, where they're hunkered down in the torrential downpour; and this letter represents everything that he is going to lose right now, everything that is very dear to him. It's important for the audience to know that at the last moment in his life all he remembers is the letter that he needs to send to his girlfriend. And this contains all the heart and soul of this young soldier and his life."

FIGURE 12.13
Actor Alex Weber provides his last look at his friend, William, who promises to give his last letter to his friend's love in a POV shot from *The Last 3 Minutes*. Hurlbut explains how, as the sun lit the actor's face and the smoke cleared, "The timing was just perfect; it was like a sunray from heaven during the death sequence."
(©2010 Hurlbut Visuals. Used with permission.)

FIGURE 12.14
Director Po Chan gives Alex Weber advice on how to reach into his pocket in *The Last 3 Minutes*.
(Photo by Kurt Lancaster.)

Po rehearses the blocking—the actions of the actor as he performs his character. She clarifies the action until it's clear that the character dying wants his friend to pull the letter out of his pocket. She then tells him what the character is thinking of when looking at the letter. It's written to "the woman you love the most. Envision her in front of you. Know that after this moment you won't see her anymore. I want you to feel that moment and then say, 'I want to go home.'"

After another take, she clarifies the action even more. "When you say, 'I want to go home,' stiffen your neck, take a deep breath." They run the scene, Po sitting in excited anticipation as she engages her entire body as she watches the scene. She squeezes the actor's finger as a way to indicate when to let go his breath. After several takes, they set off the explosions, executing the scene. Po exclaims with glee after the explosions, like a child opening a present at Christmas and getting what she's anticipated.

"I'm so happy right now; you have no idea," she says, as I ask her to comment on the latest take. "It's almost like when I'm writing [the] script at home it is just okay; it's all in my imagination. But, all of a sudden it is all in front of me. It's just so beautiful. Yeah, I almost want to cry."

Po Chan lives in the moment when rehearsing, when watching the actors live her characters' lives: "Every moment when I'm looking at my actor even in rehearsal, even through the monitor, my whole world is there. So every single inch of my skin, my muscle, is there. I'm not me anymore, I'm not Po anymore, I become *one* with my scene. That is my way to truly feel what I want for the scene."

So the detail of grabbing for the letter, of letting out the character's last breath, involves something more than just dying, or enacting a death scene, Po explains. "I want—," she sighs, searching for the words. "It's funny because to people, it's death; it is very physical. To me, death is very soulful. It is very spiritual. Life and death [are] something other than physical, to me. So what I was looking for earlier from Alex is how I want to see him suck his soul out in that last breath."

Although Po is clear she's never been in a war, she feels a strong connection to death. "My family was not very well off, and I witnessed many deaths in my family. Then I came to this country all by myself without friends and family." The theme of regret is palpable throughout the film—not only her regrets in life, but, she adds, "the regrets that belong to someone very close to me and knowing how painful it was for that someone. Because somebody you love so much and you embrace everything that is, knowing that person has to go through the pain of regret—and it is really hard, when [there's] nothing you can do and just helplessly witness it."

Getting the timing right throughout the production is an arduous task because all the scenes—except the opening—require one take in order to maintain the point of view Hurlbut and Po Chan need for the scenes. "When you do takes that are all in one, it requires everyone to be perfect," Hurlbut explains.

Typically, when you do a scene, "you do a close-up and then you do a wide shot, and you do a medium, then do a reverse. You get the performance in three, four, five takes, no problem, and you're onto the next setup. But when the camera has to be the wide shot, the reverse, the close-up, the medium shot, and the spin-around all in one, you have to translate all that into one shot." So, Hurlbut explains, "The actors' timing, my camera movement, the lighting, and performance all have to be in sync. It's nothing you can edit around. If you don't use all of it, you don't have the scene."

It's also a challenge because the scenes are so short. "Trying to do something like this when you have 8 to 15 seconds to engage the audience, inflict the emotion, and identify with a character—that's a lot to do in 8 seconds," Hurlbut laughs as he eats another piece of sushi.

BEHIND THE SCENES OF *THE LAST 3 MINUTES*

Elite Team member Tim Holterman shot and edited a series of short documentaries on the making of *The Last 3 Minutes*. See http://hurlbutvisuals.com/blog/tag/the-making-of/.

THE BATHING SCENE

One of Hurlbut's favorite scenes is the bathing scene. Originally, Po had written a scene about the mother measuring the height of William as a child

FIGURE 12.15
Actress Rachel Kolar bathes baby William in *The Last 3 Minutes*. "She had that 1940s face of being on the farm and having survived rough times," Hurlbut says. "It was a wonderful, playful scene with the splashing water, playing with her son and wiping his face." This scene was shot at ISO 160 with a Canon 35 mm L series lens, f/5.0 with a color temperature set to 5200 degrees K.
(©2010 Hurlbut Visuals. Used with permission.)

(see Appendix 5), but Hurlbut says they just couldn't find a location for it; nothing worked. "It just didn't fit." So the bathing scene "was something spontaneously created in a location that didn't really lend itself to the surroundings of the house where we were shooting. But we found an angle with trees in the background and sheets blowing on the line. The mom was so beautiful. She had that 1940s face of being on the farm and having survived rough times. It was a wonderful, playful scene with the splashing water, playing with her son and wiping his face. It was a very special moment" (see Figure 12.15).

The setup of the scene included a washtub full of water with the camera handheld by Shane Hurlbut (see Figures 12.16 to 12.19).

In the end, William dies, and the crystal rolls out of his hand. But for Po, the scene of death is more than just an ending. "The last breath of a human life means a lot," she muses. "The whole story is the last three minutes of this man's life; everything flashes back in front of him. That last breath is not just physical breath—it is the breath of the soul and the heart and the spirit of this person. So I wanted it really perfect at that moment, the right physical reactions with the eye line. Everything had to hit the right mark."

FIGURE 12.16
Shane Hurlbut handholds a Canon 5D Mark II as director Po Chan gets ready to splash water onto actress Rachel Kolar (off-screen)—the camera becoming baby William's perspective of his mother.
(Photo by Kurt Lancaster.)

FIGURE 12.17
Shane Hurlbut watches the playback of a take on a field monitor (off-screen). An assistant is ready with a reflector board in the background.
(Photo by Kurt Lancaster.)

FIGURE 12.18
The field monitor observed by director Po Chan and cinematographer Shane Hurlbut.
(Photo by Kurt Lancaster.)

FIGURE 12.19
Actress Rachel Kolar waits by the bathtub as Shane Hurlbut and Po Chan observe a take on the monitor in the background, screen left. Elite Team member Derek Edwards practices pulling focus. A reflector screen right is used to light Rachel's face with reflected sunlight.
(Photo by Kurt Lancaster.)

LESSONS LEARNED AND SCREENING RESULTS

Because the project was sponsored by Canon, Hurlbut used Canon lenses, but he was accustomed to utilizing prime lenses with a focus ring that stops, rather than the endless focus ring found in Canon glass. He admits that, "Initially, I was not a big fan of this glass because of the resolving power of their wide angle lenses and the endless focus ring. I made the wrong lens choices on the first day of the Navy SEAL movie [*Act of Valor*] and never looked back." However, he has since changed his mind. "Twelve months later and having completed a lot of research and development, we were able to solve both of these problems when using the Canon lenses with a new remote follow focus system," Hurlbut says.

Hurlbut was also pleasantly surprised by the results of Canon's L-series lenses. "I was blown away with the contrast, color, and resolving power of the 35 mm, 50 mm, 85 mm, and the 100 mm Canon macro lenses. They became my go-to lenses on the short and gave me more latitude in the under exposed areas, much more than the Zeiss. The image was creamy but sharp" (Hurlbut Visuals, "Inside Track Newsletter" March 31, 2010).

The Last 3 Minutes was placed online in April 2010. Between April 7 and April 28, 2010—in a period of three weeks—it received 146,000 plays on Vimeo. The work was also presented at NAB in Las Vegas later in the same month. Hurlbut attended NAB and discussed his experiences with the 5D Mark II to an overflowing crowd on the Canon showroom floor in the large convention center exhibit hall.

A few of the standout responses on Vimeo include this post: "The video completely took my breath away … I was captivated for the whole thing and didn't come back to the real world until it was done. Excellent work. I wish to be as good as you are one day."

D. M. Daly: "Wow … magical. Thanks for sending shivers my way, great feel!!!"

Chris Bishow: "My wife is making fun of me because I'm teary eyed, but it's probably the best piece of work I've seen with a DSLR. You owe me a tissue."

NAB 2010 became the first public screening for *The Last 3 Minutes*, and the website became a place for Shane and Po to receive written feedback. "The responses have been overwhelming, touching, and amazing," Hurlbut says. "I feel honored to have worked with Po, the Elite Team, and every person involved with the project to deliver such a heartfelt short. The story struck a nerve because it transported you on a journey through William's life, which initially appeared simple on the surface but as the memories unfold, so does the complexity of the piece. The 5D Mark II was the best tool to bring this vision to life."

Shane also realized that NAB 2010 was different. It was focused on the 5D (as well as 3D film and television): "It should have been called 5D-NAB because nearly every vendor had one—whether it was equipment to move it, monitor it, rig it, lens it, post it, color it, edit it. You name it," Hurlbut emphasizes.

But having this film projected on a large screen, first at Hdi RAWworks, and then at Laser Pacific, was the biggest reward in seeing how the look and feel of the camera paid off for this short: "What I saw could easily [have] been on a 60-foot screen," Hurlbut remarks. "I was so impressed with the image quality, color, and contrast. The only minor snafu was a little rolling shutter when I ran into the ocean due to camera vibration. Other than that, the HDSLR technology performed beautifully. This is another perfect example of a concept and story that never could have been told with this first-person intimacy without the Canon 5D Mark II."

Director Po Chan told one story where she said a Vietnam vet contacted her after seeing the film online: "You have written a wonderfully moving story. Congratulations, I expect to see your name on many more movies in the future. Everyone needs to know the technical side, but the genius lies in your creative brain. Just look at all the work and good things that spring forth as your story is born and becomes of age. You get a *gold* Star for good work!" After receiving this, she noted how deeply touched and grateful she was for this message.

It's what filmmaking's all about.

CHAPTER 13

Crafting the Film Look with Sound Design

> **The Timpanogos National Monument, Utah:** *Hansen Cave* **(2:44)**, *Middle Cave* **(2:09 min), and** *Timpanogos Cave* **(3:33 min), directed by Kurt Lancaster, United States**

Technical data: Shot on a Canon 5D Mark II with a Zeiss Contax 50 mm f/1.4 and Canon 70–200 mm f/2.8; 60D with a 50 mm f/1.8 lens. Kessler Crane Pocket Dolly Traveler. Production team: Kurt Lancaster, Shannon Sassone, Shannon Thorp, and Yfat "Yffy" Yosifor.

VIDEOS

Hansen Cave: http://vimeo.com/33791447
Middle Cave: http://vimeo.com/33621145
Timpanogos Cave: http://vimeo.com/34037288

CONCEPT: POETIC VIDEOS

The National Park Service at the Timpanogos National Monument outside American Fork, Utah put out a call to several universities and video professionals asking for someone to shoot a series of video podcasts for their website. Since the trail rises nearly 1100 feet in 1.5 miles, those with disabilities may not be able to access the wonders of the park. Martin Hansen (see Figure 13.1) discovered the first cave in 1887, while the other caves were found in the early part of the twentieth century. The first trail to the cave was built in the 1920s, and the property transferred to the National Park Service in the 1930s. In 2011, the Park Service wanted a series of videos that would include a traditional tour with a park ranger, as well as another ranger providing a scientific discussion of the colors and formations in the cave system. Lancaster[1] proposed a series

---

[1] In order to remain consistent with the voice of the book, the author refers to himself in the third person throughout this chapter.

FIGURE 13.1
Martin Hansen standing in front of the Hansen Cave entrance. The National Park Service took over the cave operations in the 1930s, opening it up to the public.
(Courtesy of the National Park Service.)

of "poetic videos" for each of the three caves, which would be shot in a lyrical style with DSLRs, a form pioneered by Philip Bloom, among others—applying cinematic techniques to everyday life and people. Within these three videos, the filmmakers decided not to edit the journey in a linear, literal way, rather juxtaposing images like memories through associative emotions.

Lancaster provided a link to a Philip Bloom piece as well as a link to work shot by Shannon Thorp, a student of Lancaster's, who shot a poetic piece in Sedona, Arizona that exemplified the kind of style he wanted to provide (see <http://vimeo.com/12095570>). After looking at several proposals, they were convinced that their budget, including the use of personal and university equipment from Lancaster's university, Northern Arizona University, as well as the poetic shooting style, would provide the proper feel for the project. He put together his team from some of the best shooters he discovered in his classes: Shannon Sassone, Shannon Thorp, and Yfat "Yffy" Yosifor.

ENTERING THE CAVES

The videos were shot over five days in August 2011, which included hikes up to the cave system each morning. The caves—comprising Hansen, Middle, and Timpanogos—each expressed their own special characteristics, each exuding a different feeling.

Hansen Cave provided that sense of disorientation occurring when walking from bright daylight into a dark cave. This was executed by a couple of dolly shots from the Kessler Crane Pocket Dolly. After entering the cave, it is much darker, but there are lights in the cave system highlighting some of its unique features. Indeed, the lowlight capabilities of DSLRs would prove useful, especially when using fast lenses. But despite that, in many cases that ISO settings would range from 640 to 1250 in order to capture the unique spaces of the cave.

As a documentary filmmaker, Lancaster and his team approached the caves as if they were characters speaking in silence, providing detailed shots intermixed with wide shots. Aristotle tells us that characters are people doing actions. A cave isn't a person, so the filmmaking team approached these cave characters through a dramatic sense of action and reaction. "A particular visual would stand out in the cave system that would impress us, as if it were speaking to us, wanting our attention," Lancaster says. "That's what we would shoot, just as if we wanted to capture a particular angle or light of a character in a documentary film."

Documentary filmmakers engage in the practice of finding the heart of characters and interpreting them through the lenses of their cameras. So for the cave system, "It was up to us to see the beauty and, yes, sometimes the creepiness of objects in the cave and interpret it through our lens," Lancaster explains. A person going on a tour will notice some details—the interpreter guide will make sure of that. However, photographers, cinematographers, and filmmakers are trained to see what others don't see—the individuality of the filmmaker will be attracted to different shot sizes, angles, light and shadow, depth of field, and movement based on how they feel about what they see. Their lens will shape the audience's experience. Timpanogos cave proved a challenge in finding these characteristics.

Initially, though, Lancaster had his doubts about submitting a proposal. "I wanted to shoot documentaries and fiction. I come from a background in theater. I like working with people, not inanimate objects," he confides. He had his doubts about doing a promotional type video, too. However, after he entered Hansen Cave, it all changed. "It's like nothing else on this planet. The features are unique to this location," Lancaster says. "I fell in love with the caves."

Cut off from the outside world by thick double-door systems in order to maintain the 100% humidity (at about 45-degrees Fahrenheit), the caves exude silence intermixed by drips of calcified water and occasional wind noises in the doorways. Drips from stalactites hit small pools of water below or against limestone surfaces.

Capturing the visuals, Lancaster and his team used a variety of shot sizes, camera movement, and static tripod shots. They maintained a similar shooting style throughout.

Shannon Sassone, a talented filmmaker who just graduated from Northern Arizona University's School of Communication, came up with the concept of how each cave system could have its character defined not through a different shooting style, but through a unique sound design.

SOUND DESIGN DEFINES THE CAVE CHARACTERS

The team extended Sassone's concept and decided that the best way to approach the sound design was to think about how they as filmmakers felt about the caves. Ultimately, the sound design would become the key tool in expressing the feeling that the filmmakers felt when going through the cave system. Although audio was recorded in different parts of the cave system with Rode NTG-2 mics and Zoom H4n audio recorders, the quality of the recording was not good enough to use in the final edit.

The team relied on sound libraries found in Apple's Final Cut Pro, as well as music by Kevin MacLeod under the Creative Commons license from his library of music at incompetech.com. Despite this, one of the National Park Service employees felt that the audio design was spot on. She mentioned that the wind sounds made her wonder if she had left a door open (since that's when you feel and hear wind in the caves). She also felt that the water dripping sounds evoked the "real sounds of the cave."[2]

---

[2] Personal notes to the author on review of the videos.

What follows is the process by which the filmmakers created the sound design for the three short films.

HANSEN CAVE

For Hansen Cave, Lancaster's filmmaking team had to capture the atmosphere through water drips and music that inspires with beauty in order to help remove the disorientation and the dark mystery found when first walking from the sunny high mountain landscape to the interior damp darkness within (see Figure 13.2).

FIGURE 13.2
A stalagmite is one of the first things visitors see when they enter Hansen's Cave. The light was placed by the National Park Service.
(Courtesy of the National Park Service.)

Through a variety of lenses, static, tilt, and dolly shots, the filmmakers reveal the space and show the details in the 2:38 minute video. The music chosen—Kevin MacLeod's "At Rest"—also presents a melancholy flavor in order to shape the coldness and closeness of the space and to remind the viewers that they have shifted into another world. Wind noise from Final Cut's sound library eases in at the end in order to provide a closing sense of finality, as well as transition to Middle Cave. "It's key that you don't use too many layers of sound," Lancaster says, "because it'll be like mixing too many colors in painting—it'll turn it into the color of mud."

As seen in Figure 13.3, 11 different audio elements were used. The opening 41 seconds reveals shots of plants and landscapes along the side of the mountain, so five audio elements of different birds were mixed into these shots in order to convey the sense of peace, warmth, and beautiful flora.

The bird songs fade down as MacLeod's "At Rest" slowly fades up as we see the mouth of the cave (see Figure 13.4). As we see the shot of the stalagmite at 48 seconds (Figure 13.2, above), the sounds of water drips rise into the sound mix, lasting for 7 seconds. The rest of the piece utilizes three other water drip designs, with the last one the longest at 13 seconds—which is mixed with wind noise entering at 2:08—with the wind lasting through the credits to 2:38.

FIGURE 13.3
The sound design layout in Apple's Final Cut Pro. The opening 41 seconds utilizes five bird song elements in the mix, before shifting to MacLeod's melancholic, "At Rest."

FIGURE 13.4
The opening to Hansen's Cave and the entrance of the tour. The bird songs fade down as MacLeod's "At Rest" slowly fades up when we see the mouth of the cave. The hole above was the original entrance before the one below was carved open.
(Courtesy of the National Park Service.)

When creating the sound design, Lancaster and his team, utilized what Hollywood sound designer and picture editor Walter Murch describes as metaphoric sound. This is a type of sound which tends to "open up the conceptual gap into which the fertile imagination of the audience will reflexively rush, eager (even if unconsciously so) to complete circles that are only suggested [providing] … the space to evoke and inspire, rather than to overwhelm and crush, the imagination of the audience" (Transom Review, Vol. 5 #1, three of his articles/interviews appear here: <http://transom.org/?p=6992, http://transom.org/?page_id=7006, and http://transom.org/?page_id=7026>).

MIDDLE CAVE

The sonic landscape for Middle Cave revolved around the theme of mystery. The filmmaking team set up a sense of disorientation and melancholy in Hansen Cave. They felt that by this point, they'd have gotten used to the enclosed space, and now they're entering the heart of the cave system, so the sound design evokes a sense of the mystery of what's around the corner. This time, the natural audio elements of several different wind sounds and extended moments of audio drips (with no music) would evoke the feeling of Middle Cave (see Figure 13.5).

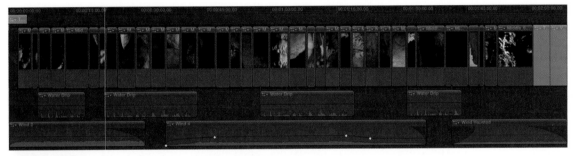

FIGURE 13.5
Wind sounds transitions us from Hansen Cave into the mystery of Middle Cave. Three different wind sounds and extended water drips make up the sound design for this cave.
(Courtesy of the National Park Service.)

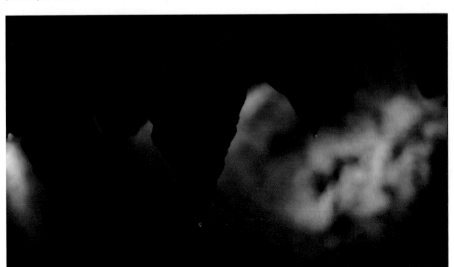

FIGURE 13.6
The tips of stalactites bead up with water and the sound design helps evoke the dripping sounds of water throughout the cave system. Notice the shallow depth of field caused by the open aperture and fast lens on the Canon 5D Mark II.
(Courtesy of the National Park Service.)

Close-ups, rack focus shots, details of water drops at the end of stalactites (see Figure 13.6) comprise the visuals as we hear wind fade in and out and we see and feel the atmosphere through pools of water comprising the first 25 seconds of the work. The wind fades to silence for 5 seconds before we hear a different kind of wind sound.

(In actuality, there is no wind in the caves, except in the passage ways as the inner and outer doors of the caves are opened and closed. However, for the purpose of the video, the atmospheric sounds of the wind evoke the feeling of the dampness and humidity the filmmakers felt in the cave and they felt that this was the best way to bring that feeling across to the audience—along with the wetness of the water drip sounds.)

This second wind lasts for a minute and heightens the atmospheric beauty of the space, tunnels, rocky crags, and the scale of a large cavernous space, along with a slowly spinning shot (0:53–0:55) that reveals the ceiling and archways with helictites colored formations, like organs in the bowels of a giant (0:55–1:08). Within these segments water drips fade in and out and the silence in between the drips causes a sense of emotional release, a sonic shift that places the audience into a different mindset that engages a different kind of imagination.

The wind fades out to silence at 1:35 to more drips accompanied with some tracking shots, then another type of mysterious wind ends the piece with thrusting move-in shots and glistening water on a dark cave ceiling (1:41–2:08).

TIMPANOGOS CAVE

Timpanogos Cave is the largest and most complex cave of the three, containing some of the strangest and fascinating formations of the entire system. Therefore it required a more complex sound design with a mix of water drops, wind sounds, and three different pieces of music from Kevin MacLeod ("Symbiosis," "Impact Lento," and "Sad Trio") in order to reveal the awe and majesty of this cave (see Figure 13.7).

FIGURE 13.7
The sound design layout from Final Cut Pro for Timpanogos Cave. It contained some of the most complex and fascinating formations of the entire system, so it utilized the most varied and strongest musical elements to evoke this journey of majesty.

The piece opens with a solo piano in MacLeod's "Symbiosis," accompanied by no other sound for 20 seconds. It's a bit pensive, but acts as a counterpoint to the experience of seeing the beauty of more complex formations. At 20 seconds there is a slow fade in of two segments from MacLeod's "Impact Lento"—which extends to the end of the piece at 3:32. As "Impact Lento" begins, it's so soft that we can just begin to hear it at 40 seconds and to add a bit of complexity to the design, the filmmakers fade in the sounds of water drips at 46 seconds, which last for 18 seconds. As the water drips fade, the solo piano from "Symbiosis" begins to fade out, lasting until 1:13. At this point "Impact Lento" with choral elements builds loudly for 30 seconds or so as we enter and leave Chime Chamber, a location with tiny formations like straws and twisting choral-type rock growth, and rich colors of greens, whites, and reds (see Figure 13.8).

FIGURE 13.8
The intricate beauty of Chime Chamber. The choral elements of MacLeod's "Impact Lento" builds throughout this segment, while at the same time a slow build-up of underwater sounds heightens the tension.

As we move through Chime Chamber, sounds like thunder crunching in the deep (in actuality, an underwater recording from Final Cut's sound library), enter as we push down a rock tunnel (see Figure 13.9).

As we move out of this segment, the second water drip effect is utilized at 2:09–2:21, in order to release the tension created in the previous section. At the same time, "Impact Lento" has shifted from an awe-inspiring choral theme to a low end bass tone and string instruments. The underwater rumble slowly fades out at 3:02, while MacLeod's "Sad Trio" fades in at 2:27, maintaining its presence to the end simultaneously with the slow fade out of "Impact Lento."

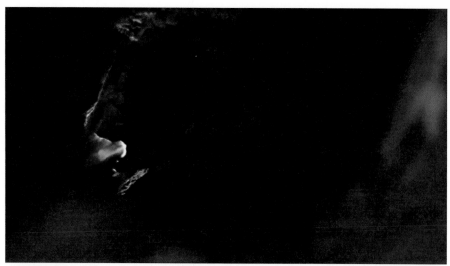

FIGURE 13.9
A push-in shot created by mounting the 5D Mark II onto the Kessler Crane Pocket Dolly down the axis. "Impact Lento" and underwater sounds evoking thunder accompanies this moment shaping a climatic moment of visual aural energy. The foreground is out of focus due to the shallow depth of field of the DSLR.
(Courtesy of the National Park Service.)

FIGURE 13.10
The heart of the cave, a unique stalactite in the shape of a heart. We push onto the object as we simultaneously push through the sonic atmosphere of MacLeod's music.
(Courtesy of the National Park Service.)

As "Sad Tio" builds its beat and heightens its lofty tune, another wind design fades in at 2:39 (carrying through to the end)—this helps evoke two major shots in this section, the heart of the cave (a uniquely shaped stalactite, see Figure 13.10) and a rare albino-like cave cricket (see Figure 13.11). To key us to the emotional close or dénouement of the piece, the final segment of water drips fade in at 3:06–3:13, the wind and two pieces of music slowly fading out as we see shots of chime chamber.

FIGURE 13.11
A rare white cave cricket helps reveal the beauty of the cave system, alive with different wonders, evoked by MacLeod's music. The 5D's limited depth of field helps define the space of the cricket.
(Courtesy of the National Park Service.)

The entire sound design—and especially the elements of water drips and wind, was purposely designed to evoke Walter Murch's metaphoric sound, where the audio isn't literal: "Synchronization of sight and sound, which naturally does not exist in radio, can be the glory or the curse of cinema. A curse, because if overused, a string of images relentlessly chained to literal sound has the tyrannical power to strangle the very things it is trying to represent, stifling the imagination of the audience in the bargain. Yet the accommodating technology of cinema gives us the ability to loosen those chains and to re-associate the film's images with other, carefully-chosen sounds which at first hearing may be 'wrong' in the literal sense, but which can offer instead richly descriptive sonic metaphors" (Transom Review, Vol. 5 #1).

The music, wind, and water drips become the sonic metaphors that allow us to shape the characters of the caves, the thematic elements comprising the mystery and darkness of Hansen's Cave, the mystery of Middle Cave, and the majesty and awe of Timpanogos Cave.

CHAPTER 14
Crafting the Film Look with Puppets and Miniature Sets

Gods of the Flies (2012), directed by Danger Charles, United States, 5:53 min

Technical: Canon 60D, 18–135 mm f/3.5–5.6 lens, tripod, cinema slider.

http://vimeo.com/41331304

Danger Charles fell in love with the dark side of Jim Henson's puppetry—specifically *The Dark Crystal* (1982), and he's wanted to make a film with puppets ever since. But he thought it took itself too seriously and after watching *Kung Pow: Enter the Fist* (2002), and listening to how they made this martial arts spoof—he decided that there's a way to have fun making movies. The`y "just sounded like they were having so much fun making this movie," Charles says in an interview. And that's when he decided he wanted to make films.

Attending the University of Rhode Island, Charles transferred to Northern Arizona University to complete his degree. He wanted to follow in Henson's footsteps and make a movie with puppets. "Gods of the Flies" was based on Argentinian author, Marco Denevi's short story, "The Lord of the Flies," in which the author imagined a heaven for flies made up of "a hunk of rotten meat, stinking and putrid," while the fly's hell is "a place without excrement, without waste, trash, stink, without anything of anything; a place sparkling with cleanliness and illuminated by a bright white light; in other words, an ungodly place."[1] After reading the story, Charles imagined a short, easy project, "but then it developed into something that was a lot more involved," he adds.

Like an Aesop's fable, Charles' film engages universal themes, but doesn't really examine a particular "hero's journey" of a character, but rather utilizes tropes and metaphors, as well as visual cues—such as the portrait of a fly family—to tap into the human connection (see Figure 14.1). At the same time, he doesn't take the film "itself too seriously, but it also lends itself to this type of puppetry." There's a certain amount of fun watching the movie.

---

[1] Denevi, Marco (2000.) "The Lord of the Flies" Translated by José Chávez in *El libro de la brevedad/The Book of Brevity*, Trilce Editores, Bogotá. Cited in The Café Irreal. Assessed May 14, 2012. <http://cafeirreal.alicewhittenburg.com/denevi.htm>

FIGURE 14.1
A fly reaches over and picks up a family portrait. These elements imbue the film with a "human" touch, bridging the fly world with metaphoric power in Charles' *Gods of the Flies*.
(Still courtesy Danger Charles. Used with permission.)

This was the first short film Charles shot with a DSLR, although he and a friend shot "a couple little documentary spots over the summer" with a 60D and fell in "love the way they look," Charles says. He doesn't like the over use of the rack focus, so he "avoided that at all costs" in *Gods of the Flies*. He liked how the sensors of the cameras "pick up color so well"—especially when you're "carefully crafting every color" in the mise-en-scène.

FIGURE 14.2
Danger Charles works on a set from Gods of the Flies.
(Photo courtesy Danger Charles (2012). Used with permission.)

FIGURE 14.3
Jon Goodrich sets up miniature lights as a fly looks at an Egyptian tomb. A Canon 60D on a cinema slider is used for the shot in *Gods of the Flies*.
(Photo courtesy Danger Charles (2012). Used with permission.)

Charles and his team would build sets over the weekend and then bring them in to shoot on Mondays (see Figures 14.2 and 14.3).

Charles likes to challenge himself. He had never worked with miniatures or puppets before, but he took on the challenge, so he "would have to learn a lot of new things," he says. He utilized foam latex to build the puppets, because that's the material Jim Henson used when building his puppets. He explains the process:

> You have to mix all these ingredients and weigh them out, and then there's a schedule, like a certain temperature and humidity. You have to mix at this speed for seven minutes, this speed for five minutes, this for four, this for three, and then you only have thirty to forty-five seconds to pour the material into a mold or paint it onto a body before it starts curing. […] And then you have to bake it in an oven for three or four hours. And if you leave it in there for thirty minutes too long, it gets, like sort of rigid and not very flexible, and if it's in there for not long enough you'll squeeze the material and it won't spring back to its intended shape.

See Figures 14.4–14.6.

FIGURE 14.4
A fly head ready to be molded.
(Photo courtesy Danger Charles (2012). Used with permission.)

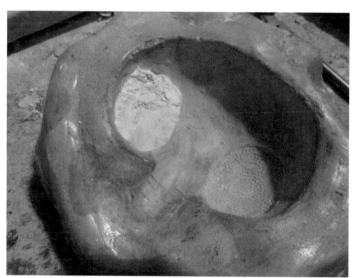

FIGURE 14.5
Fly head mold.
(Photo courtesy Danger Charles (2012). Used with permission.)

Before actually going into production, Charles engaged a Kickstarter campaign (<http://www.kickstarter.com/projects/dangerhuman/gods-of-the-flies>), and raised $631 of the $600 goal—materials to build the puppets. In addition to raising funds, Charles liked the built-in audience factor with Kickstarter: "It's

FIGURE 14.6
After the mold is created a series of different heads were built. Here is a completed model in a nightgown.
(Photo courtesy Danger Charles (2012). Used with permission.)

a really cool way to promote your movie," he explains, "because you have all these people who give you nominal donations of five, ten dollars, which really isn't a vested financial interest in your film, but they've got a vested interest in your film, already. So we've got thirty people online who really want to see my movie." He gave them first looks on the cut of the film and listened to their feedback before making it public. "Getting all this feedback from them is really interesting and fun," Charles says.

As he entered production, Charles started with the "least complicated to most complicated and important" scenes, because "I figured we'd be learning along the way. So I shot a series of still shots of just sets where we push in. We shot all those first because there are no puppets." These are the shots of the various gods mentioned in the script (see Figures 14.2 and 14.3). "We got comfortable lighting everything in the studio, and how everything felt, and then we shot puppets next, and more complicated scenes after that with more puppets." They started with a Lowell light kit, but switched to photo soft lights.

A complex scene would take them hours to set-up. They would get into the studio around eight in the morning, then begin shooting around noon or one. It took that long "to get everything right, because the puppets break, and you have to fix them, and then you realize, 'Oh, we forgot to put this in, we need to set this up,'" Charles says. "Fly heaven" was one of the most complex scenes. What would fly paradise look like?

I was just trying to think of little images we could show of fly paradise. So I was trying to make a comparison [to a human heaven], so I'm like, "oh, we could put flies in a hot tub," and "we'll make the hot tub just be nasty brown water." And so we had this grand idea of putting them in these tubs, so we found these oil pans that we were going to use, and we were like, "it'll be perfect." And we were going to snake in a tube so somebody could blow bubbles in it, and of course, you know, two or three people didn't show up who were supposed to operate puppets that day, so it was just three of us, me and two of my friends, so I was like, "okay, I'll do camera, two puppets can be moving." And we set this all up. And of course, we're going pour the water in, and there might be a little leak, so we'll just shoot it fast. We pour the water in and it just starts gushing out the bottom in the studio. I don't know what happened. I have two of my friends under the table getting completely soaked with this nasty water, and I'm saying, "we're going to shoot it! We're going to shoot it right now!" It was a three hour setup, and I wasn't going let my actors manipulating the puppets getting wet compromise the shoot. And we ended up using it, which was funny. Because I thought that we wouldn't even end up using that shot, because I didn't really like it. (See Figures 14.7 and 14.8.)

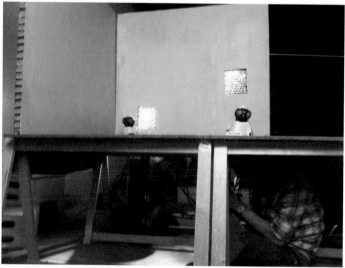

FIGURE 14.7
Performers sit under a table to manipulate puppets in the mosque scene from *Gods of the Flies*.
A similar setup for the fly heaven scene resulted in the performers getting wet as water was poured into hot tubs.
(Photo courtesy Danger Charles (2012). Used with permission.)

FIGURE 14.8
Flies enjoying their time in heaven as they bask in the warmth of hot tubs.
(Photo courtesy Danger Charles (2012). Used with permission.)

Charles would edit scenes as they got completed so he had a running cut by the time they entered post. They spent two weeks editing the film. "I had been dropping scenes in and editing them as we shot them," Charles explains, "which really helped because I could do little things and tweak things and even reshoot in some cases. So I edited as I went, resulting in a rough cut minus two or three scenes three weeks before it was done, and then we shot for another week." And then he taught himself Adobe After Effects, using a trial version to learn it and eventually removed all of the wires from the puppets. "As I learned the program," he continues, "I realize that I could do this, and try this out, like putting the rain in was really helpful. And then I just brought it back over into Final Cut and trimmed everything up how I wanted it."

The final part of post was the sound design, which Charles admits as being "the most important part of the editing." He explains:

> We got a local musician named John Whipple, who I discovered after putting out an ad for a narrator on Craigslist, and he responded. So I went to meet him, and he was playing a gig at Mother Road Brewery in Flagstaff, and he had this sweet slide guitar, and he was putting it through a synth, and it was just really cool music and I tell him, "We'll have you record narration, but I really want you to record music, too," and he's a super cool guy so he just came in and did music. He had an accordion and a slide guitar that we used, and it turned out really well. We ended up going with a different narrator, but we got our music!

Final thoughts Charles has about his film stems from the idea of building a universe. What stands out in the film is its reality, its complexity of a real world extending beyond the edge of the frames, which he says comes about during writing, and then visualizing it later in the production design. At the same time, the sound design "creates an atmosphere," Charles says, that helps build the reality of that universe.

The final cut of the film was screened at the Orpheum Student Film Festival in Flagstaff, Arizona, where it received a faculty award for best student film—a reward that will allow the film to be screened at the Sedona International Film Festival, in February 2013.

PART 3
Getting the Gear

THE FUTURE OF DSLR GEAR

Hybrid DSLRs started a cinematic revolution four years ago. Thousands of film-makers, journalists, event videographers, and film students have utilized them beyond what the original designers at first conceived. Many purchased the camera and found the ergonomics a tad difficult to wield. Shooting outdoors, the LCD screen is nearly impossible to see, and since you can't look through the viewfinder in live view (except for the Panasonic Lumix GH1, because it's a 4/3 system and not an SLR camera), you would need to throw a jacket over your head to see.

Video cameras don't have such issues. You can go out and buy a video camera, and in most situations, that's all you need (aside from spare batteries and a tripod). Prosumer models have built in neutral density filters (electronic), many of the higher end cameras have XLR connectors with manual control of audio—and most have fixed lenses.

DSLRs are of a different breed. They're stills cameras and if you want it to have the ergonomics and capabilities of a video camera (such as manual control of audio), you may need additional gear to make it work for you. Dozens of companies have sprung up to meet the need of filmmakers wanting better ergonomics. From Redrock Micro to Zakuto creating handheld and shoulder mounted rigs, from BeachTek to juicedLink building XLR audio adapters with a microphone preamp and manual gain control, and Zeiss designing prime lenses specifically for the DSLR market, companies understand the needs and wants of DSLR shooters.

Indeed, because of the popularity of DSLRs being used as cinema cameras, the video camera industry has taken notice. Both Sony and Panasonic have released video cameras that not only include interchangeable lenses, but also Super 35 mm sensors. They've taken notice and stepped up to help make video more cinematic. Canon put the gloves down with the C-300 in fall of 2011, followed by their 4 K cinema cameras, the C-500 and the HDSLR, EOS-1D C.

But they're expensive for independent filmmakers, video journalists, and students—pushing past $15,000.

DSLR shooters share a secret. The Canon 7D, 60D, 5D Mark II, and even the $600 Rebel T2i (550D) shoots much better images than old-style video cameras costing thousands more. Can they compete in a 4 K world? If you tell a good story, these cameras will provide a cinematic image on a low budget.

Professionals may buy these new video cameras, and other companies will come out with video cameras with larger sensors and interchangeable lenses—but they likely won't be of the same quality when compared to the much lower price point of DSLRs.

DSLRs are not going away. As Philip Bloom noted when talking about these new video cameras coming down the pike, DSLRs are not just a fad:

> Is this fad over? No Chance. Video DSLRs will be with us for a hell of a long time to come. Students, indie filmmakers, event videographers and so many more simply won't be able to afford these new cameras. The tech will improve and some of the issues will go away. Some will be here for a long time to come though. But of course we are working with these limitations right now and incredible work is being done by so many despite them. This will continue for many years. Also, take this job I am on now. I am shooting lots of timelapses as well as video. I can easily put 3 or 4 bodies in my carry on luggage and it takes up no space and is less that the cost of, probably, one of these new video cameras with large sensors. The small size is a massive plus for me. I can also see the day soon when I travel with a new large sensor video camera and still bring a couple of DSLRs with me, second and third angles etc.—it simply makes sense.
>
> So when you hear people say, "is this the end of that DSLR fad then?", tell them no. This "fad" is only just beginning. It's just going to get better and better. Yes, I cannot see "House" or other

major players choosing to shoot on DSLRs if affordable ($10K is affordable to pro companies) cameras are out there that do the job much better. But for the rest of us, DSLRs will be our main cameras for many years to come.[1]

Technologies evolve with demand. What was the hot ticket last year will be subsumed by new models coming out in 2013. Ikonoskop, Black Magic Design, and Digital Bolex are releasing cameras that shoot 16mm cinema RAW in Adobe's standardized DNG format. BMD and Bolex are pricing their cameras around $3000, but require a lot more space and postproduction color correction, and are not suitable for run-and-gun shooters. But DSLRs are here to stay and what follows is a minimal list of some of the gear priced for students, video journalists, and low-budget indie filmmakers.

[1] Bloom, P. (August 8, 2010). The future of video DSLRs. *PhilipBloom.net.* <http://philipbloom. net/2010/08/13/the-future-of-video-dslrs/.>

CHAPTER 15

DSLR Cinema Gear for Low Budget Shooters

DSLR CINEMA GEAR: AN OVERVIEW

This chapter provides a list of recommended gear for low-budget filmmakers, students, video journalists, and documentary filmmakers. But rather than include a lot of different gear priced by a variety of categories, I'm only going to describe the minimum needed for a student, video journalist, and independent filmmaker. *Most of this is my recommended list based on actual use in the field by myself and/or working professionals I've encountered while writing this book.*[1] It is not even close to an exhaustive list of everything available—far from it. This is my recommendation and there are many websites and companies that offer a variety of gear for different needs. I'm sorry that the list only includes Canon DSLRs, but those are what I have field tested with my students, so that's my recommendation based on experience. I have never shot with a Nikon, so I don't have the experience to recommend their DSLRs.

Before you start shooting, it's recommended that you test equipment to make sure it's what you want and it does what it needs to do to meet your needs.

A lot of companies manufacture a variety of body and shoulder mount rigs with follow focus gear and matte boxes. I'm not going to make these recommendations in order to keep the prices down. The monopod and/or tripod I list below is more than adequate for most situations. If you want to attach additional gear to the camera, then getting a cage might be useful. Furthermore, unless you can afford it, I don't recommend any of the large sensor video cameras at this time. If you can purchase a 5D Mark II for half the price of a Sony FS-100 (with a $5000 body), then I don't see any reason for spending the extra money. The 5D Mark II will provide a better image. Once large-sensor cameras drop to $3500 and under will be the time to consider such a purchase. I'm also not including the Black Magic Design Cinema camera or the D16 Digital Bolex, since I'm currently writing a separate book on 16mm cameras that shoot in DNG cinema RAW, requiring a different workflow than what's covered in this book.

Go to the author's website to access links to the gear listed: <www.kurtlancaster.com>.

---

[1] Please note that any prices listed in this chapter were based on known prices at the time this book was being written. No guarantees of similar pricing models can be made.

STUDENT PACKAGE (REBEL T2I/550D OR 60D): ~$2500–$3000

For shooters on a budget. Remember, this entire package costs about the same as getting a prosumer video camera, such as JVC GY-HM150U!

I've included the kit lens, as well as other necessary accessories. You may decide that you don't want the Rode VideoMic Pro and only use the Tascam DR-40 with the Rode NTG-2, in which case you'll save more than $200.

Canon Rebel T2i (550D) with 18–55 mm f3.5–5.6 lens: ~$650

For the money, this is the best buy out there for capturing images, cinematically. It doesn't contain all of the features of the 60D, but it does do the job, putting out quality better than video cameras costing thousands more. Put Magic Lantern on it, and you'll be rocking, making it a powerful video camera that can shoot cinematically. The camera is discontinued, so if you can't get one, then get the T3i/600D—you just won't be able to use the audio features in Magic Lantern.

Canon 50 mm f/1.8: ~$120

The best buy Canon has—this is a "fast" lens, meaning the aperture opens to f/1.8, so you can get a shallow depth of field and shoot in low light situations. This should be your go-to lens for most of your shooting situations. Use the kit lens as a wide angle lens (18–25 mm).

Light Craft Neutral Density Fader Filter (52 mm for 50 mm f/1.8 lens): ~$75

An ND fader is essential when you're shooting outdoors. You can get up to eight stops from this rotating filter if you want shallow depth of field for an outdoor shot with the f/1.8 50 mm lens. This means you can prevent the highlights from blowing out and still get a shallow depth of field.

Rode VideoMic Pro (use for gathering ambient audio): ~$220

Useful for on-camera ambient sound and backup if your external recorder fails (always have a backup). Be sure to get the furry "dead cat" windmuff for another $39 to help prevent wind noise when shooting outdoors.

Tascam DR-40: ~$200

This is an inexpensive version of the Tascam DR-100. For the price, it delivers high quality audio. Put it in the Petrol pouch and hook it on your belt, and you'll be able to handhold a shotgun mic with a pistol grip. Eats up the batteries quickly in phantom power mode.

Petrol PS615 Deca Audio Pouch: ~$50

Hook this on your belt and you'll be able to go into the field holding a shotgun mic with a pistol grip (or mount a shotgun mic on the camera's hot shoe with a shockmount) and you'll be able to get the audio you need.

Rode NTG-2 shotgun mic: ~$270

Rycote Pistol Grip: ~$120

Transcend 32GB SDHC class 10 memory card: ~$45

A 32GB card will give you about 90 minutes of recording time. Be sure to get a Class 10 card (no less than 6), otherwise the camera will choke on all the video data and stop recording.

A quality pistol grip designed to absorb sound from your hand as you mount a shotgun mic. Good for documentary work. Use a boompole when shooting fiction dialog.

A solid shotgun microphone that can be powered with an AA battery, so you can save battery power on the external recorder (Tascam DR-40).

Aluratek SDHC card reader: ~$10

LowePro DSLR video pack 250AW: ~$120

Impact 5-in-1 Reflector 32″: ~$39

A tried and true card reader.

An easy way to pack your gear and go into the field. It'll hold the DSLR, a couple of lenses, audio recorder, a laptop, among other equipment.

It's good to have a reflector and diffuser on hand so you can control where light falls on your subject in close-up and medium shots (not useful for wide shots).

G-Technology G-Drive 750GB 7200 rpm FireWire 800 ~$150

A great portable hard drive with FireWire 800 and USB cables. Useful for dumping footage in the field (since it's powered by the computer).

Manfrotto 561BHDV monopod with mini legs: ~$250

If you need stability and movement, portability and run-and-gun capability, then this monopod will become one of the best tools you can get for your camera. It allows for stable shots as well as slight push-in and pull-out shots due to its ball joint on the legs. A powerful tool used often by Patrick Moreau of Stillmotion.

Canon 60D with 18–135 mm f3.5–5.6 lens: ~$1200

If you prefer the more robust 60D, then subtract the Rebel from this list and go with this solid camera. It's sturdier and has such features as manual control of audio, a flip-out LCD screen, rear dial for adjusting the aperture (the Rebel requires you to press a thumb button and index finger dial at the same time), and you can dial in manual color temperature. Great with Magic Lantern, too.

VIDEO JOURNALISM/DOCUMENTARY PACKAGE (CANON 5D MARK II)

This package is for professionals with a fairly large gear budget. A video journalist or documentary filmmaker can easily use a 60D or even a Rebel and it'll still look better than a professional small sensor video camera. But I recommend the 5D Mark II, since it's the gear of choice for many photojournalists—due to its full frame sensor (equivalent to 70 mm cinema film). I don't recommend the Canon 7D, because it can't use Magic Lantern.

Canon 5D Mark II with 24–105 mm f/4L lens: ~$2900 (~$2200 body)

Canon 50 mm f/1.8: ~$120

Light Craft Neutral Density Fader Filter (77 mm for the 24–105 mm f/4 lens): ~$130; get the 52 mm thread size for the 50 mm lens.

The one that started the DSLR cinema revolution due to its full frame sensor. Very few cameras—even ones costing thousands more—have a hard time achieving the unique look of the 5D. It's been replaced by the Mark III, but at an additional $1300, you're probably better off getting extra lenses, but if you can afford it, see the Mark III below. The kit lens here (costing over $1100 if buying separately) is a great go-to lens for video journalists, who need to get close but still have an ability to go wide, when needed. The L-series lens is Canon's top of the line lens.

The best buy Canon has—this is a "fast" lens, meaning the aperture opens to f/1.8, so you can get a shallow depth of field and shoot in low light situations. This should be your go-to lens for most of your shooting situations. Use the kit lens as a wide angle lens (18–25 mm).

An ND fader is essential when you're shooting outdoors. You can get up to eight stops from this rotating filter if you want shallow depth of field for an outdoor shot with the f/1.8 50 mm lens. This means you can prevent the highlights from blowing out and still get a shallow depth of field.

Rode VideoMic Pro (use for gathering ambient audio): ~$220

Tascam DR-40: ~$200

Petrol PS615 Deca Audio Pouch: ~$50

Useful for on-camera ambient sound and backup if your external recorder fails (always have a backup). Not good when shooting outdoors on a windy day, but it works well under most conditions.

This is an inexpensive version of the Tascam DR-100. For the price, it delivers high quality audio. Put it in the Petrol pouch and hook it on your belt, and you'll be able to handhold a shotgun mic with a pistol grip. Eats up the batteries quickly in phantom power mode.

Hook this on your belt and you'll be able to go into the field holding a shotgun mic with a pistol grip (or mount a shotgun mic on the camera's shot shoe with a shockmount) and you'll be able to get the audio you need.

Rode NTG-2 shotgun mic: ~$270

A solid shotgun microphone that can be powered with a AA battery, so you can save battery power on the external recorder (Tascam DR-40).

Rycote Pistol Grip: ~$120

A quality pistol grip designed to absorb sound from your hand as you mount a shotgun mic. Good for documentary work. Use a boompole when shooting fiction dialog.

Transcend 32GB compact flash 400x memory card: ~$58

A 32GB card will give you about 90 minutes of recording time. There are more expensive cards out there, but I've never had an issue with the 400 speed Transcend card.

Transcend USB 3 card reader: ~$16

Haven't used it, but with the USB 3 capabilities, it'll be useful for fast transfers.

LowePro DSLR video pack 250AW: ~$120

An easy way to pack your gear and go into the field. It'll hold the DSLR, a couple of lenses, audio recorder, a laptop, among other equipment.

Impact 5-in-1 Reflector 32″: ~$39

It's good to have a reflector and diffuser on hand so you can control where light falls on your subject in close-up and medium shots (not useful for wide shots).

G-Technology G-Drive 750GB 7200 rpm FireWire 800 ~$150

A great portable hard drive with FireWire 800 and USB cables. Useful for dumping footage in the field (since it's powered by the computer).

Manfrotto monopod 561BHDV with mini legs: ~$250

If you need stability and movement, portability and run-and-gun capability, then this monopod will become one of the best tools you can get for your camera. It allows for stable shots as well as slight push-in and pull-out shots due to its ball joint on the legs. A powerful tool used often by Patrick Moreau of Stillmotion.

Sennheiser EW112 wireless lav system (use for interviews): ~$600

This is one of the best wireless microphone systems on the market. For documentary and video journalism work, its one of the best pieces of gear you'll get for your audio.

Zacuto Z-Finder: ~$375

When shooting outdoors, this is the best gear you'll have in order to see the LCD screen. It also magnifies the screen (2.5X or 3X depending on the model you get). In addition, when using the monopod, it provides an extra point of contact on your body (the eye), giving a bit more stability to your shots.

Manfrotto 190CX3 carbon fiber tripod legs: ~$250 and 701HDV fluid head: ~$140

This package will allow you to travel light (carbon fiber sticks) and utilize a solid fluid head.

Kessler Crane Pocket Dolly Traveler: ~$630

A must for tracking dolly shots. Face the camera out for a tracking shot. Face the camera in for push in and push out shots. You may want to get a small head to place on the pocket dolly, so the camera can clear the end for push in and pull out shots, lifting the camera above the end piece, otherwise it may get into the shot.

INDEPENDENT CINEMA PACKAGE (CANON 5D MARK III):

For those needing an inexpensive professional camera for independent film projects.

Canon 5D Mark III body only: ~$3500

The upgrade to the classic 5D Mark II, The Mark III does much better in low light and using a different compression codec. This is the crème of the crop for DSLRs in this price point. In addition, it includes a headphone jack and audio meters. With it's full frame sensor, you cannot go wrong with this choice.

Canon L-Series lenses: 35 mm f/1.4 L ~$1400 50 mm f/1.2 L ~$1500 100 mm f/2.8 L ~$1000

Light Craft Neutral Density Fader Filter (price varies based on thread size of lens).

An ND fader is essential when you're shooting outdoors. You can get up to eight stops from this rotating filter if you want shallow depth of field for an outdoor shot. This means you can prevent the highlights from blowing out and still get a shallow depth of field.

Shane Hurlbut shot *The Last Three Minutes* using L-series lenses, the top of the line for Canon DSLRs (unless you use their cinema series lenses). When shooting cinema, prime lenses is key and this set of lenses for about $4,000 will do the trick for most situations. They're all fast lenses and so they'll deliver good rendition in low light as well as providing a shallow depth of field when needed.

If this is too much, check out KEHphoto.com and purchase a set of used Zeiss Contax lenses with a Fotodiox adapter. A set of 35 mm, 50 mm, 100 mm costs about $1200 and delivers the Zeiss quality glass.

Sound Devices MixPre-D: $750

The MixPre-D is an essential tool for getting clean audio in the field. Hook up a digital audio recorder, such as the Tascam DR-100, and you'll be able to achieve unparalleled sound quality with its quality microphone preamps and unclippable audio feature. In addition, it includes an output to a DSLR, so you can take the audio coming through this device and have it record to your camera.

Tascam DR-100mkii: ~$330

The upgrade to Tascam's DR-100. Aluminum housing with two XLR and 1/8" TRS input and output. Put it in the Petrol pouch and hook it on your belt, and you'll be able to handhold a shotgun mic with a pistol grip or boompole. Get the battery extender for extra field life (~$25).

Petrol PS615 Deca Audio Pouch: ~$50

Hook this on your belt and you'll be able to go into the field holding a shotgun mic with a pistol grip (or mount a shotgun mic on the camera's shot shoe with a shockmount) and you'll be able to get the audio you need.

Sennheiser ME62/K6 omnidirectional microphone and power capsule: ~$450 ME66 shotgun mic capsule: ~$210

For under $700, this is a rock solid microphone setup. Includes the omni dialogue microphone for indoor scenes, and also get the additional shotgun capsule for outdoor scenes.

Rycote Pistol Grip: ~$120

A quality pistol grip designed to absorb sound from your hand as you mount a shotgun mic. Good for documentary work. Use a boompole when shooting fiction dialog.

Transcend 32GB compact flash 400x memory card: ~$58

A 32GB card will give you about 90 minutes of recording time. There are more expensive cards out there, but I've never had an issue with the 400 speed Transcend card.

Transcend USB 3 card reader: ~$16

Haven't used it, but with the USB 3 capabilities, it'll be useful for fast transfers.

LowePro DSLR video pack 250AW: ~$120

An easy way to pack your gear and go into the field. It'll hold the DSLR, a couple of lenses, audio recorder, a laptop, among other equipment.

Impact 5-in-1 Reflector 32″: ~$39

It's good to have a reflector and diffuser on hand so you can control where light falls on your subject in close-up and medium shots (not useful for wide shots).

G-Technology G-Drive 750GB 7200 rpm FireWire 800 ~$150

A great portable hard drive with FireWire 800 and USB cables. Useful for dumping footage in the field (since it's powered by the computer).

Manfrotto monopod 561BHDV with mini legs: ~$250

If you need stability and movement, portability and run-and-gun capability, then this monopod will become one of the best tools you can get for your camera. It allows for stable shots as well as slight push-in and pull-out shots due to its ball joint on the legs. A powerful tool used often by Patrick Moreau of Stillmotion.

Sennheiser EW112 wireless lav system (use for interviews): ~$600

This is one of the best wireless microphone systems on the market. For documentary and video journalism work, its one of the best pieces of gear you'll get for your audio.

Zacuto Z-Finder with EVF: ~$950

When shooting outdoors, this is the best gear you'll have in order to see the LCD screen. It also magnifies the screen (2.5X or 3X depending on the model you get). The external monitor (EVF) is another necessary piece of gear for helping to view footage. The viewfinder flips up so you can view the screen directly. If you want to use the Z-Finder separately, then you'll need to get a gorilla plate to attach it to the camera.

Manfrotto190CX3 carbon fiber tripod legs: ~$250 and 701HDV fluid head: ~$140

This package will allow you to travel light (carbon fiber sticks) and utilize a solid fluid head.

Kessler Crane Pocket Dolly Traveler: ~$630

A must for tracking dolly shots. Face the camera out for a tracking shot. Face the camera in for push in and push out shots. You may want to get a small head to place the camera, so you can clear the end of the pocket dolly for push in and pull out shots, lifting the camera above the end piece, otherwise it may get into the shot.

GEAR IN THE FIELD

This next section will cover the types of gear you might need in particular situations. Different types of shots require a variety of equipment, but this section will show the type of gear that worked for these projects.

Marketing Commercial/Promo Projects

For promotional videos I've completed for Northern Arizona University's marketing department, my student team and I went with a two camera setup (two Canon 5D Mark II's allowed for two angles to be shot at once saving setup times) along with a Kessler Crane Pocket Dolly Traveler attached to a tripod, and the Manfrotto monopod with the ball joint legs. We also used Canon's 50mm f/1.8 lens, and 85mm f/1.8 lens, a Zeiss Contax 50mm f/1.4 lens, and 35mm f/2.8 lens. We shot with a neutral picture style. The project was shot in two hours.

Recommended gear:
Camera: Two 5D Mark II
Audio: Zoom H4n with Rode NTG-1 (synced with Final Cut Pro); Magic Lantern on one of the Mark II's connected to the Sennheiser ME62/K6 dialogue mic; dedicated sound person monitoring audio.
Support: Tripod for Kessler Crane Pocket Dolly Traveler, Manfrotto monopod with fluid head and ball joint leg support for quick setup of shots.

FIGURE 15.33
A still from a marketing video for Northern Arizona University by Javeon Butler, Kurt Lancaster, and Jenna Lyter. In this particular shot, a Canon 5D Mark II was attached to the Kessler Crane Pocket Dolly traveler for a tracking shot moving screen left. All lighting natural with neutral picture style.
(Image courtesy of NAU Marketing.)

Video Journalism and Documentaries

For documentaries and video journalism, traveling light and being unobtrusive is essential. Therefore, whether you choose to shoot with a 5D, 60D, or a Rebel, the key element is being light—therefore using Magic Lantern with a good microphone will provide the smallest footprint and portability available. With Magic Lantern you can monitor audio with headphones, see and adjust levels, and use focus peaking so you can adjust focus quickly. In my *Occupy Wall Street* video, I used a 5D Mark II, Magic Lantern, and the Sennheiser ME62/K6 setup attached to a shockmount on-camera (with a XLR to minijack step down cable). I did not have the Manfrotto monopod with me, so I shot the project handheld, keeping the camera about two feet from the subject so they were close enough to the microphone to get good levels (see Figure 15.34).

Recommended gear:
Camera: 5D Mark II (or any other DSLR based on budget)
Audio: Magic Lantern with a Sennheiser ME62/K6 or ME66 shotgun mic; headphones and adapter to monitor audio. If the project is crucial, always have a backup, so using a Tascam DR-40 and belt pouch with a wireless lav or shotgun microphone (and pistol grip) is a good idea, but if you're running and gunning for your shots, it can be done with just Magic Lantern.
Support: Manfrotto monopod with fluid head and ball joint leg support for quick setup of shots. Take advantage of the ball joint mini-legs to do some push-in and pull out shots, as well as small tracking type shots. Use movement, as long as you keep the movement slow and micro.

FIGURE 15.34
A subject holding up a sign out of frame discusses his reasons as to why he's occupying Wall Street in New York City. A Canon 5D Mark II is about two feet from him in order to record a strong audio signal, along with the Zeiss Contax 50 mm f/1.4 and a Light Craft ND Fader to help maintain a shallow depth of field.
(Image courtesy of Kurt Lancaster.)

Fiction Projects

Any large sensor camera will deliver a decent cinematic image if lit properly. If you want the unique look and the strongest look for the price point, the Canon 5D Mark II or III will be one of the best tools you can invest in when shooting fiction projects on a micro budget. Shane Hurlbut, ASC, chose the 5D Mark II for *The Last 3 Minutes*, as well as for the action sequences in the feature, *Act of Valor* (2012).

FIGURE 15.35
Still from *The Last 3 Minutes*. Canon 85 mm L with f-stop at 3.5; color temp: 2800 degrees K; ISO 320.
(©2010 Hurlbut Visuals. Used with permission.)

Recommended gear:

Camera: 5D Mark II or III

Audio: Tascam DR-100mkii with Sennheiser shotgun and dialogue mic attached to Sound Devices MixPre-D with a line out attached to the camera; dedicated sound person monitoring audio.

Support: Tripod for Kessler Crane Pocket Dolly Traveler, Manfrotto mono-pod with fluid head and ball joint leg support for quick setup of shots and to allow for a little bit of the handheld look.

In the end, the gear you choose to buy or rent isn't nearly as important as the story you want to tell with this gear. Some gear will help with your storytelling needs better than others. Use the right tool for the job, but don't get caught up with the latest and greatest—there are many people out there with gear but few who know how to tell a good story. If you tell a great story, a $600 Rebel T2i will be better than a 5D Mark III, if the person using the 5D has a bad or poorly executed story.

CHAPTER 16

Conclusion

From Film to Low Budget Large Sensor Cinema

Large sensor cinema snuck up on us all. My first short movies were shot on the Canon L2 Hi8 mm video camera. When I was doing doctoral work at NYU's Tisch School of the Arts in the mid- to late 1990s, I enrolled in the NYU boot camp one summer, and we shot on 16 mm black and white film with no sync sound—Arriflexes that had three fixed lenses that you could rotate into position. After that, I purchased the first generation Panasonic DVX100 24p miniDV camera and shot two fiction shorts and several documentary projects. When I consulted with reporters in Spring 2008 at *The Christian Science Monitor*, our budget allowed only for consumer HD cameras (a mix of Panasonic and JVC tapeless cameras), and they cost around $1,200. Before shifting to DSLRs, I shot my latest festival documentary on a Sony A1U HDV miniDV camera, a $2,200 camera, nearly the price of a Canon 5D Mark II body! And *none* of those cameras matched the image quality of the Canon Rebel T2i for $600!

I know digital video.

None of my footage from these cameras looked as good as the two-minute rolls of film I shot on that Arriflex at NYU. Not even close. The smooth, creamy shots were unlike anything I've ever seen on video. The sharpness of the glass was incomparable. But I lived with shooting on video because it was affordable, and artistic sensibility—that cinematic feel I had previously seen in 16 mm film—was compromised due to budget.

Until now.

Once I picked up the Canon 5D Mark II, there was no going back. The footage coming out of the camera—if not the same as those shorts I shot with an Arriflex—was the best thing I've seen since then. It was cinematic. I, like Philip Bloom, dismissed the camera at first because of the lack of controlling aperture.

But in the fall of 2009, I started watching videos on Vimeo by DSLR shooters. The stuff looked good. I wanted one. I did more research and convinced my colleagues at Northern Arizona University's School of Communication to get one—the Panasonic GH1 (the only other serious contender at the time for around ~$1300). One of my students, Shannon Sassone, shot her short fiction project with it in my intro video production class. She was amazed at the quality of the image. And I became convinced that DSLRs could be used in the classroom.

Later, I decided to write a book proposal that would address the cinematic needs of these student shooters, as well as for independent filmmakers and video journalists who saw the potential of these cameras but didn't know where all the resources were to make effective use of DSLRs as cinema cameras. I wanted to bring together some of the best thinkers and practitioners practicing this form of cinema—from Philip Bloom, who pioneered the sharing of information about DSLRs on his blog; to Rii Schroer, who is primarily a photo journalist who wanted to make movies with this camera; to Shane Hurlbut, ASC, who had access to nearly any camera in the world but wants to shoot films with the Canon 5D Mark II.

It's one thing to ignore shooters who get excited about putting up test shots online. It's another thing to look at Philip Bloom's *San Francisco People, Cherry Blossom Girl*, or *Skywalker Ranch*, or even his *Salton Sea Beach* (shot on a Canon Rebel T2i), and not realize that there's something going on here—something different from the kinds of video we've seen over the past 15 to 20 years.

Then Philip Bloom announced 10 million views on his website as of June 1, 2010, and we're not talking about a celebrity site, but a working man's view of HDSLR cinema and how he's doing it (see <http://philipbloom.net/>). Other blogs sprouted up (which I highly recommend checking out): Shane Hurlbut: Hurlbut Visuals (<http://www.hurlbutvisuals.com>), Jared Abrams: Wide Open Camera (<http://wideopencamera.com/>), PlanetMitch's blog: <http://blog.planet5d.com/>, Vincent Laforet: <http://blog.vincentlaforet.com/>, and Dan Chung's DSLR News Shooter (<http://www.dslrnewsshooter.com/>). All of these sites reveal a democratization of the cinema look, an inside peak at how to do good work.

And when Lucasfilm jumped on board, the tremor became an earthquake. As Shane Hurlbut, ASC, is fond of saying, Canon knocked over the applecart, burned it up, and decided to make applesauce. How cinema and television are being done is starting to change. Hollywood has embraced the new aesthetic offered by these cameras.

The season finale of *House MD* (2010) was shot on a Canon 5D Mark II. "We started testing on episode 19, which I was directing," Greg Yaitanes says in an interview with Philip Bloom.[1] "We would run the 5D next to our film cameras just to see how the 5D was reacting to our lighting, what our sets looked

---

[1] Bloom, P. Greg Yaitanes 'House' Interview transcription. *Transcription by Oli Lewington.*, <http://philipbloom.net/other-stuff/case-studies/greg-yaitanes-house-interview-transcription/, accessed July 2010>.

like, how actors looked, anything we needed to be aware of. And we were very happy with these tests." Everyone was surprised by how good the image looked. Everyone on the production and postproduction team agreed—including those handling special effects; even the studio executives said it was good enough for broadcast, Yaitanes explains.

In the end, Yaitanes said it looked "gorgeous … It allowed us to tell a story that we never told before." The HDSLR camera changed how the story was told. There was no examination of test charts. There was what they saw on-screen, and there was the emotion of the story.

> I'm not trying to create a film aesthetic. I'm trying to create its own aesthetic. I want it to be its own look, its own style.

Yaitanes embraced the aesthetics of the camera. And despite banding issues—which does tend to occur when the camera overheats—he and his team didn't let that bother them. "We struggled a bit with banding … That was every once in a while and frankly it's part of a look," Yaitanes says to Bloom. "You can try and fight these things away and wish they weren't there, but then you're just comparing that aesthetic to something else. I'm not trying to create a film aesthetic. I'm trying to create its own aesthetic. I want it to be its own look, its own style. If there's some banding … some motion blur, then for me, who cares? I feel like the story trumps all. These are, again, tools. These are, again, things that give you a look."[2]

If anything, I hope this book shows how you can develop that cinematic look—if not the look of film, then something else that looks as cool. When Yaitanes went to film school, there was only film. But he wished that it "was not the only medium in which people would look at [motion pictures]. Back then no one would take something you shot on video seriously in terms of a narrative." Conventional video just didn't have an alternative look that felt aesthetically strong.

But that has now all changed. The DSLR cinema movement embraced a new kind of digital video aesthetic, a cinema aesthetic made possible by an HD codec combined with a large sensor, small form factor, and interchangeable lenses. Now we have many choices of large sensor cameras. Some of these are DSLRs, some are video cameras with Super S35 mm or micro 4/3 sensors—all with interchangeable lenses and all manufactured because of the DSLR cinema movement (and perhaps with a bit of influence from RED cameras). But what began as a 30 fps video on a stills camera (Canon 5D Mark II) designed for print journalists needing the convenience of shooting "a little bit of video" to supplement their in-the-field assignments for newspaper websites has now become a tool for cinema.

---

[2] Bloom, P. (April 19, 2010). In-depth interview with Greg Yaitanes, Executive Producer and Director of 'House' Season Finale shot on Canon 5DmkII, http://philipbloom.net/2010/04/19/in-depth-interview-with-executive-producer-and-director-of-house-season-finale-shot-on-canon-5dmkii/, accessed April 20, 2010.

With the release of 4 K cameras and professional large sensor cameras over $10,000, many professionals will likely steer away from DSLRs, but many independent filmmakers, students, video journalists, and documentarians will all continue to use DSLRs because the price is right and the cinematic image is comparable to the higher-end pro cinema cameras costing thousands more.

At the same time as these higher priced cameras become predominant, the next cinematic evolution will be what many of us have asked for in the original RED Scarlet (announced in spring 2008) and later in DSLRs (fall 2008)—shooting RAW on a budget (under $3,500). This next year is when it's happening. Joe Rubinstein and Elle Schneider created the Digital Bolex camera (<http://www.digitalbolex.com/>), announced at the SXSW film festival in Austin, Texas in March 2012—the Kickstarter campaign hoped to raise $100,000 to get the first 100 production models built. Within a day or two of the announcement – with a nudge from Philip Bloom – they received over $260,000! This indicates a strong desire on the part of independent filmmakers to shoot RAW. Schneider's short film, *One Small Step* (2012) was shot on an early preproduction model and premiered at Cannes Film Festival (Short Film Corner) in 2012 (see Figure 16.1).

FIGURE 16.1
A still from Elle Schneider's *One Small Step*, a short film shot on an early pre-production model of the Digital Bolex D16, a 16 mm camera that shoots in RAW.
(Image courtesy of Digital Bolex, trailer at < http://www.digitalbolex.com/videos/trailer-one-small-step/ >.)

The camera is based on the original 16 mm Bolex (made in Switzerland) so popular in the 1960s and 1970s. In addition, they're using a CCD sensor designed by Kodak, a similar chip Rubinstein discovered in the Swedish company's sleek Ikonoskop 16 mm camera. The telling sign of the oncoming RAW revolution occurred when Philip Bloom tweeted a picture of himself holding an Iknoskop and stating that his "favorite image from a camera at the show? Probably the ikonoskop. Lovely! Hope to shoot with it soon!"

(<https://twitter.com/#!/ikonoskop>). The video I saw on monitors at the Ikonoskop booth at NAB certainly revealed a strong film aesthetic. A promotional video directed by Thomas Gangalter, for clothing design company, Co was shot on an Ikonoskop (see Figure 16.2).

FIGURE 16.2
A still from Thomas Bangalter's poetic promotional for the clothing company, Co. Take note of a wide range of latitude in the desert landscape, with exposure on the face as well as on a blue sky and detail in white clouds.
(video at: http://co-collections.com/ss12.php)

It reveals a wide range of latitude in a desert landscape, with exposure on the face as well as on a blue sky and detail in white clouds. But for over $9,000 it's still in the same price range of the higher end cinema cameras. Rubinstein and Schneider, however, want a simple camera priced at the right price. They plan to release their digital Bolex in fall of 2012, with a wider market in 2013 for under $3500.

Just a month or so after the South-by announcement, Black Magic Design—the maker of quality production and postproduction hardware and software (such as DaVinci Resolve)—announced their own cinema camera that shoots 2.5 K RAW for under $3,000. The promise of RAW includes a wide latitude of exposure ranging from 12 to 14 stops—the same as film (see Figure 16.3 for RAW production still comparison).

And more recently, Weisscam announced their own version of a RAW camera, the T-CAM (<http://www.weisscam.com/products/t-cam/features_t1.html>).

The future will be about the film look, rather than being limited by the amount of exposure needed. The gloves are being thrown down and new technologies are coming out that make filmmaking cheaper and cheaper.

> The DSLR cinema movement embraces a new kind of digital video aesthetic, a DSLR cinema aesthetic made possible by an HD codec combined with a large sensor, small form factor, and interchangeable lenses.

Common DSLR Shot   RAW Wide Dynamic Range   Final Color Graded Shot

FIGURE 16.3

Black Magic Design's promotional material includes a series of stills comparing the lower range of exposure latitude on a DSLR to their RAW camera. Take note of the gradual shadow falloff in the color graded shot, as well as the details found in the highlights in the background in contrast to the blown-out highlights and sharper falloff of shadows in the DSLR shot. This is what reveals the power of RAW when utilized for a cinematic look.

(Image courtesy of BlackMagic Design <http://www.blackmagic-design.com/products/ blackmagiccinemacamera/>).

Because of the cheaper costs, filmmaking is no longer just for the Hollywood elite, but for you and me, the independent filmmakers, as well as event video shooters, students, video journalists, documentary filmmakers—the do-it-yourselfers who have been desiring cinematic quality on an affordable camera but had to simply make do with miniDV and prosumer HD cameras that just didn't cut it due to their fixed lenses and small sensors.

We can now gear up for a cinema-type project for as low as $2,000 or less and not worry that our vision's being compromised. There is no excuse to shoot crappy-looking movies. You can still shoot bad images with these cameras, but that'll be due to a lack of skill, and not the camera.

I hope this book helps you make the best-looking movie on the lowest possible budget.

It can be done. And you can do it.

Image Resolution

Resolution is measured in lines and pixels—the microdots on a computer's LCD screen, which you can see with a magnifying glass, or when you accidentally spit on the screen and notice little red, blue, and green dots in each pixel. Each of these three colors changes value, shaping the hues you see on-screen. The more pixels you have on-screen, the more detail you can see. These pixels are arranged in lines. Lines are measured top to bottom, whereas pixels are measured along the lines, left to right. As a point of comparison, the miniDV format contains about 480 lines of resolution with about 720 pixels per line, whereas 1080 HD video contains 1,080 lines with 1,920 pixels per line. In addition, the P in 1080 P indicates a progressive scan (where the image is presented fully), as opposed to a 1080i (which indicates alternating interlaced scan lines used in broadcast television).

In film, 35 mm provides about six times the resolution of HD video in its original negative (6,000 lines of resolution), whereas a projection print has about 2,000 (for 2 K projectors). The figure varies; one source places film resolution at 3,112 lines with 4,096 pixels per line. So 1080 × 1920 high-definition video provides just over 2 million pixels of resolution, whereas film contains 12 million pixels of resolution!

The exposure index (the optimum ISO setting to expose the image) for miniDV is about 200, whereas HD is around 300. Film contains an exposure index of 800.

Filmmakers interested in digital film find the RED Scarlet and Epic cameras fascinating because their resolution and exposure index approaches the quality of film. The resolution of the 3 K Scarlet contains 3072 × 1728 pixels (that's 5.3 million pixels, over twice that of standard HD).

It must also be mentioned that one of the main debates circulating around DSLRs are some manufacturers' slow CMOS chips (requiring "line skipping" in the sensor's signal processing, resulting in line bending during camera pans). The RED company, which created one of the first digital cinema cameras, the RED, followed by the new Epic and Scarlet models, did tests comparing its Mysterium-X sensor to the Canon 7D and Sony's F35 (see Figure A1.1).

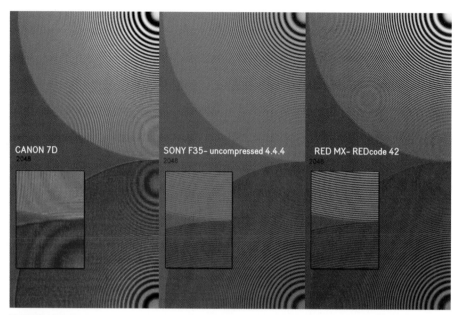

FIGURE A1.1
As can be seen, the zone test reveals high amounts of pixilation in the Canon, with less in the Sony F35, while the RED provides nearly a flawless image. Debate went back and forth on Reduser.net, some stating that it's an unfair test and that professional work is being shot with Canon 5Ds and 7Ds, for example. RED owner Jim Jannard weighed in by stating that he's just putting facts out there and wants camera users to decide: "I guess the proliferation of misinformation about what the DSLRs can and can't do triggered a bit of frustration. I just believe that 'good enough' isn't a professional mindset." He, among others, feel that professionals should be concerned with image resolution.
(*<http://reduser.net/forum/showthread.php?t541220&page53>, accessed February 25, 2010*)

Barry Green, testing the image quality of several DSLRs by recording resolution charts (see Figure A1.2), argues on DVXuser.com that many DSLRs are cheating their resolution:

> [T]he [Panasonic] GH1, the [Canon] 7D, and the 5D Mark II all look like they're rendering incredibly sharp, highly detailed images, but they're not. In reality, according to the resolution charts, they're rendering images that fall somewhere around a standard-definition camera, and maybe a 720P camera. Any additional "sharpness" you see in the image is fake—it's aliasing, it's smoke and mirrors, it's image contamination.
>
> Rarely will you see such obvious image contamination as on a resolution chart. In a real-world image, it may be much harder to spot what's "real" and what's aliased "fake" detail. To *an untrained eye, a heavily aliased image might even look good.* Before you had the chart explained to you, which image looked

"sharper"—the one with the blur, or the one with the vertical lines? Granted, neither of them is a perfect representation of what they're supposed to look like, but which of these images looks more like an accurate representation of the third chart?

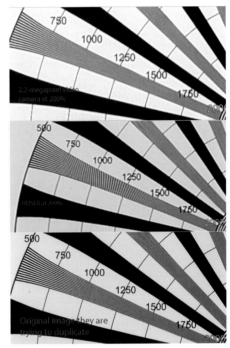

FIGURE A1.2
Barry Green's resolution chart comparing the resolution of a video camera to a DSLR. The third image reveals the original chart.

Similar to the arguments found on Reduser.net, users on Prolost.com argued back and forth about the merits of shooting HD with DSLRs. Some claimed (correctly) that they're first and foremost stills cameras with video added as an afterthought.

Ted Schilowitz, the number two person at RED, said in a personal interview that RED is concerned about resolution because it wants to create digital film, a form that's designed to replace analog film. "Our world is not about making sacrifices, our world is giving people the tools to make really, really good pictures. So, the Scarlet, with a 3 K sensor in it, the body is under three thousand bucks. A set of prime lenses, they're super fast, are under five thousand for the whole set. And the Scarlet is a real RED camera right? It's not an SLR that is cheating and doing video scaling to get your 1080 P image. This is doing 3 K RED code raw, just like its bigger brother the RED One." They're setting themselves up for the 4 K projection world of future cinema.

However, despite resolution tests, the most important point to make out of this argument is not the resolution of the camera or whether or not it's aliasing, but what the image feels like to the audience. And because the Scarlet hasn't been released at the time writing was completed for this book in early summer 2010, it's really a moot argument. Cameras are tools for storytelling. Stephen van Vuuren, who created the film *Outside In* (a movie on Saturn composed of still imaging techniques), noted on the Prolost.com site how he was concerned about the resolution tests, and debated whether or not to get a Canon 7D. However, after seeing Vincent Laforet's *Nocturne*,

I pulled the trigger. I absolutely knew about the [resolution-aliasing] issues and found it easy to figure out when the problem occurs (see my test clip [http://vimeo.com/sv2studios]). Shoot fine horizontal detail stopped way down with high shutter speed handheld—yowza.

However, after hours of shooting with my 7D, I've yet to see this again. Occasionally I see some mild aliasing.

But here's the most important thing to me—non-technical and technical people I've worked for years watching my Canon XL-1, DVX100a, HV30 and other footage respond "Wow" upon seeing 7D on a native 25" 1080P monitor.

I personally have not been this excited in a camera since I bought [a] top-of-the-line Chinon Super 8 camera in 1988. I love it—the camera excites me. People who watch the footage go "wow." It cost $1,900 with a lens, ready to shoot 24p 1080p images with Super 35 mm DOF with lovely low light and dynamic range. Yeah, it has a few technical issues. But who cares. I don't, nor do the people watching.

Van Vuuren, like many DSLR shooters, really doesn't care that much about resolution tests, and the minutia of such geek details are really lost on them because they understand that the story comes first and if the weaknesses can be overcome, then good-quality cinema projects can be created. Philip Bloom and Shane Hurlbut, ASC, use Canon DSLRs to make their movies despite such limitations because, for them, like van Vuuren, clients are wooed over by the wow factor of the image. They feel the image *is* good enough for professional use—even George Lucas.

When Philip Bloom was invited to Skywalker Ranch to show off the capabilities of DSLR cameras, he shot around the ranch using a Canon 5D and 7D, and then screened the results on a 40-foot screen for Rick McCallum and George Lucas. They did not complain about the footage, but were impressed.[1] Lucasfilm used DSLRs in some of their work for *Red Tails*, a World War II film focused on an African American fighter squadron.

One of the reasons people like to shoot on HD DSLRs as compared to standard HD cameras is their ability to shoot in low light. Matt Buchanan, a reporter for Gizmodo.com, discusses how camera companies marketed the quality of their image by pixel count but have since changed: "However it began, 'amazing low-light performance' is now a standard bullet point for any camera that costs more than $300 (even if it's not true)."[2] In either case, pixel resolution in DSLR cameras is only for still-image mode; the pixel count in 1080P is the same, no matter the high megapixel count advertised, because when cinema makers shoot in video mode, it'll be 1920×1080 (for 1080 resolution). The ISO exposure capabilities for low-light sensitivity and low signal-to-noise ratio are advantages with DSLR cameras.

---

[1] Bloom, P. The tale of Lucasfilm, Skywalker Ranch, Star Wars and Cnon DSLRs on a 40 foot screen! <http://philipbloom.net/2009/12/12/skywalker/?, accessed February, 25.2010.

[2] Giz Explains: Why ISO Is the New Megapixel. <http://gizmodo.com/5470334/giz-explains-why-iso-is-the-new-megapixel>, accessed March 2010.

It comes down to this: someone shooting on a RED Scarlet, for example, can shoot a project that doesn't look that good, whereas someone shooting on a standard HD camera can get a cinema look if he knows what he's doing. The resolution doesn't create a cinematic look; the cinematographer's eye does that. That's why many cinematographers look at the lighting in the world around them and study master painters because they know how to use light and color to set the mood of the image. When shaping the mood with light and shadow, the cinematographer crafts an illusion of beauty on-screen, which results in what we call the "film look." The film look, in other words, is subjective. It's what we see in cinema, shot by cinematographers who are helping to shape the mood of the story by using light and shadow, lenses, filters, and so on to be able to craft the cinematic mood of a scene.

ISO Tests for the Canon 5D Mark II and 7D

Shane Hurlbut, ASC, and his team conducted a comparison ISO test between the Canon 5D Mark II, 7D, and the 1D, showing how the 1D manufactured more noise than the 7D or the 5D (see Figure A2.1).

Canon's 1D revealed high levels of noise, far more than the 7D or 5D Mark II. The test confirms the native settings of ISO 160, 320, 640, and 1250. The Canon Rebel T2i has all of its settings native.

The more noise in the test shot for the ISO shows how the 7D matches up to the 5D Mark II (see Figure A2.2).

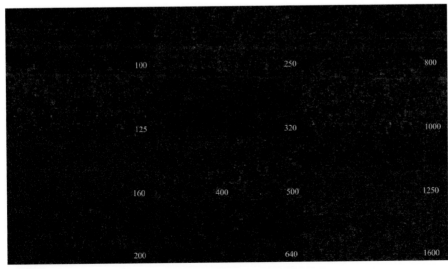

FIGURE A2.1
ISO test for the Canon 5D Mark II. Hurlbut Visuals newsletter, January 29, 2010.
(<http://www.hurlbutvisuals.com/newsletter_archive.php>, accessed March 26, 2010; <http://hurlbutvisuals.com/images/isotest/5D_ISO_Test.png>)

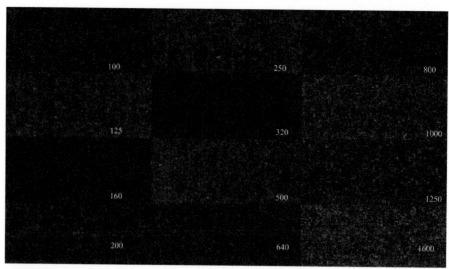

FIGURE A2.2
ISO test for the Canon 7D. Hurlbut Visuals newsletter, January 29, 2010.
(*<http://www.hurlbutvisuals.com/newsletter_archive.php>, accessed March 26, 2010; <http://hurlbutvisuals.com/images/isotest/7D_ISO_Test.png>*)

Exposure and Dynamic Range

Technically, video exposure works differently than film exposure. Aside from the obvious chemical properties of film that allow for the emulsion process, film has a smooth "characteristic curve," whereas video has a sharp curve, leading to sudden drop-offs on the curve and toe (see Figure A3.1). The characteristic curve is simply the amount of chemical density on the film activated based on the intensity of light. This density can be plotted on a graph as a relatively straight line with a curve on the top (shoulder) and bottom (toe). The slope of this curve is called the *gamma*, and it essentially determines the contrast of the scene. Changing the gamma curve changes the contrast value of the shot. You can alter the curves some in postproduction, but you can also manipulate it in-camera before shooting (see Chapter 4).

Film has about 8 to 10 zones of dynamic range or a 512:1 contrast ratio. Standard video has only a 25:1 contrast ratio. DSLR cameras, with their larger sensors, have a much greater latitude than standard HD video cameras. According to Shane Hurlbut, ASC, the Canon 5D Mark II contains the smoother film-like curve in the toe (see Chapter 3).

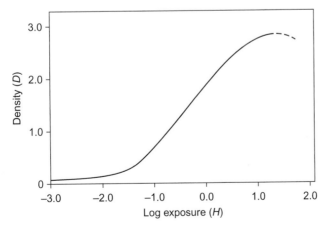

FIGURE A3.1
The characteristic curve of film presents a rounded toe and shoulder, indicating a smooth exposure latitude. Video typically lacks this quality, resulting in more sudden drop-offs in the shadows and clipped highlights.
(Image from <http://www.answers.com/topic/characteristic-curve-2>, accessed March 1, 2010.)

The ISO setting determines the dynamic range of the image (see Figure A3.2). The higher the ISO setting, the lower the contrast ratio of the dynamic range.

Notice that as you increase the ISO setting, the dynamic range rapidly falls off—with 11 when setting the ISO at around 100 and just about 7 at 6400 (see Figure A3.3).

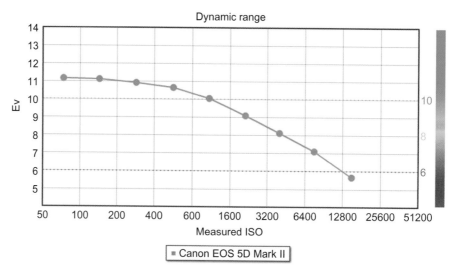

FIGURE A3.2
Dynamic range of the Canon 5D Mark II compared to the dynamic range of the Panasonic GH1 (below). (<*http://www.dxomark. com/index.php/eng/Image-Quality-Database/Canon/ EOS-5D-Mark-II>*).

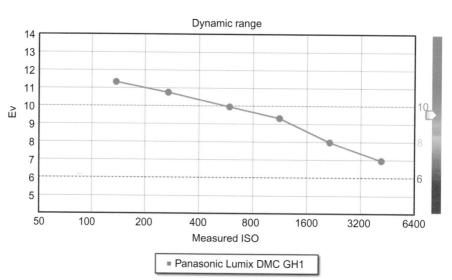

FIGURE A3.3
"Dynamic range or light sensitivity range of a sensor indicates the ratio of light exposure between the highest brightness a camera can capture (saturation) and the lowest brightness it can effectively capture (typically when noise becomes more important than signal, i.e., SNR<0dB). This range indicates the maximum contrast that can be effectively captured by the sensor. The larger the dynamic range, the better, as the sensor is able to capture higher-contrast scenes. Note that dynamic range is expressed on a logarithmic scale in EV (same as f-stop), thus an increase of 1 EV corresponds to a doubling of dynamic range."
(<*http://www.dxomark.com/index.php/eng/Image-Quality-Database/Canon/EOS-5D-Mark-I.>*)

Luminance and Chrominance Compression

The number 444 refers to the luminance (light) and chrominance (color) compression (brightness and color) (see Figure A4.1).

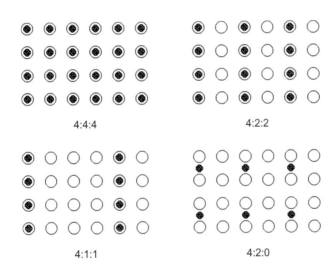

FIGURE A4.1

Chroma-luminance bandwidth illustration, where a 4:4:4 has no subsampling (each pixel contains the full luminance and chrominance value). In a 4:2:2 subsampling, half the pixels contain full luminance and chrominance value, while the remaining half contain luminance.

(http://lea.hamradio.si/~s51kq/V-BAS.HTM.)

Story Treatment to *The Last 3 Minutes* by Po Chan

(Each scene was accompanied by a photo capturing the feeling of each scene. The photos are not reproduced here for copyright reasons. —Kurt Lancaster)

THE LAST 3 MINUTES

The story of the last three minutes of William Turner's life and his beloved CRYSTAL, by Po Chan

William Turner

(Scene # 1)

William Turner, a weary 68-year-old office janitor who lives alone in a rusted trailer, with no family and friends. He is known to the employees as a quiet old man with few words. Never likes to interact with others. Keeps everything to himself.

One night William is working in the office alone as usual. Suddenly he feels a lightning pain in his chest. He drops to one knee, bead of sweat starts to run down his forehead. Fear in his eyes. As the pain intensifies, a crystal ball falls out from his pocket and rolls onto the floor. He desperately tries to reach the crystal, but he loses his balance and falls to the ground...

The Crystal

(Scene # A1)

He falls to the ground next to the crystal. His shaking hand struggles to reach for it, he slowly holds it up to his eye. He looks deep into it. He always loves to see the world around him through this crystal, but this time, he sees more than he expected. His whole life starts to flash back in front of him, in reverse, through this crystal.

Camera as William's POV looks deep inside the crystal, we see a woman's face suddenly appear ...

Transition to ...

Transition

We are using transition effects throughout the film, which are the reflection of his next memory that are layered over his previous memory.

From transition into ...

The memory of his wife leaving him

(Scene # 2)

Transition back in time when William was 35 years old. Everything after this point does not even register in his mind. His memory stopped after his wife, who is carrying his unborn child, walked out the door.

William's POV through the crystal. He sees his pregnant wife's face close to the crystal. She is crying. He pulls the crystal away and his wife walks off…

The memory of his wife leaving him

(Scene # 2 continues)

His wife walks to the bed and picks up a suitcase on the left side of frame. We see a bottle of whiskey come into the right side of frame.

William is drinking. His wife looks at him one last time; tears continue to fall. She walks out of the door. As she walks out, a dress drops on the floor. William picks it up.

Transition to ...

The memory of his wife and her dress

(Scene # 3)

Transition back in time when William was 30 years old…

William's POV sees his wife wearing the same dress. She seductively takes off the dress and crawls under the sheet with William…

Transition to ...

The memory of the good time with his wife on the beach

(Scene # 4)

Transition back in time when William was 30 years old…

William's POV sees his wife lying next to him on the beach. A hyperfocus view of the sea water and sand on his wife's beautiful skin, the water dropping down from her wet hair, her smile, her beautiful face, her lips. Setting sun flares behind her. She gets up and runs into the water.

William follows. Waves splash into the lens, cut to …

The memory of his best friend dying in his arms during the Vietnam War

(Scene # 5)

A bomb blast …back in time when William was 26 years old…

Dirt, grass, fire … William's POV as he crawls to his best friend and sees him covered with blood. His best friend struggles to pull out an unsent letter to family from his uniform pocket… His friend dies in William's arms.

CU of the letter, we transition to …

The memory of seeing his best friend writing the letter

(Scene # 6)

Transition back to two days before his best friend died.

William's POV sees his best friend using the flashlight on his helmet, writing a letter back home in the dark. He turns to William; the flashlight flares the camera (William's eyes); we still can see the silhouette of his best friend's face, sadness in his eyes.

The flare transition to …

The memory of marrying his wife with soda can tabs

(Scene # 7)

A flare transitions back in time when William was 18 years old…

William's POV of him and his wife exchanging soda can tabs as wedding rings. William leans in for a kiss. Focus blurs out.

Transition to …

The memory of his Jr. Varsity baseball game

(Scene # 8)

Transition back in time when William was 13 years old…

William's POV as he slides into home plate. His team wins. Teammates rush to the camera and cheer.A teammate offers him a hand to get up…

Hands, transition to …

The memory of his father

(Scene # 9)

Transition back in time when William was 10 years old…

William's POV of CU of his father's rough hands working in the field on the family farm. His father gets up; William's POV follows. His father takes off his hat, wipes off sweat from his sun-drenched face. He looks at William with a smile. Playfully puts his hat on William's head, covers the lens …

The memory of the first street fight he got himself into

(Scene # 10)

Transition back in time when William was 10 years old …

William's POV as he is about to start a fight with a kid; a girl tries to separate them. The kid pushes the girl away, then pushes William (camera). He falls backward …

Cut to …

The memory of migrant farmers on the road

(Scene # 11)

Transition back to when William was 5 years old…

William's POV as he rides in his father's truck. He sees a couple of migrant farmers walking on the side of the road, with everything they own on their back. The farmers sadly look at William when the truck passes by them.

Time is suspended as William makes eye contact with one of the migrant farmers.

The memory of the good time with parents

(Scene # 12)

The movement of the truck transitions to …

William's POV as his parents spin him around on the family farm.

Camera spins into …

The memory of wonderful things in his childhood

(Scene # 13)

The weather vane spinning.

The memory of his mother measuring his height

(Scene # 14)

Transition back to …

William's POV sees his mother measuring his height by the wall. He turns around and looks at the markings.

The memory of the wonderful things in his childhood

(Scene # 15)

Transition back to …

William's POV of the grass dancing in the gentle wind; he touches the grass.

He looks up and sees …

The memory of watching a sunset with his parents

(Scene # 16)

William's POV sees his parents arm in arm watching a sunset.

The memory of the wonderful things in his childhood

(Scene # 17)

The sound of the wind chime.

The wind blowing the white curtain …

Transition to …

The memory of his mother and the clean laundry under the sun

(Scene # 18)

Transition back in time when William was one year old …

William's POV as he stares at the white sheet dancing in the wind in front of him; he looks at his mother's face and the clean laundry under the sun. She bends down, gives him a smile.

A white sheet wipes the frame into …

The memory of the day he was born

(Scene # 19)

White fade into when William was born …

William's POV as newborn child. This is the first time he sees his father and mother.

A midwife wraps him in a towel and hands him to his mother. His father looks at him, overjoyed. He reaches into his pocket and takes out the crystal. He slowly puts it into William's eye (the lens). The crystal is the thread; it was a gift from his dad at birth.

Cut to …

A look inside the crystal

(Scene # A19)

Newborn William's POV, looks deep into the crystal.

Cut to…

Back to present time

(Scene # 20)

We cut to a close-up of William's hand as the crystal rolls out of it.

His life ends.

Twelve Steps for HDSLR Shooting

1. Choose and attach the lens.
2. Choose a picture style (use Neutral or load or create a user-defined picture style, such as SuperFlat or ExtraFlat or other "flat" style if you're planning to do postproduction color grading).
3. Set the color temperature (white balance).
4. Attach and turn on the XLR adapter and/or microphone and set audio levels.
5. Set the frame rate (24 P, etc.).
6. Set the shutter speed to 1/50 (or 1/40); don't use 1/60 in order to avoid a video feel.
7. Set the ISO (for the 5D Mark II and 7D, use the native ISOs: 160, 320, 640, 1250, and 2500).
8. Set the f-stop.
9. Focus.
10. Meter and adjust the f-stop and/or ISO (push the shutter button halfway down).
11. Examine the histogram for tonal range to make sure your blacks are not crushed or your highlights blown out.
12. Press Record (press the Info button if you want to see the time lapse for recording).

Index